W9-CDN-248

BATHROOM
UPGRADES

EDITORS OF
FineHomebuilding

The Taunton Press

FOUNTAINDALE PUBLIC LIBRARY

300 West Briarcliff Road
Bolingbrook, IL 60440-2894
(630) 759-2102

© 2016 by The Taunton Press, Inc.
All rights reserved.

The Taunton Press
Inspiration for hands-on living®

The Taunton Press, Inc.
63 South Main Street, PO Box 5506
Newtown, CT 06470-5506
e-mail: tp@taunton.com

Editors: Christina Glennon, Tim Stobierski
Copy editor: Nina Rynd Whitnah
Indexer: Heidi Blough
Cover design: Alexander Isley, Inc.
Interior design: Carol Singer
Layout: Amy Griffin | A is for Design
Cover photographers: Front cover (clockwise from top left): David Hiser, Mike Kaskel, Charles Bickford
Back cover (left to right): Charles Bickford, Justin Fink

The following names/manufacturers appearing in *Bathroom Upgrades* are trademarks: 3form®, 3M®, Amba®, AmCork®, American Olean®, American Standard®, Amiga®, Amma®, Amtico®, Ann Sacks®, Armstrong®, Axor®, BainUltra®, Bed Bath & Beyond®, Belle Foret™, Blue™, Blum®, Bobcat®, Bondo®, Bricor®, Brizo®, Cadet®, Caesarstone®, California Faucets®, Camber®, Canyon Creek Cabinet Company®, Carlisle Wide Plank Floors®, Carlyle®, Casa Dolce Casa®, CertainTeed®, Chicago Faucets®, Colorbody™, Congoleum®, Cor-Ten®, Crossville®, Custom Building Products®, Custom® Building Products, Daltile®, Dens-Shield®, DeWalt®, Diamondback®, Dow Corning®, Duravit®, Durock®, Dynametric®, Eco Promenade®, Enduro®, Energy Conservatory®, EverClean®, Evolution®, Expanko®, Fiberock®, Flushmate®, Forbo®, FreeStyle Linear Drains™, Frigidaire®, Gacoflex®, Gaggenau®, GE®, General Finishes®, GreenGlass®, Green Squared®, Häfele®, HardieBacker®, Hercules®, Hydro Ban®, HydroRight®, IceStone®, Infinity Drain®, Island Stone®, Jaclo®, Jacuzzi®, johni-ring®, Kallista®, Kathryn®, Kendal Slate™, Kerdi®, Kohler®, KraftMaid®, Laticrete™, LG Electronics®, Linens-n-Things™, Loewen™, Lugarno®, Lumber Liquidators®, Mannington®, Mansfield®, Mapei®, Mapelastic™, Marmoleum®, Marshalltown®, Marvin®, Megaloc®, Miller Paint®, Mountain Lumber Co.®, Mr. Steam®, MTI®, National Gypsum®, Niagara Conservation®, NobleSeal®, Nuheat®, Oceanside Glasstile®, One2Flush™, Panasonic®, Pella®, PermaBase®, PermaGrain®, Pfister™, Phenoseal®, Porcelanosa®, Pottery Barn®, Princeton®, Prism®, ProPanel®, Purist®, Ram Bit™, Rejuvenation, Inc.®, Restoration Hardware®, Rev-A-Shelf®, Rhythm®, Robern®, Safety Tubs®, Samsung®, San Raphael®, Satinglo™, SaunaFin®, Schlüter®, Serif®, Sharpie®, SharpShooter®, Sheetrock®, Shelf Genie®, Sikaflex®, Sioux Chief®, Sloan®, Smart Faucet®, Smooth-On®, Solutions®, Spark™, Speakman®, Stealth®, Sterling®, Stone Forest®, Styrofoam®, Subway Ceramics®, Tarkett®, Tea-for-Two®, Teflon®, The Container Store®, The Hardware Hut®, The Home Depot®, Tile America®, Toto®, Tri-Max™, Tribeca™, USFloors®, USG™, Util-a-Crete®, Vintage Tub & Bath®, Vyta-Flex®, WaterSense®, Waterworks®, Wedi®, WhisperGreen Select™, WhisperSense™, WonderBoard®, Zen Bathworks®

Library of Congress Cataloging-in-Publication Data

Names: Taunton Press.
Title: Bathroom upgrades / editors of Fine Homebuilding.
Other titles: Fine Homebuilding.
Description: Newton, CT : Taunton Press, Inc., [2016] | Includes index.
Identifiers: LCCN 2016027698 | ISBN 9781631866548
Subjects: LCSH: Bathrooms--Remodeling--Amateurs' manuals.
Classification: LCC TH4816.3.B37 B385 2016 | DDC 643/.52--dc23
LC record available at https://lccn.loc.gov/2016027698

Printed in the United States of America
10 9 8 7 6 5 4 3 2 1

About Your Safety: Homebuilding is inherently dangerous. From accidents with power tools to falls from ladders, scaffolds, and roofs, builders risk serious injury and even death. We try to promote safe work habits through our articles. But what is safe for one person under certain circumstances may not be safe for you under different circumstances. So don't try anything you learn about here (or elsewhere) unless you're certain that it is safe for you. Please be careful.

ACKNOWLEDGMENTS

Special thanks to the authors, editors, art directors, copy editors, and other staff members of *Fine Homebuilding* who contributed to the development of articles in this book.

Contents

Have a Solid Plan

When you compare the square-foot costs of all the spaces in your home, the bathrooms are very likely at the upper end of the cost scale. The fixtures, finishes, cabinetry, and materials used to construct a beautiful and durable bath are inherently expensive. A truly custom bathroom—one that is tailored to the rhythms of your life and outfitted with all of the fixtures and finishes you've been dreaming about—can very quickly and very easily overwhelm your remodeling budget. It's important to keep those costs in check, and you'll certainly have to make compromises on some aspects of your bathroom design. One area where you can't afford to compromise is the planning of your new space. Wandering into a remodeling project like this without a comprehensive plan is asking for trouble.

It's easy to get lost in the aesthetic options when setting out to upgrade a bathroom. But don't forget that where you place the outlets is just as important as selecting the type and color of the vanity top.

Truly successful design is rooted in logic through and through. That perspective has driven the collection of information in this book. Here, we outline strategies for planning the most comfortable and functional bathrooms possible, we shed light on the latest material options on the market, and we identify what to consider when choosing products for your new bathroom. Above all, we arm you with the information you need to execute the remodel yourself. Not only does this afford you the opportunity to remodel a bathroom that's truly all your own, but it allows you to take the savings in labor and apply them to the finishes that make for a standout bathroom. If you look to this book as the first step in your design process—which I encourage you to do—you can feel confident that a solid plan will emerge. You can then begin demolition on your bathroom, knowing that success is not too far away.

Rob Yagid, Editor, *Fine Homebuilding*

PART 1

Planning and Layout

Bathroom Sightlines for Privacy and Grace

BY KURT LAVENSON

Sometimes the smallest rooms are the most difficult to get right. Bathrooms are a prime example. Within their small footprints, we must satisfy a multitude of mechanical, code-imposed, and client-requested conditions. It is tempting simply to pack the fixtures into the room, satisfy the necessary clearances, and move on. With the exception of some master baths that aspire toward being spas—at roughly the same acreage—the utilitarian nature of bathrooms can lead to some unfortunate design results. I have been in many houses where I was greeted by the powder-room toilet as I stood in the formal entry, or have been directed to a guest bathroom that was so closely connected to a living area that the homeowners might just as well have hung a curtain in the corner of the room and installed a toilet behind it.

The bathroom is not just about the toilet

Clients chuckle when I say this, but indoor plumbing is still one of our greatest achievements. It deserves respect. I like to celebrate it by making bathrooms as delightful as possible. Many beautiful fixtures are available in the marketplace, but I believe they are secondary to the approach and layout of the bathroom. In other words, a toilet should be afforded some privacy, even if it costs $2000 and looks like it has no tank.

I pay attention in my design work to the sightlines and travel routes within houses. Bathrooms are no exception. Through careful arrangement of circulation paths, doorways, and windows, we can control the views into and inside bathrooms as well as the sequence of arrival to get there. My rule of thumb is that the bathroom plays a supporting role to the adjacent spaces and that the toilet plays a supporting role within the bath. Maintaining this hierarchy keeps the plumbing in harmony with other activities in the house.

Most bathrooms, however, are engineered outward from the toilet. It requires the largest drainpipe and typically establishes the location of the bathroom as well as potential framing or slab changes to accommodate it. These days, we have more freedom to alter and engineer the floor to relocate drains, but it is still essential to consider the structure below when planning a new bathroom or a remodel. A big beam can foil the best design by limiting drain locations, and a thick slab with waterproofing below is troublesome to breach.

Thoughtful components make a great bathroom

Once the structure is worked out, the rest of the bathroom, above the floor line, becomes an interactive puzzle that can be solved in multiple ways. Each fixture requires a minimum clearance side-to-side and in front (consult your local codes), and each affects the others' locations. In residential construction, we are allowed to overlap the clear spaces in front of fixtures because the bathroom is not required to be accessible to multiple users simultaneously. This gives some freedom to compress the bathroom footprint when necessary. It also can be the key to a more pleasant layout within the bathroom, because fixtures can be rotated in or out of view. Extending countertop and floor surfaces also can help to make a small bathroom feel larger. The following examples use design moves like this to correct flaws in bathroom/living-space connections commonly found in today's homes.

Unlike some amenities, bathrooms are not expendable. A house will always need at least one, and probably more. So why not design these rooms to be special to arrive at and to see through as well as to use? That way, we leverage the utilitarian into the realm of the delightful and turn a requirement into an opportunity.

AN INVITING VIEW. Avoid placing the toilet so it will be the first thing you see upon entering. Here the window offers an inviting look beyond the room, drawing you in.

A BATHROOM THAT OPENS OFF AN ENTRY

SHUFFLING THE FEATURES within an existing space can change sightlines dramatically. A door opening on axis with a toilet at the opposite wall below a window is too utilitarian. By rotating the toilet to a perpendicular sidewall, adding a half-wall to screen it, and enlarging the window, the room is transformed. The vista into and through the bathroom becomes an inviting view out of the window. In this example, a similar alignment was used for the front door.

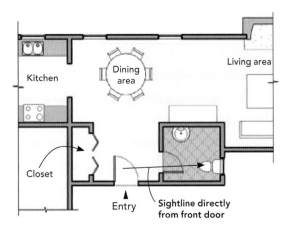

BEFORE
Bathroom and closet open directly to the entry. Many midcentury homes have front entries that deliver visitors right to the bathroom, where the toilet takes center stage.

AFTER
Closet shift allows bathroom privacy and a view. A new coat-closet hallway creates privacy and separation. Repositioning the toilet behind a half-wall obscures the view from entry to toilet. Doors align with windows.

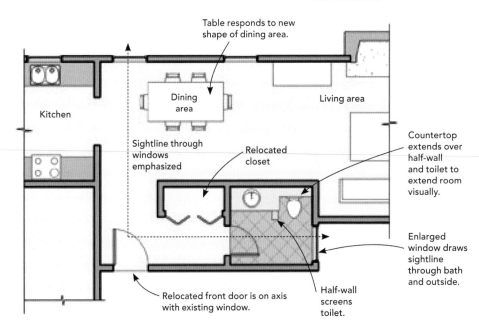

A BATHROOM THAT OPENS OFF A PUBLIC ROOM

THE PLACEMENT OF THE DOOR into the bathroom has a powerful effect on sightlines. For example, the typical situation of a door leading from a main room into a guest bath can be improved substantially by creating a small pocket of new buffer space en route to the bathroom and then rotating the bath doorway to open into it. Add a window to capture views from outside where possible. Once inside the bathroom, the presence of clutter and mass at eye level makes us feel constricted; reducing tall cabinetry, partition walls, and soffits makes the room feel larger and more inviting. Use clear tempered glass instead of walls where possible. Where the eye is directed within the room is as important as the vista from outside.

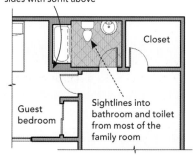

Full-height tiled enclosure at tub sides with soffit above

Closet

Guest bedroom

Sightlines into bathroom and toilet from most of the family room

BEFORE
Bathroom door opens directly into family room. Tub area is surrounded by structures. Guest bedroom is nearby but has no direct connection.

Built-in tub and enclosures are replaced with a freestanding bathtub.

Closet is reduced.

Sightlines into bathroom now limited to one corner of family room near the closet

Bath door is moved to perpendicular wall.

Floor extends under the bathtub to increase the visual sense of space.

Guest bedroom

Family Room

AFTER PLAN #1
Pocket space boosts privacy. The closet is reduced, and the bathroom doorway is rotated 90° to the perpendicular wall, deflecting views into the bathroom. Clutter around the tub is removed. There is no change at the guest room.

Toilet-nook space taken from bedroom

Tile or stone shower with clear-glass enclosure and high window for light and ventilation

Bench

Closet

Guest room gets own door to bathroom.

Primary-view axis through new window

Arched opening separates nook.

Guest bedroom

Family room

AFTER PLAN #2
More privacy, plus light and convenience. The creation of a deeper bathroom entry nook and addition of a new window not only increase the privacy for the bathroom but also create a pleasant transition space. A second door to the bathroom provides access from the guest room.

A BATHROOM THAT OPENS OFF A HALLWAY

AS IN THE FIRST EXAMPLE, this bathroom, even though it opens off a hallway, is uncomfortably close to a public space—in this case, the kitchen and dining area. This can be improved by moving the doorway to the other side of the bathroom and creating an adjacent minor hallway. Although this involves changing or taking space from adjacent closets, it provides an opportunity to leverage those changes to improve the circulation and privacy of nearby rooms.

BEFORE
Bathroom opens right off the kitchen. In a situation typically found in older homes, the bathroom lacks separation from the dining area and the kitchen, even though the hallway where it is located is long. The office/guest-room door opens directly into the living room.

Office/guest room

Kitchen

Closet

Door opens into living room.

Dining area

Door too close to dining area and kitchen

AFTER
Circulation and privacy are improved at the bathroom and beyond. The dining area and kitchen are separated from the bathroom by adding a hallway nook. The office/guest-room door is moved, and the closets are changed. A bench seat is added under the office/guest-room window.

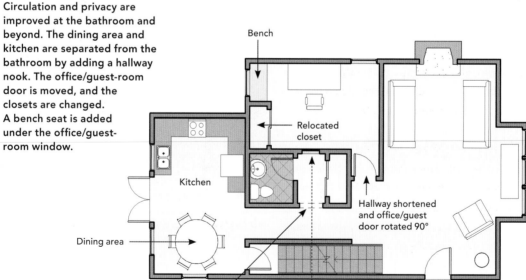

Bench

Relocated closet

Kitchen

Hallway shortened and office/guest door rotated 90°

Dining area

Arched opening

Wall-niche focal point

Remodel a Bath for Accessibility

BY DUNCAN MCPHERSON

Remodeling an existing house presents many design challenges. Modern living requires different functions and spaces from those in a house built 50, 20, or even 10 years ago. Designing homes and remodels that consider long-term livability has become a priority in residential design as we embrace an aging baby-boomer population.

Whether you're looking to age in place in your current home, to accommodate aging family members, or simply to consider resale value and market appeal, issues of wheelchair access and accessible design are critical. Even if you don't require accessible spaces today, you can design spaces that are functional, comfortable, and flexible enough to accommodate any accessibility needs that arise in the future.

Recently, I was charged with redesigning the existing full bath in the *Fine Homebuilding* Project House to create a more accessible master suite. This 1950s ranch has a floor plan common to many homes of a similar style and vintage. By looking at the problems with the existing bath and the solutions in the new bath, you'll easily be able to recognize the flaws and opportunities in your own projects.

ACCESSIBLE TO ANYONE. Bathrooms such as this one incorporate elements of universal design, including a barrier-free shower entry, grab bars in the shower, and an open toe-kick space under the sink.

Identify problems with the existing bathroom

The existing bathroom in *Fine Homebuilding's* Project House (floor plan below) has several problems. A narrow doorway leads to a claustrophobic space only 3½ ft. wide at its widest point. All the services—the toilet, the tub, and the sink—would be difficult to access if the user had limited mobility or were using a wheelchair. Adding grab bars to improve the functionality of this bath would be a hit-or-miss proposition because blocking is missing from the appropriate locations. Also, despite the need for it, the bathroom doesn't contain storage for toiletries or towels.

A A bathtub is difficult and dangerous to navigate into and out of if mobility is limited.

B A narrow doorway inhibits easy access into and out of the bathroom, especially if a thick threshold is in place.

C A narrow floor plan prevents wheelchair-bound users from being able to turn around.

D A toilet in a narrow nook without grab bars is difficult to access from a wheelchair.

E A linen closet is outside the bathroom, but storage should be integrated into the bath space.

F The hallway is too narrow to navigate easily in a wheelchair and is unnecessary in the new master-suite plan.

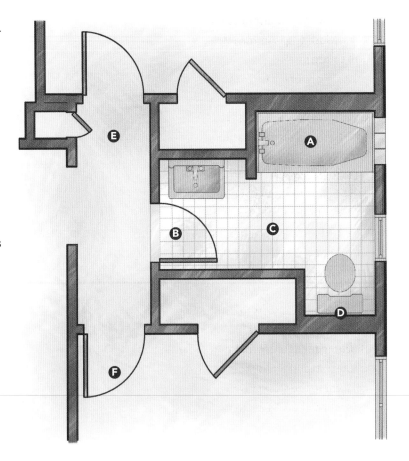

Create an accessible plan with integrated solutions

The first step in designing flexible spaces is determining which design elements need to be included initially and which can be installed later if they are needed. For example, building a bathroom with access to a 5-ft. clear turnaround area that improves wheelchair maneuverability should be incorporated initially, because it would be difficult and expensive to make accommodations for such a space later. Below are the elements that make this new bathroom accessible while still maintaining an aesthetic that is comfortable and style appropriate.

Ⓐ Doorways have a minimum 32-in. clear width to accommodate wheelchairs.

Ⓑ Swinging doors with levers, not knobs, are used instead of pocket doors because they're less challenging to open from a seated position.

Ⓒ Hallways and passageways are 48 in. wide to improve access.

Ⓓ A 5-ft. clear turnaround circle integrated into the floor plan of the bath is best. If this isn't possible, create a turnaround circle outside the bathroom, as shown at right.

Ⓔ A removable shower screen/partition provides better access to the shower if necessary in the future.

Ⓕ Blocking for a future fold-down seat is integrated into the shower wall adjacent to the shower controls. Typical seat height is 18 in. above the floor.

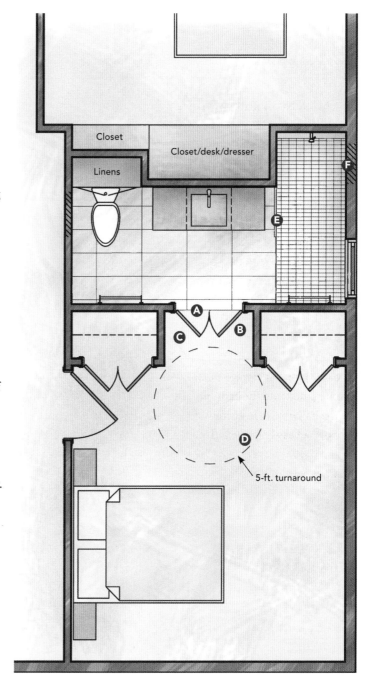

Design an elevation that can adapt to change

The psychological influence a home can have on its residents is profound. Having a fully accessible bathroom before it is needed can be a looming reminder of aging and the loss of mobility. Well-designed spaces can create more positive responses, however.

Like all properly designed accessible spaces, this bathroom is meant to be adaptable to change. For example, a vanity that is in tune with the modern style of the bath is built so that its middle cabinet can be removed, allowing easier wheelchair access to the sink. Until that need is necessary, the vanity reads as a contemporary cabinet fit for any home.

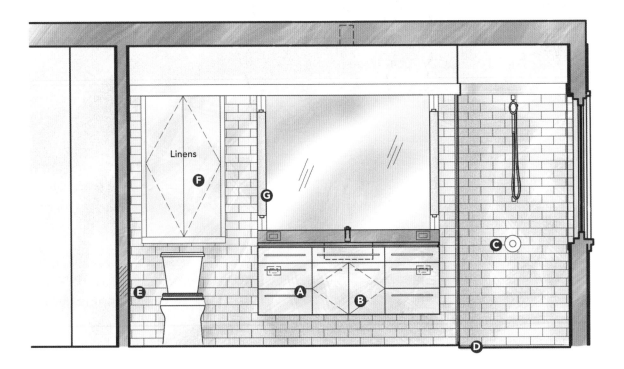

A Vanity provides plentiful storage that can be used from both seated and standing positions.

B Vanity is built so that the middle cabinet is removable to allow for knee space below the sink.

C Shower valves, light switches, and thermostat controls should be from 38 in. to 48 in. above the floor.

D There is less than a ½-in. transition between the bathroom floor and the shower floor to enable roll-in access.

E Blocking is integrated into the walls so that grab bars can be installed around the toilet and shower in the future. Typical grab-bar height is from 33 in. to 36 in.

F A linen cabinet integrates additional storage opportunities in the bath where none had existed previously.

G Two light fixtures mounted at eye level provide adequate illumination at the vanity.

Better Bathroom Storage

BY JAMIE GOLD

The house I grew up in had only one full bathroom, which my parents, sister, brother, and I shared. Somehow, we made it work, but any bathroom will work better with a little more storage. The best time to maximize a bathroom's storage capacity is at the design stage, but you can explore storage-boosting options while remodeling or making other updates.

Whether incorporated into the original design or added after the fact, bathroom-storage expansion fits into three categories: (1) increasing the capacity of traditional storage areas like vanity cabinets; (2) maximizing existing floor and wall space with new storage options; and (3) identifying storage possibilities in spaces that are not traditionally used for storage. These approaches are outlined on p. 16, and strategies from all three are used in the illustrated examples.

Store it where you use it

The key to good bath storage begins by identifying all the items that are kept in the bathroom according to their point of use, which could be at the vanity, the commode, the tub, or the shower. Items to be stored also can be sorted into one of three use categories: daily, backup, and occasional.

Daily-use items like shampoo in the shower require space at their point of use. Backup items are extras of daily-use necessities, like the remaining five bars in the soap package. They need not clutter the point-of-use area; instead, they can be kept in their own storage space. Occasional-use items like cold medicine can be kept in the bathroom, where they'll probably be used, but they also can move outside the bathroom for storage.

Once a bathroom's storage needs have been identified, the storage solutions can be designed based on the point-of-use and non-point-of-use opportunities.

THE FULL-FUNCTION VANITY

It's common even for large vanity units to fall short on functional storage. In this example, the space between the sinks is wider than 30 in., allowing a stacked 24-in.-wide butt-door cabinet pair. The double doors and lack of a center stile allow access from both sides. The lower unit is backless and contains a wall outlet, making it useful for housing and charging electric shavers and electric toothbrushes. The 12-in.-deep space above houses daily-use items too large for the medicine cabinets.

False panels in the sink bases have been converted to tilt-out trays for toothpaste and dental-floss storage. Doors are equipped with storage racks, including one for hair dryers. If extra storage is needed, U-shaped shelves can double the capacity of the sink cabinets. The center drawer's functionality is increased with a tiered divider, while the basic linen tower has been made more useful with a quartet of roll-out trays in the lower section.

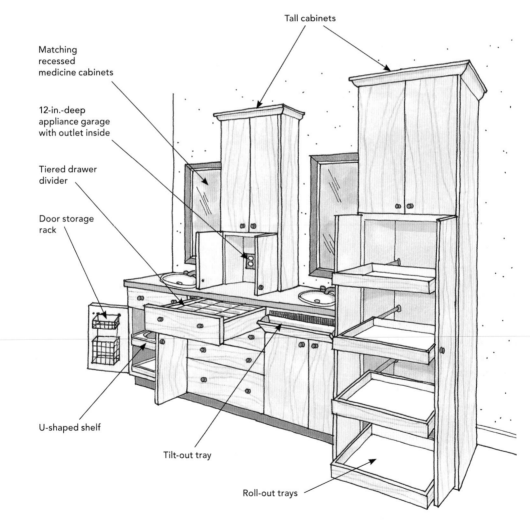

Tall cabinets

Matching recessed medicine cabinets

12-in.-deep appliance garage with outlet inside

Tiered drawer divider

Door storage rack

U-shaped shelf

Tilt-out tray

Roll-out trays

THE COMPACT BATH

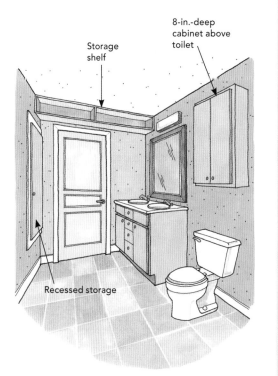

Storage shelf

8-in.-deep cabinet above toilet

Recessed storage

THIS TYPICAL, SMALL MASTER BATH offers occupants two sinks and a shared drawer bank but not much more in the way of storage. National Kitchen & Bath Association design guidelines recommend 30 in. of clearance (or a minimum of 21 in.) in front of the vanity and toilet, eliminating the opportunity for floor storage on the opposite wall. However, a 12-in.-deep shelf runs the length of the wall above the entry door to hold occasional-use items. The shelf can be supported by L-brackets or decorative supports, as long as they don't interfere with the door swing below. Taking advantage of otherwise unusable space behind the in-swing door is a tall, shallow cabinet installed between the wall studs. It holds occasional-use items that might otherwise be stored in a recessed medicine cabinet, freeing that valuable point-of-use space for daily needs. An 8-in.-deep cabinet above and within reach of the toilet offers point-of-use storage for spare rolls of tissue and other items.

THE MAXIMIZED MASTER BATH

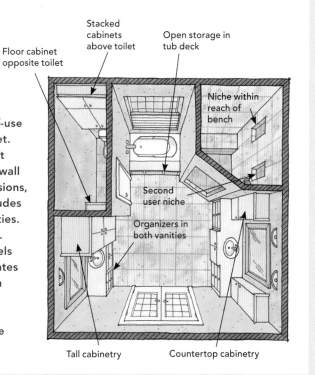

Floor cabinet opposite toilet

Stacked cabinets above toilet

Open storage in tub deck

Niche within reach of bench

Second user niche

Organizers in both vanities

Tall cabinetry

Countertop cabinetry

THIS REMODELED BATH MAXIMIZES daily point-of-use space in all three functional areas: tub, vanity, and toilet. The water closet features a floor cabinet for extra toilet paper, a toilet brush, and toilet-cleaning supplies. The wall cabinets above the toilet, only 8 in. deep to avoid collisions, hold supplies within reach of the user. The shower includes double niches to hold each occupant's bathing necessities. One is within 15 in. of the shower bench for easy reach. The tub deck is extended with storage in front for towels and other bath essentials. The deeper deck also facilitates a safer sit-and-swivel entry. In the vanity area, the linen tower offers space for a roll-out hamper in the bottom section. The opposite vanity takes advantage of an extrawide countertop to offer additional storage above for small electric devices with access to an outlet.

THREE WAYS TO BOOST BATHROOM STORAGE

1. INCREASE THE CAPACITY OF TRADITIONAL AREAS

- Add two-tiered organizers to any 4-in. or taller vanity drawer boxes, thus creating extra half-drawers without altering the existing cabinet.
- Install a storage rack on the back of every vanity base-cabinet door. Special racks are available for space-hogging hair dryers.
- Add roll-out trays to the bottom of base cabinets, and use them in place of shelves in linen towers, making what's stored in the back more visible and accessible.
- Use pull-out base cabinets fitted with storage compartments for blow dryers, curling irons, shampoo, and other beauty essentials.
- Wrap a U-shaped shelf around under-sink plumbing to add an extra level of storage.
- Convert the false panel below a vanity counter-top to a tilt-out tray.

2. MAXIMIZE EXISTING FLOOR, SURFACE, AND WALL SPACE

- Take advantage of unused floor space to create a built-in furniture armoire, floor cabinet, or storage bench for backup and occasional-use items. Remember to allow for clearances when adding storage of this type. National Kitchen & Bath Association (NKBA) design guidelines recommend 30 in. in front of a vanity, commode, or shower. NKBA guidelines are often more stringent than building codes, but be sure to check local requirements to ensure that you're in compliance whenever undertaking a bathroom project.
- Maximize point-of-use vanity storage with countertop cabinetry. Use 12-in.-deep cabinets, keeping them at least 3 in. from the sink edge to prevent water damage. The cabinets can extend to the ceiling with a decorative crown molding, or stop a foot lower if there's a vent or light above. Regardless of height, they should be finished with a topcoat that protects against moisture and should be kept as dry as possible to prevent moisture damage at the point of contact with the vanity top.
- Increase the point-of-use commode storage. If the toilet is not under a window, install a single or stacked cabinet to the ceiling above it. The cabinet

should be placed low enough for a seated user to be able to reach inside and extend no farther out than the toilet tank to avoid causing injury.

■ If there is a window directly above the toilet, space might still exist for a short cabinet or shelf to be installed between the window and the ceiling for backup supplies. Ensure that the bottom is finished because it will be highly visible.

3. IDENTIFY STORAGE POSSIBILITIES IN NONTRADITIONAL SPACES

■ Add a finished shelf above the bathroom entry door to take advantage of otherwise unused space for occasional-use items. Whenever possible, run it wall-to-wall.

■ Take advantage of the forgotten space behind an in-swing door by building a tall, shallow cabinet into the wall between studs.

■ Plan built-in, open wall-shelving units at one or both ends of a tub-only enclosure for daily point-of-use bathing items in storage baskets.

■ Plan open-storage cubbies for towels or bath supplies on the front end or exposed side of a new tub deck.

■ Create a shower-wall niche for each bathroom occupant to accommodate daily point-of-use bathing items. At least one should be built within 15 in. of the shower bench for seated access.

SOURCES

POTTERY BARN®
www.potterybarn.com

THE CONTAINER STORE®
www.containerstore.com

BED BATH & BEYOND®
www.bedbathandbeyond.com

REV-A-SHELF®
www.rev-a-shelf.com

NO DRILLING REQUIRED
www.nodrillingrequired.com

ARMSTRONG® SALONCENTER
www.armstrong.com

LINENS-N-THINGS®
www.lnt.com

ORGANIZE-IT
www.organizeit.com

ORGANIZED A TO Z
www.organizedatoz.com

SOLUTIONS®
www.solutions.com

SHELF GENIE®
www.shelfgenie.com

SHELVES THAT SLIDE
www.shelvesthatslide.com

THE HARDWARE HUT®
www.thehardwarehut.com

KRAFTMAID®
www.kraftmaid.com

Invisible Ventilation for a Better Bath

BY RUSSELL HAMLET

I t bothers me to walk into a nice bathroom and see a randomly placed exhaust grille on the ceiling or wall. In a small room full of fixtures and accessories, a sense of visual order is important—and a haphazardly positioned grille shouts for attention. Thoughtfully placed ventilation, on the other hand, is virtually invisible.

Of course, aesthetics is not the only consideration in positioning bathroom vents. Exhaust grilles perform best when located high on the wall or in the ceiling and as close as possible to the source of water vapor (over a shower, for example). Proper installation of the system is also essential.

TYPICAL EXHAUST-VENT LOCATIONS

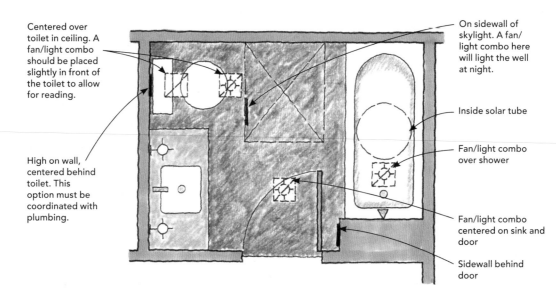

Centered over toilet in ceiling. A fan/light combo should be placed slightly in front of the toilet to allow for reading.

High on wall, centered behind toilet. This option must be coordinated with plumbing.

On sidewall of skylight. A fan/light combo here will light the well at night.

Inside solar tube

Fan/light combo over shower

Fan/light combo centered on sink and door

Sidewall behind door

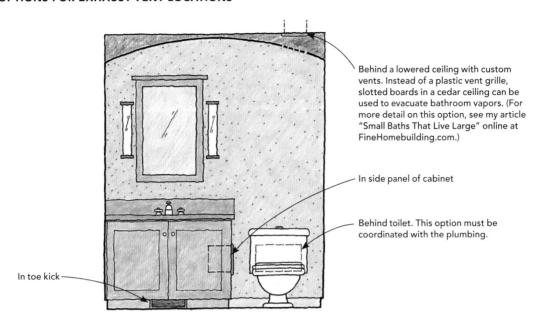

Behind a lowered ceiling with custom vents. Instead of a plastic vent grille, slotted boards in a cedar ceiling can be used to evacuate bathroom vapors. (For more detail on this option, see my article "Small Baths That Live Large" online at FineHomebuilding.com.)

In side panel of cabinet

Behind toilet. This option must be coordinated with the plumbing.

In toe kick

Different bathrooms, different needs

Choosing the ventilation system that is right for your bathroom is important. Follow code requirements and industry recommendations, and consider the frequency of use and the source and amount of moisture you expect will be generated. Proper placement of the exhaust grille is critical in a bathroom with a steam shower, but not so critical in a powder room by the front entry. A powder room or a small bathroom could meet code with just an operable window consisting of a 3-sq.-ft. glass area with a minimum 1.5-sq.-ft. opening (IRC 2009, 303.3). If a window is not an option and/or mechanical ventilation is used, the location of the vent is worth some design thought.

As a side note, it is important to allow intake air into the bathroom so that the exhaust system works properly. I usually specify that the door be undercut ½ in. to ¾ in. above the finished floor to provide space for this makeup air.

There is usually no code requirement governing grille placement, so we can get creative here. If the room's aesthetics are a priority—if it's a showpiece powder room, for example—you can locate an exhaust vent low on the wall, in a cabinet side panel, in a toe-kick space, or behind the toilet tank (drawing above).

Once you have a location planned for the exhaust vent, it's vital that this be communicated to the builder and subcontractors so that they can adjust the framing, plumbing, and electrical layouts to accommodate the vent where you want it. Too often, the framing is completed and the plumbing installed before the exhaust-vent location is considered. At this point, the extra labor and expense to move the framing, plumbing, and electrical is prohibitive, and the exhaust-vent location is compromised.

If you are planning a bathroom remodel, seriously consider upgrading the exhaust-ventilation system. There are many "quiet" exhaust units on the market now (look for units with a sound rating of 1 sone or less). Additionally, locating the fan motor away from the grille will reduce fan noise significantly. This is also the time to consider the grille's placement in the room. If you are opening the ceiling or walls, look for an opportunity to locate the vent grille in the best place possible.

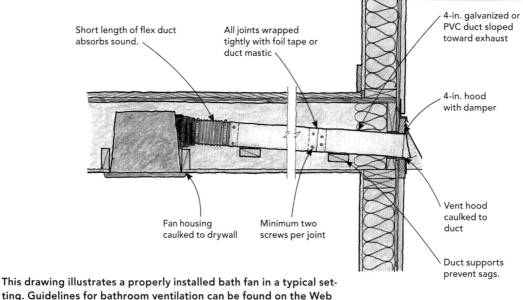

Short length of flex duct absorbs sound.

All joints wrapped tightly with foil tape or duct mastic

4-in. galvanized or PVC duct sloped toward exhaust

4-in. hood with damper

Fan housing caulked to drywall

Minimum two screws per joint

Vent hood caulked to duct

Duct supports prevent sags.

This drawing illustrates a properly installed bath fan in a typical setting. Guidelines for bathroom ventilation can be found on the Web site for the Home Ventilating Institute (www.hvi.org).

THE BEST LOCATION FOR VENTILATION

HERE ARE SOME GUIDELINES I use when considering where to locate a bathroom vent:

- Keep it subtle and out of the way. Locate grilles where they will receive the least amount of visual attention. Avoid a location in the center of the bathroom, unless it is a small bathroom and a fan/light combination unit is used.
- Hide the vent by painting the grille to match the color of the surrounding surfaces.
- Consider many grille-design options. This may take some research, but different designs can work with a bathroom's aesthetics and style.
- Keep the grille away from ceiling lights and other fixtures and devices so that it doesn't compete for attention. Incorporate lighting into the ventilation system by installing a fan/light combination unit.
- Locate the exhaust vent in a skylight well, if that's possible. Not only do vents perform well there, but they also are largely hidden from view.
- Align the vent grille with plumbing fixtures (sink, toilet, tub, shower), lighting fixtures, windows, and/or doors.
- Consider centering the vent over the toilet, typically a good location.

Finishes for a Master Bath

BY DUNCAN MCPHERSON

Renovating the *Fine Homebuilding* Project House bath into a master bath was a great opportunity to investigate how to improve functionality and durability in an older home. In "Remodel a Bath for Accessibility" (p. 9), I looked at how to make a limited bathroom space accessible to a homeowner for years to come. Here, I'll focus on finishing that bath with durable materials from a classic palette that, like the bath's accessibility features, will enhance the space for today and beyond.

Per square foot, bathrooms are the hardest-working rooms in a house and take a beating from everyday use and high moisture levels. These small spaces require big-time maintenance, so a thoughtful renovation that lasts generations should include a variety of finishes that embody classic-style, easy-to-clean surfaces, and durable materials. Because materials play such an important role, I've included thumbnail photographs of materials I'd consider in outfitting this bath.

Keep it simple

Simple finishes that don't rely on trendy color accents help a room to feel timeless and prevent the space from becoming outdated. Tile is a highly durable material that can last 100 years or longer, so using a classic, subtle color improves the chances that it won't need to be replaced for a long time.

I believe a bathroom should be a calming space, so I avoid a lot of colors, textures, and patterns. For this bath, I suggested off-white and light neutral tones for the walls and ceiling, including the tile, window trim, and wall color. That goes for the commode as well—I almost always choose a white toilet, either a dual-flush or ultra-low-flow model. I would also paint the linen cabinet to match the wall tile so that it blends in. Together, these neutral surfaces create a clean canvas that allows other elements of the room, such as the vanity, to stand out.

The vanity serves as the main focus of the room. You don't want more than one accent element competing for your attention in a bathroom of this size. I suggested a maple vanity cabinet, with a countertop of a complementary tone and color. This acts as the "paint" on the canvas of the room and highlights the natural variation of the wood grain against the more solid-toned walls. Alternatively, a darker walnut tone would provide a higher contrast and more modern look.

Again, for simplicity's sake, I recommend such classic metal finishes as chrome or stainless steel on faucets, showerheads, cabinet hardware, and bath

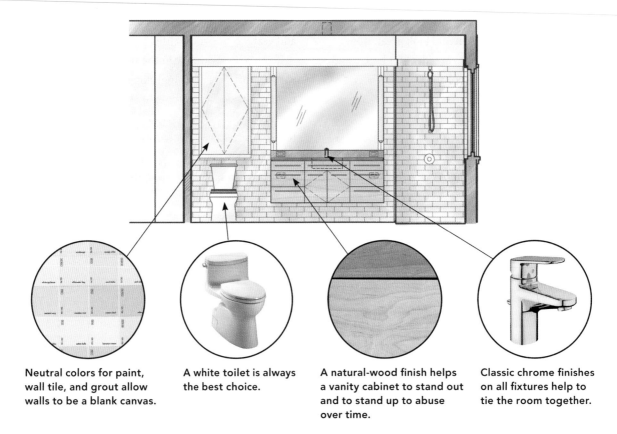

Neutral colors for paint, wall tile, and grout allow walls to be a blank canvas.

A white toilet is always the best choice.

A natural-wood finish helps a vanity cabinet to stand out and to stand up to abuse over time.

Classic chrome finishes on all fixtures help to tie the room together.

accessories. All these metal finishes should match so that they tie the room together. Don't experiment with brushed nickel plumbing fixtures and polished chrome for your bath accessories. Ideally, any metal on the light fixture will match as well. If this palette seems a bit boring, consider adding more color or interest to the room with your towels, soaps, and other objects, rather than doing so with the fixtures, paint, or tile.

Choose your tile wisely

To help the room feel larger, the shower floor tile should match the floor tile of the bath itself, but in a smaller size to minimize the risk of slipping. Through-body porcelain tile with a slight texture works well because it can be cut into smaller sizes, is slip resistant, and has edges that can be ground down if chamfering is needed at corners. A linear floor drain (see p. 94) at the edge of the shower creates a single-direction slope to the floor and an easier floor-tile installation. It also moves the drain out of the standing area of the shower.

Lately at my firm, we've been using larger tiles (12 in. by 24 in. or larger) for both walls and floors in a lot of our projects, and I really like the look of fewer grout joints. Having less grout to clean is a major plus, too. At the wall tile, I like to use thin "toothpick" joints for the grout and a grout color that matches the tile color as closely as possible. Grout on the floor tile should generally be darker to help hide dirt, and I usually match the floor-tile color so that the floor doesn't create potentially distracting grid lines. I recommend a "calm" tile that does not have a busy pattern or dramatic variations in color or tone. For floor tile, choose a neutral, mid-to-dark tone to help hide dirt, but make sure the color works well with the color of the vanity cabinet.

Think durability

Water is always present in a bathroom, so durable, nonporous finishes that are easy to wipe down will help the room to stay clean and look great. Both ceramic and porcelain tiles are ideal for baths, and we like to use smooth or polished tile on walls for long-term durability and ease of cleaning.

Vanity cabinets with a natural-wood finish hide scuffs and age better than those with a painted finish. I recommend that you use a catalyzed lacquer for a durable finish, although your local cabinet-maker may prefer an alternative. Wood surfaces are often the first things that need to be replaced in a bathroom, so consider a high-quality finish that can add years to the wood's life.

If you have a window in the shower, be sure to waterproof its sill framing, slope it to drain, and finish it with the countertop material or wall tile. The shower wall tile should wrap the jamb of the window to minimize exposed wood in the shower. I recommend epoxy paint or marine-grade paint for wood window sashes in the shower area.

DURABLE MATERIALS IN SIMPLE PATTERNS

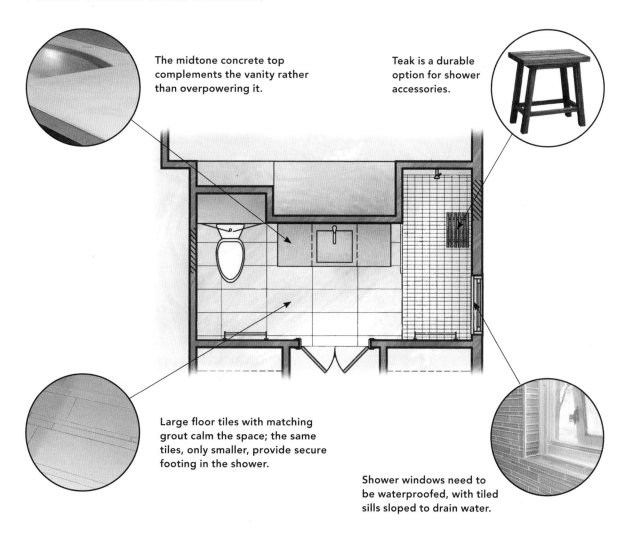

The midtone concrete top complements the vanity rather than overpowering it.

Teak is a durable option for shower accessories.

Large floor tiles with matching grout calm the space; the same tiles, only smaller, provide secure footing in the shower.

Shower windows need to be waterproofed, with tiled sills sloped to drain water.

Light a Bathroom Right

BY RUSSELL HAMLET

On a cost-per-square-foot basis, a bathroom is pretty darned expensive, which might account for people's tendency to skimp on bathroom lighting. But it's in the bathroom, in front of the mirror, where you begin and end each day. The bathroom should be an enjoyable and functional space.

In too many bathrooms, a single overhead light fixture provides all the light. Unfortunately, this isn't a good strategy. It casts unflattering shadows on your face and in corners of the room, and it's not adequate for tasks like shaving and applying makeup.

Light the surfaces

One of the most important things to remember about lighting is that you are not lighting the space bounded by the bathroom walls; you are lighting surfaces. Light bounces off walls, ceilings, floors, mirrors, and cabinets, and it is this reflected light that illuminates the room.

The corollary is that surfaces are important elements; their texture and color affect the quality and amount of light. It's important to consider whether a color will absorb or reflect light. I like to use warm, light colors in bathrooms because they reflect light and add a comfortable hue. Not only do dark colors absorb light, but in a small bathroom, they shrink the space visually.

Textures in a bathroom should create interesting shadow lines but not objectionable dark spots. Regardless of a textured surface's effect on the quality of light, choose materials that continue to feel and look clean over time despite the large amount of moisture in the room. (For example, some unfinished wood surfaces will look and feel mildewy, and deep reveals in tongue-and-groove boards might appear to harbor mold.)

GOOD LIGHTING DEMANDS A FIVE-PART STRATEGY

- Use layers of light.
- Consider the reflected light that bounces off surfaces.
- Use plenty of light where it's needed the most.
- Choose appropriate colors for the walls, ceilings, and fixtures.
- Take the size and shape of the room into account.

USE NATURAL LIGHT
ANY WAY YOU CAN

DURING THE DAY, the skylight and the window let the sun stream in. Privacy glass in the door and a transom window allow the bathroom to borrow light from the hallway or an adjacent room. These "relites" are an effective way to bring light into the room and establish a connection with other spaces. This also makes the bathroom feel a bit more expansive.

There are two sources of artificial ambient light: the overhead fixture and secondary cove lighting, which are both dimmable to supplement sunlight at dawn and dusk.

At night, a skylight becomes a black hole. To counteract this, a dimmable cove light bounces light into the well, replicating the feeling of natural light streaming though the skylight. The skylight well is also a good place to put the fan. It's hidden from view when you enter the bathroom, and the integrated light tucked high up makes a great night-light.

In this bathroom, the light-green colors help to reflect light and reinforce the outdoor connection that's made through the window and the skylight.

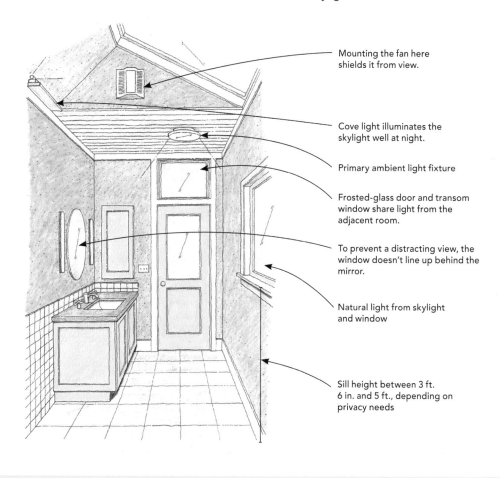

Mounting the fan here shields it from view.

Cove light illuminates the skylight well at night.

Primary ambient light fixture

Frosted-glass door and transom window share light from the adjacent room.

To prevent a distracting view, the window doesn't line up behind the mirror.

Natural light from skylight and window

Sill height between 3 ft. 6 in. and 5 ft., depending on privacy needs

LIGHT EACH BATHROOM ACTIVITY

GOOD LIGHTING IS PART FIXTURE LOCATION and part bathroom design. In this case, the glass enclosure lets task lighting above the shower and tub spill across boundaries. The soffit houses the task lights for the vanity and toilet, and it also creates a shadow along its intersection with the ceiling. By compressing the space above these task areas and creating a border of shadow and light between the task zones and the rest of the bathroom, the toilet and vanity areas feel warmer and the scale more comfortable. The overhead vanity light is directed at the mirror, so it doesn't cast shadows on the face. The vertical lights provide cross illumination. When you choose trim kits for recessed cans,

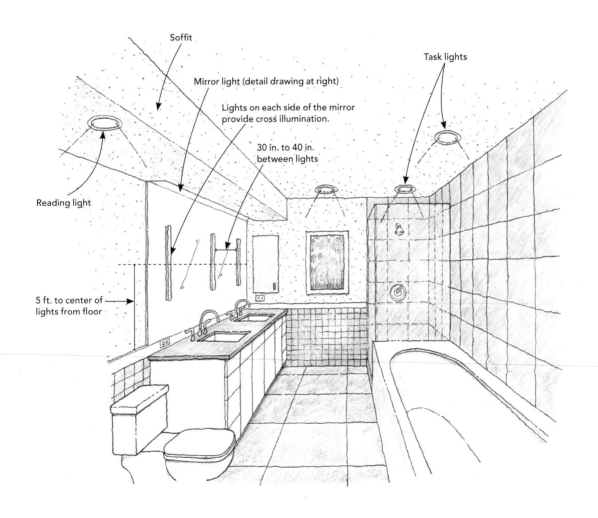

Soffit

Task lights

Mirror light (detail drawing at right)

Lights on each side of the mirror provide cross illumination.

30 in. to 40 in. between lights

Reading light

5 ft. to center of lights from floor

skip the white step baffle because it'll be too bright and pull your eye to the ceiling. A gold baffle enhances wood cabinets and skin tones by casting a warm glow. A black baffle reduces glare and helps to camouflage the can, and a clear baffle works in modern baths with white and metallic finishes.

OVERHEAD FIXTURE THAT LIGHTS THE MIRROR, NOT YOUR FACE
A canted fixture and a curved reflector aim light at the mirror.

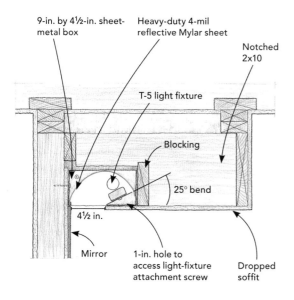

9-in. by 4½-in. sheet-metal box

Heavy-duty 4-mil reflective Mylar sheet

Notched 2x10

T-5 light fixture

Blocking

25° bend

4½ in.

Mirror

1-in. hole to access light-fixture attachment screw

Dropped soffit

As with the other rooms in a house, light the bathroom with layers, using ambient, task, and accent lights. Layering the light helps to eliminate unwanted shadows, ensures that there is enough light for specific jobs or functions, allows for different intensities of light to suit different users and activities, and creates a sense of drama.

Bathrooms are often too small for the fourth layer of lighting, dedicated decorative lights. However, a beautiful or interesting fixture providing ambient, task, or accent light might also serve as decorative lighting. Controlled by a dimmer, the fixture can switch between its primary role and a decorative role.

Start with ambient light

Ambient lighting is general illumination. Ideally, this nondirectional light comes from a combination of natural and artificial light. You should look to daylight as your first lighting choice. That can be tough in a bathroom; many lack an exterior wall. Even with an exterior wall, window space is limited by privacy concerns and the need to pack a sink, shower and/or tub, and toilet into the space.

I often look skyward to bring in natural light. Skylights, traditional and tube types, supplement windows and bring light to landlocked rooms. While tubular skylights are compact, flexible, and virtually leakproof, I find the lightwell of a traditional skylight especially useful in the bathroom. Sunlight reflects off the sides of the well, creating even light around the room. I typically splay the lightwell to allow more light into the bathroom.

As important as it is to have good daylighting, the bathroom receives the heaviest use on the shoulders of the day, so artificial light is required. It can come from an overhead fixture, recessed cans, wall sconces, cove lights, valances, or a combination of these choices. For small and moderate-size bathrooms without alcoves or L-shaped layouts, you might find that a single overhead fixture works well for ambient

CREATE DRAMA WITH LIGHTS AND SHADOW

IN THIS BATHROOM, LIGHTS CALL ATTENTION to the curved tongue-and-groove ceiling, the wall tile, and the artwork above the toilet. There is no dedicated ambient-lighting fixture. Rather, accent and task lights combine for general illumination.

Recessed lights with a wall washer or gimbal ring trim create pockets of light on the wall to call attention to artwork or surfaces, in this case the tile. Don't be afraid to think outside the box: An outdoor sign light highlights the framed artwork.

Because this bathroom has no natural light, a pale-yellow color is used on the walls to reflect light and add a warm hue. Lighting the arched wood ceiling with uplights and strip cove lighting also adds warm tones to help replace the sense of natural light.

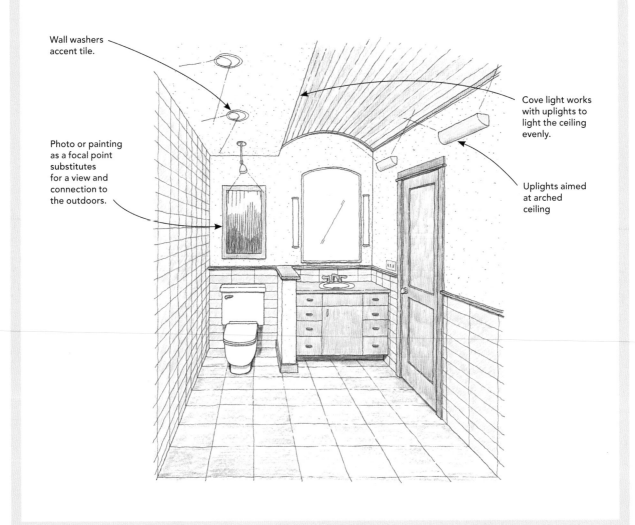

Wall washers accent tile.

Photo or painting as a focal point substitutes for a view and connection to the outdoors.

Cove light works with uplights to light the ceiling evenly.

Uplights aimed at arched ceiling

light. In large or irregularly shaped bathrooms, you'll need additional fixtures like recessed cans or cove lights.

For ambient light, designers use the rule of thumb of 1w of incandescent light, or its compact-fluorescent equivalent, for each square foot of floor. Put ambient lights on a dimmer so that they can account for daylight and for your mood. (Consider the amount of light you'd want for an evening bath versus the workweek morning routine.) Adjustable light levels also let older and younger folks find the precise level of light they need for nighttime trips to the toilet. Finally, dimmers let you mix the level of ambient light with task and accent lighting to create patterns of shadow and light, an interplay that adds interest and drama.

Avoid shadows at the mirror

Vanity lighting is the most important task lighting and can make or break your bathroom experience. A light, or row of lights, above the mirror to light your face creates shadows under your eyes, cheekbones, nose, and chin that make you look tired, heavier, and older. Cross illumination is much more flattering. By placing vertical lights at eye level on both sides of the face, you eliminate shadows. Generally, use lights with some sort of shielding here, whether it's frosted glass, acrylic fabric, or some other material. Especially if it's a fluorescent bulb, this softens the light and adds warmth. Be sure to choose a light fixture with a finished look to the back if it will be reflected in the mirror.

Other areas that require task lighting are the tub and/or shower, as well as a light at the toilet for reading. Often, these lights will be recessed cans, which have a wide range of trim kits available. Because the lights over the tub and shower have to be vaporproof, I generally use a diffuser on all task lights for consistency. Plastic lenses yellow over time, so use glass.

Highlight beauty

Accent lighting emphasizes an object or a surface; the fixture itself is discreet. Typically, I use accent lights in two ways: One is to call attention to beautiful surfaces, and the other is to highlight artwork. You might be thinking, "Wait a minute. Artwork in the bathroom?" But if there are no windows, a photo or painting can replace the connection to the outdoors. Lighting framed art or something sculptural creates depth and shadow that the eye welcomes. You can accomplish the same thing by highlighting the materials you splurged on, whether it's the wall tile or a tongue-and-groove ceiling.

Layering three lighting types means that you could be using different light technologies. It's important that the quality of light—the temperature and color-rendering ability—match regardless of its source. The color temperature of incandescent light is 2700 kelvin, a warm (yellowish) hue that makes skin look good. If you use fluorescent, LED, or halogen bulbs, their color temperatures must match each other and should be the same as an incandescent lamp. Plus, they should have a color-rendering index of at least 82—higher if it's available.

How to Daylight a Bathroom

BY CATHY SCHWABE

When I was in middle school, my family moved into our first house. It was a beautiful, modern, one-story home in Northern California built in the late 1950s and designed by a local architect who was clearly interested in daylight and solar design. Like many modernist houses of that era, the bathrooms were small, efficient "machines for living" and were also all interior rooms. One memorable and unusual feature of these bathrooms was the low, flat ceiling, whose surface was an off-white, semi-translucent plasticlike sheeting. The sheeting was set in a lay-in frame and hung below roof-mounted skylights. The effect was to bring diffused daylight into the space during the day without the heat gain that was the mainstay of our summers. Many years later, I still find myself thinking about those bathrooms.

As an architect, one of my goals when designing a bathroom is to introduce daylight into the space so that it is balanced within the room and so that the contrast in illumination from one area to another is minimal. I try to control the shadows.

If at all possible, I try to bring daylight into a bathroom from more than one opening and from more than one orientation. Daylight can be introduced to a bathroom from three key perspectives: from the side, from the top, or from both. Each has its advantages and disadvantages.

1. DAYLIGHTING FROM THE SIDE

Daylight brought in from the side of a bathroom is mostly accomplished through windows, but it can be done with glazed doors as well. Ideally, the room will have two outside walls so that the light can be brought in from two different orientations. This is not always possible, and in these situations, more care has to be taken about the placement of the openings, the use of adjacent surfaces, and the layout of the bathroom itself.

A key advantage of bringing daylight in from the side is that it's easier to adjust the window or door location so that the daylighting illuminates the space where it is most needed—in the mid- to upper-body range. Daylighting a bathroom from the side works well only in small bathrooms where the distance between the window or door and the opposite wall is minimal. In large bathrooms, the light levels fall off quickly, and the space is more apt to be underlit.

The bathroom on the facing page, an addition and remodel in Palo Alto, Calif., sits adjacent to a semiprivate second-floor deck and is a good example of daylighting from the side.

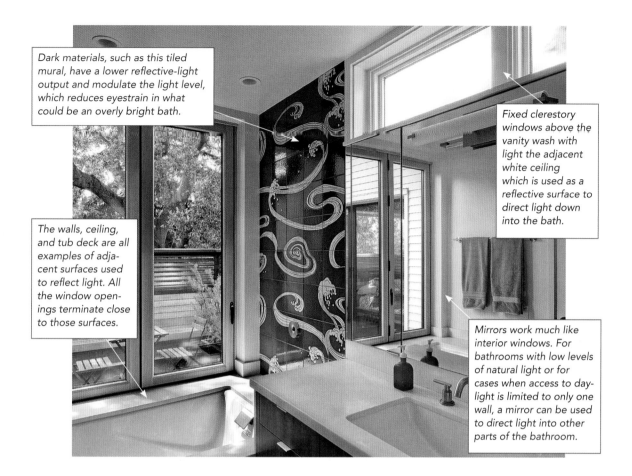

Dark materials, such as this tiled mural, have a lower reflective-light output and modulate the light level, which reduces eyestrain in what could be an overly bright bath.

Fixed clerestory windows above the vanity wash with light the adjacent white ceiling which is used as a reflective surface to direct light down into the bath.

The walls, ceiling, and tub deck are all examples of adjacent surfaces used to reflect light. All the window openings terminate close to those surfaces.

Mirrors work much like interior windows. For bathrooms with low levels of natural light or for cases when access to daylight is limited to only one wall, a mirror can be used to direct light into other parts of the bathroom.

PLACE LIGHT SOURCES STRATEGICALLY

WHEN PLACING A WINDOW, DOOR, OR SKYLIGHT in a bathroom, it's important to consider inline and adjacent surfaces. Understanding the difference between these surfaces helps you to balance the daylight within a space more successfully.

Adjacent surfaces run perpendicular to a daylight source. The closer you can place the edge of a window, door, or skylight to an adjacent surface, the more it is washed with light and the better it reflects light into the room. Inline surfaces lie in the same plane as the daylight source, rarely receive direct

light, and are naturally in shadow. To balance the light, they require illumination, ideally with reflected daylight.

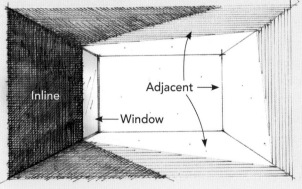

Inline

Adjacent →

Window

NATURALLY LIT SPACES
ARE HEALTHY SPACES

DAYLIGHT OFTEN COMES WITH A VIEW and with opportunities to provide natural ventilation. I take advantage of these benefits any time I can. However, there are additional benefits associated with naturally lit spaces.

The circadian rhythm, often called the internal biological clock, is our daily physical, mental, and behavioral response to light and darkness. The natural production of certain biochemicals that control and regulate our learning and intelligence, our impulse control and muscle coordination, our focus and moods, and our management of stress is triggered by appropriate amounts of either darkness or light. Artificial lighting can stimulate, and in some instances overstimulate, this biochemical production. The absolute best and most self-regulating stimulus is the natural daily cycle of daylight followed by the true darkness of night.

There are additional reasons for ensuring that our bathrooms have good daylighting. The most obvious is the reduced energy usage resulting from naturally lit spaces. Another is the increased safety that comes when we are able to see more clearly in a room that is evenly lit and where contrast in light levels is controlled. Finally, good daylighting gives us a stronger sense of comfort and confidence; we can be certain that how we look in the natural light at the mirror is also how we will look as we venture out for the day.

The room has mechanical ventilation, but the skylights, which are set high above the bath due to the steep roof, provide strong passive ventilation through the stack effect.

A glass wall in the shower permits the light from the skylight to flow fully into the rest of the room.

2. DAYLIGHTING FROM THE TOP

On occasion, the ceiling can be the only surface available for introducing daylight into a bathroom. When a bathroom is landlocked in a layout and the ceiling sits just below the roof, I always add a skylight. A skylight or multiple skylights can be used to balance the daylight in the space below.

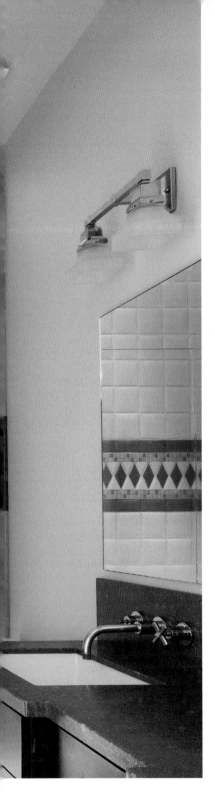

Because the skylights in the bath are so high, light levels fall off as they approach the floor. This effect is less significant, however, because the area of the upper torso is still evenly lit.

The angled skylight's shaft walls are designed to spread light as it enters the bath so that it falls across the whole room. As a result, the contrast between surfaces in the bath is reduced.

The skylight was positioned so that sunlight entering the bath is directed away from the sink and vanity mirror, which reduces the potential for glare and eyestrain.

Although it's difficult to daylight a bathroom fully with a single skylight, a skylight with a well-placed shaft can concentrate light in the upper level of the space. The falloff in light intensity will be downward and not as noticeable. However, a drawback to skylights is that they are sometimes difficult to orient correctly to the path of the sun.

In the bathroom in the photos above —a 50-sq.-ft. bathroom located on the second floor of a house in Atherton, Calif.—two venting skylights were placed at each end of the room to daylight the space fully, to provide small views out, and to offer passive ventilation.

3. DAYLIGHTING FROM THE SIDE AND THE TOP

Bathrooms that have only one exterior wall and window can be a challenge to daylight properly. However, when the bathroom's ceiling is set just below the home's roofline—in a second-story bathroom, for example—I add a skylight to help balance the daylight.

It's much easier to balance the daylight in a bathroom when light enters the space from both the side and the top. When the skylight is operable, there also is a great opportunity for passive ventilation.

In the photos on this page and the facing page, a 50-sq.-ft. bathroom in a historic house in Palo Alto, Calif., daylight enters from two directions—through large windows and a large skylight—which provide a high, even level of natural illumination without any high-contrast shadows.

Daylight from the high window head illuminates the ceiling, which reflects light back down to the vanity and shower area.

The angled ceiling plane receives reflected light from the opposing shower wall and bounces light into the other areas of the bathroom. Even though this ceiling plane is in shadow, it's evenly lit, so contrast within the space is minimal.

A glass shower surround permits all parts of the room to benefit from the sources of daylight.

The artificial light in this bathroom, especially at the sink counter, parallels the high, even level of illumination provided by daylight.

The windowsill is set deliberately high so that views into and from the adjacent one-story house and garden are well blocked.

The placement of the mirror in this bathroom allows it to be one of the adjacent surfaces for the window. It then can reflect and direct daylight onto other surfaces in the space.

Constructing the skylight shaft so that it is slightly smaller than the skylight frame allows an uninterrupted view of the sky. The skylight frame is hidden atop the shaft walls.

The skylight is positioned so that two of the shaft walls are extensions of the adjacent walls below, which allows the shaft to draw light as deep into the room as possible.

Inoperable skylights are easier to maintain because they don't have screens that need to be cleaned. A chain-operated louver provides natural ventilation.

SOLVING THE PRIVACY EQUATION

LOTS OF WINDOWS IN A BATHROOM can enable public spaces to encroach on private spaces. You can consider several options when trying to retain privacy while still allowing daylight and views into your bathroom.

In a window with multiple lites, you can mix glass. Take the windows in the bath below, for instance. For the lower lites, use translucent glass such as narrow reed, or use laminated glass with Japanese paper; for the upper lites, use clear glass. The translucent glass will diffuse the sunlight and obscure the view, while the clear glass will allow daylight and views to enter the bathroom.

Fixtures and Materials

Low Flow

BY SEAN GROOM

Here's a look at fixtures and appliances that can save you money, improve community health, and help the climate. And yes, your toilet will still flush.

In areas of the West, mandatory water conservation is the price for enjoying 300 sunny days a year. East of the Mississippi, conservation has become increasingly important as droughts affect areas not used to water shortages. And regardless of where you live, public water supplies are increasingly unable to meet demand for healthy water or to treat the volume of wastewater they receive. Consequently, conservation isn't just about reducing your water bill; it's an issue of water quality, public health, energy, and the environment.

Every day, we use water in toilets, showers, faucets, washing machines, and dishwashers. For every one of these points of use, there are both best-in-class and reasonable conservation targets to help you trim water waste. In the following pages, you will find some examples.

A GALLON SAVED GOES FARTHER THAN YOU THINK

Because water and energy are relatively cheap in the United States, the monthly savings from conserva-

MANY BENEFITS. Fixtures and appliances that conserve water not only save you money but also improve community health and help the climate.

tion can seem small, and the payback period can be several years. You may ask, "What's the point?"

The point is that water is increasingly scarce, and using it requires energy. Running cold water for five minutes consumes as much energy as a 60w lightbulb does in 14 hours. It also requires energy to treat the water afterward. Nationally, it takes an average of 0.0033kwh of electricity to supply and treat each gallon.

To see how this adds up, I'm going to make some conservative assumptions. First, I'll consider only detached, single-family homes; second, I'll assume that all these houses have fixtures and appliances that meet current plumbing standards (1.6-gal.-per-flush toilets, 2.5-gal.-per-minute showerheads, etc.). If they accomplished the modest goal of reducing household-water consumption by 20%, they each would save an average of 9670 gal. of water and around $100 in heating costs annually.

Sounds paltry. Nationally, however, that's more than $6 trillion saved, 774 billion gal. of water unused and that won't require treatment, and a 35-million-ton reduction in CO2 emissions. That CO2 reduction would be equivalent to taking 11.5 coal-fired 500-megawatt electricity plants offline. These numbers also drastically understate the savings. There are hundreds of millions of fixtures and appliances that don't meet today's minimum-efficiency standards, and I didn't factor in apartments, town houses, or condos.

A COMMONSENSE STARTING POINT

Akin to its Energy Star program for electric appliances, the EPA launched WaterSense® to recognize products that meet heightened standards for water conservation. Critics of past water conservation efforts argued the measures demanded large performance sacrifices, so WaterSense includes a performance component to weed out clogging toilets and impotent showerheads.

Unless a product is pressure-compensating, its advertised flow rate depends on water pressure. If water pressure is high, say 100 psi, then a fixture is going to use more water. If you use a public water supply, the provider can tell you the static pressure. If it's greater than 60 psi, you should install a pressure-regulating valve (www.watts.com).

Toilets

A huge chunk of your water bill literally is money down the toilet. Nearly 30% of indoor water use in the average American household stems from toilets. Replacing an older toilet will put a big dent in household water consumption.

A 1992 federal standard restricts new toilets to a maximum of 1.6 gal. per flush (gpf), but the best estimate is that there are still 100 million nonconforming toilets using 3.5 gpf or even 5 gpf. WaterSense-labeled toilets are a 20% improvement over the standard. A qualifying commode must be a single-flush type using a maximum of 1.28 gpf or a dual-flush toilet using a maximum of 1.6 gal. for solids and 1.1 gal. for liquids. New high-efficiency toilets use between 0.8 and 1.28 gpf and rely on either gravity or compressed air to move water and waste out of the bowl.

New toilets: Traditional toilets rely on gravity to wash waste through the trapway and into the waste lines. With 16 years of engineering behind them, gravity-flush low-flow toilets work fine at 1.28 gpf. WaterSense-qualified toilets flush at least 350 g of uncased soy balls, a tougher simulation than the voluntary test manufacturers use.

Pressure-assist toilets rely on air pressure in a sealed plastic water tank hidden inside the porcelain tank to create a forceful flush with relatively little water. (The tank-within-a-tank design means no sweating.) The flush system is the heart of a pressure-assist toilet, and the top-performing Sloan® Flushmate® IV can be found in pressure-assist toilets across the price range. For the uninitiated, the loud swooshing flush of a pressure-assist toilet can be startling. Redesigning the pressurized tank to create a vacuum-assist flush allowed Niagara

Conservation® to develop a 0.8-gpf, nearly silent toilet, called the Stealth®.

Retrofit: You can squeeze greater efficiency from your 1.6-gpf toilet by displacing water in the tank with a toilet-tank bank (a sealed plastic bag filled with water) or a plastic bottle with some pebbles in the bottom. A sexier way is to convert it to a dualflush commode with the MJSI HydroRight® dual-flush converter kit or the One2Flush™ 200 dual-flush retrofit kit. Relatively simple to install, these kits replace the flapper and flush lever with a new mechanism allowing for a small- and a large-volume flush. The volume of water used for both flush types can be adjusted to find the lowest volume that successfully removes waste.

Washing machines

After the toilet, the washing machine is the greatest consumer of water in the house. Most manufacturers don't quantify water usage, but the Energy Star Web site provides that data for all qualified washers (www.energystar.gov).

Washing machines come in different sizes, so a straight-up comparison of gallons per cycle is apples to oranges. A small 2.7-cu.-ft. washer might use less water per cycle than a 4.1-cu.-ft. washer, but it's also cleaning fewer clothes. (If you have to do an extra three loads a week, you're not saving water or electricity.) For a fair comparison, Energy Star calculates an integrated water factor (IWF), the number of gallons used per cycle per cubic foot of clothes-washer capacity. The lower the IWF, the more water efficient the washer.

The federal government now restricts water usage for washers to an IWF of 8.4 for standard top-loading washers and 4.7 for standard front-loading washers. Energy Star requires an IWF of less than 4.3 for standard top-loading washers and less than 3.7 for standard front-loading washers. While this improvement is significant over older models, you can easily find washing machines with an IWF in

VACUUM ASSIST MEANS HALF THE WATER

THE STEALTH RELIES ON SLICK ENGINEERING to get by with only 0.8 gpf. As the toilet fills, rising water compresses air in the sealed inner tank. A tube transfers the compressed air to the trapway. This pressurized-air pocket raises the water level in the bowl for a larger water surface and cleaner bowl. Flushing the toilet quickly drains water from the bottom of the tank and sucks the trapway air pocket into the tank, creating a momentary vacuum. Water from the bowl rushes to fill the vacuum, sucking the waste in the bowl through the trapway.

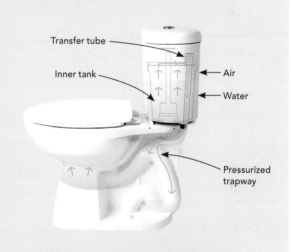

Transfer tube
Inner tank
Air
Water
Pressurized trapway

the 2.9 to 3.5 range, and these washers are among the most energy efficient available.

Larger capacity machines tend to generate lower IWF scores, which is great for families with consistently full laundry loads. But if you know that you'll frequently run less-than-full loads, look for a model with loading-sensing technology, like the three shown here. They adjust the water level to the amount of clothing.

Showerheads

Your showerhead delivers almost 20% of your indoor water use, and most of that water is heated. A new showerhead is relatively inexpensive and an easy way to reduce both water and energy bills. Today's showerheads are limited to 2.5 gpm. But for each half-gallon per minute you reduce the flow rate, you'll reduce your water heater's annual energy consumption by about 150kwh of electricity or 750 cu. ft. of natural gas.

WHERE DOES ALL THE WATER GO?

ONE OF THE REAL SURPRISES ABOUT WATER use is that leaks account for nearly as much water as bathroom faucets. Generally, the sources are easy-to-ignore dripping faucets or unseen toilet flappers allowing water to seep from the tank to the bowl.

To prioritize the fixtures and appliances in your conservation efforts, compare your device's flow rate to WaterSense standards and consider its contribution to household consumption—that is, don't replace an 8-gal.-per-cycle dishwasher if you still have 5-gal.-per-flush toilets.

You don't always need to replace items to make a dent in consumption. In many cases, you can retrofit accessories, like the Smart Faucet® on p. 42, that help you to use water smarter for the cost of a pie at your local pizzeria.

WATER CONSUMPTION LIMITS		
	FEDERALLY MANDATED MAXIMUM	**NEW WATERSENSE STANDARDS**
Toilet	1.6 gpf	1.28 gpf
Washing machine	8.4 IWF top-loading standard 4.7 IWF front-loading standard	4.3 IWF top-loading standard** 3.7 IWF front-loading standard**
Shower	2.5 gpm	2.0 gpm
Bathroom faucet	2.2 gpm	1.5 gpm
Leaks	0	0
Dishwasher	6.5 gal./cycle	3.5 gal./cycle*

*Energy Star standard as of January 2016
**Energy Star standard as of March 7, 2015

CUSTOM-DRILLED FOR YOUR WATER PRESSURE. The aerating metal showerheads from Bricor® come in three flow rates: 0.625 gpm, 1 gpm, and 1.25 gpm. Intended for drought-stricken areas, the 0.625-gpm Ultramax is a bit reminiscent of a camp shower, but the other two versions mimic the feel of a more luxurious 2.5 gpm.

DIAL YOUR FLOW RATE. Twisting the black ring on Niagara Conservation's Tri-Max™ showerhead switches the flow rate. The company asks you to think of the 0.5-gpm setting as soaping mode, the 1.0-gpm setting as soaking mode, and the 1.5-gpm setting as an option for high-pressure shampoo rinsing.

LESS WATER, SAME FORCE. The venerable showerhead manufacturer Speakman® offers low-flow nonaerating versions of its classic Anystream 32-, 48-, and 50-spray models in 1.5 gpm, 1.75 gpm, and 2.0 gpm. A pressure-compensating device matches the force of the original and offers the same variable spray patterns.

Despite the savings potential, people fear that less water means weak spray and poor coverage. This has been an obstacle for the adoption of low-flow showerheads, especially because you can't try one before you buy it. To overcome this hurdle, WaterSense includes testing protocols to ensure reliable, strong pressure, and an even, well-dispersed spray. Fortunately, plenty of showerheads in the 1- to 2-gpm range have a nice spray pattern and plenty of force. (If you have a tankless water heater, be sure the flow rate is enough to activate it.)

Low-flow showerheads come in two varieties: aerating and nonaerating. One is not better than the other, but each produces its own type of spray. Aerating showerheads are the most common. They inject air into the water stream, in essence creating bigger, plumper droplets. By increasing the water volume, the flow is reduced, and the steady pressure and even, full spray create the impression of a more ample 2.5 gpm. The downside is that the air cools quickly, which means you'll notice the temperature drop at your feet.

Instead of pumping water droplets full of air to increase the volume of water, nonaerating showerheads use a pressure-balancing flow constrictor to increase force. The shower will be stronger, but the water may be too needlelike with some models. On the plus side, these showerheads allow water to retain heat longer.

The other way to conserve water in the shower is to shut it off when it's not necessary. If you're hearty enough for a "Navy shower," a shutoff valve between the showerhead and shower arm lets you turn off the flow when you're lathering.

A less miserly but more comfortable approach reduces the amount of water wasted before you enter the shower. If you turn on the shower and then brush your teeth while the cold water is flushed from the pipes, you're wasting both water and energy. Installing an aftermarket device like the Evolve between your shower arm and showerhead shuts down the flow as soon as hot water reaches the showerhead.

Faucets

Like other fixtures, bathroom faucets come in low-flow varieties. The maximum flow rate for the industry is 2.2 gpm, while WaterSense-labeled faucets top out at 1.5 gpm. You should look at a low-flow faucet if you're redoing the bathroom, but there's no need for that kind of cash outlay to save water. Faucets work fine at less than full volume. You can cut water use immediately with every faucet's integrated flow restrictor: the handle. Because old habits are tough to break, though, spend a few bucks for a new low-flow aerator to ensure water savings. These inserts screw onto faucet threads, control the stream type and shape, and are available in low-

RETROFIT YOUR FAUCET. The cheapest on-demand faucet solution is a simple, spring-loaded retrofit valve that replaces the faucet aerator (for example, Smart Faucet). Set the handle(s) once at the preferred volume and temperature. Place your hands under the faucet, apply pressure to the weighted lever with the back of your hands, and water will flow. A sliding disk allows the arm to be locked in the on position.

flow rates of 0.5 gpm, 1 gpm, and 1.5 gpm. (Kitchen faucets aren't included in WaterSense because higher flow rates make things like filling pots easier, but you can add an aerator if you like.)

Do you turn off the water when you're scrubbing your hands and then back on again to rinse them? Probably not, so regardless of flow rate, most of the water coming out of a faucet is unused, and heated. For bigger water and energy savings, limit water flow to when it's really needed by adding an on-demand device.

Foot pedals are a higher-tech (and higher-priced) means of hands-free faucet control. Used in the kitchen or bathroom, the pedals mount in the kick space and give you control of both the hot and cold water. One pedal controls hot water, one pedal controls cold water, and stepping on both provides warm water. They are great in the kitchen when you're preparing meat and you'd normally be fumbling to turn on the faucet without actually touching it. Plus, with the elimination of the sink-

TOUCHLESS FAUCETS REQUIRE AN ELECTRICITY SOURCE. Sensor-operated faucets typically come with a battery pack that becomes a backup power source if you purchase an add-on plug-in or hard-wire kit. A battery pack powers EcoPower from Toto®, but it's recharged by an inline turbine every time you turn on the water, increasing battery-life expectancy to 10 years.

STEP ON IT. Does it bother you that you have to touch the faucet with clean hands to turn it off? Or that heated water is pouring down the drain while you're scrubbing? Foot pedals address both concerns. Chicago Faucets® makes 15 different styles (model 625 pictured above).

top controls, you get a really clean countertop installation. In the bathroom, you need some sort of cabinet to hide the pedals' mechanicals.

Another hands-free option is an electronic faucet. When the infrared beam aimed into the basin is broken, a solenoid opens water flow and closes it one second after your hands leave the sensor field.

Note that many electronic faucets don't include the mixing valve, which you need for tempered water. You'll also need to decide whether you want a set-and-forget temperature control or an external control so that you can adjust the temperature with each use.

Faucets typically have a maximum running time between 10 and 60 seconds before they shut off, regardless of whether your hands are still in the basin. If the faucet times out while you're still washing, remove your hands from the sensor field for a second to reset the faucet, then resume washing.

Dishwashers

It's a misconception that hand-washing dishes saves water. If you want to use water frugally, run the dishwasher. WaterSense doesn't rate dishwashers, but Energy Star incorporates water consumption in its qualifying criteria. Now, an Energy Star dishwasher must use less than 3.5 gal. per cycle.

It's important to recognize that not all Energy Star products are created equal. As a product line, you can't go wrong with Bosch. With the exception of a few Gaggenau® models with matching performance, all of Bosch's models are head and shoulders above other brands when it comes to water and energy usage. Remember that efficiency figures are for normal cycles. Heavy-duty wash cycles can use significantly more water and energy.

Price generally tracks features, not efficiency. Of course, loading flexibility, cycle options, cleaning performance, and appearance all factor into a dishwasher purchase, but you can improve efficiency and performance by choosing one with clean-sensing technology.

LESS WATER MEANS LESS ENERGY. Heating water to 130°F accounts for most of a dishwasher's energy consumption, so engineering it to use (and heat) as little water as possible saves electricity. Sensors that evaluate the size and dirtiness of the load to reduce water volume and running time further boost savings.

During each segment of a wash cycle, the dishwasher uses an allotted amount of water several times. As wash water collects in a sump at the bottom of the tub, a light beam measures turbidity—the volume of particles in the water and the water's opaqueness—throughout the cycle and uses that information to adjust the length of the wash segment. If more cleaning is needed, the water is filtered (so that food particles don't get pasted back on the dishes) and returned to the spray arms. Another water- and energy-saving feature is half-load cycles that can either reduce water use for the load size or wash only one rack.

SOURCES

TOILETS

American Standard®
www.americanstandard-us.com

Mansfield® Plumbing Products
www.mansfieldplumbing.com

Niagara Conservation
www.niagaraconservation.com

SinkPositive
www.sinkpositive.com

Sloan
www.sloan.com

WASHING MACHINES

Frigidaire®
www.frigidaire.com

LG Electronics®
www.lg.com

Samsung®
www.samsung.com

SHOWERHEADS

Bricor
www.bricor.com

Evolve Technologies
www.thinkevolve.com

Niagara Conservation
www.niagaraconservation.com

Oxygenics
www.oxygenics.com

Speakman
www.speakman.com

FAUCETS

Bricor
www.bricor.com

Chicago Faucets
www.chicagofaucets.com

Niagara Conservation
www.niagaraconservation.com

Smart Gadgets Inc.
www.water-saver-faucet.com

TOTO USA, Inc.
www.totousa.com

DISHWASHERS

Bosch
www.bosch.com

Gaggenau
www.gaggenau.com

GE®
www.ge.com

Bath Sinks with Style and Sense

BY MARIA LAPIANA

Running the gamut from spalike minimalism to sybaritic decadence, today's bathrooms bear little resemblance to the no-nonsense washrooms of old. If this is apparent anywhere, it's in the stunning array of bathroom sinks—or lavatories, as they are known in the trade—available today.

These artful fixtures include vessels of natural stone, copper, bronze, and blown glass as well as ceramic basins that distinguish themselves through designs that are sleek, curvaceous, carved, outsize, or edgy. It may seem that function has given way to form, with designs so stunning we're likely to forget that bathroom sinks even have a purpose. Consider this a reminder that there are practical considerations to weigh when choosing a new sink.

If you're designing a bath, your first task is deciding the type of sink suitable for the space. After you've settled on one of those seven essential types—

GV-100 by Kraus

pedestal, wall mount, integral, drop-in, under-mount, top-mount, and console—there are plenty more decisions to be made.

This is partly because the bathroom sink has evolved from a hardworking fixture the whole family uses to a luxury item designed to call attention to itself. Still, the sink needs to fit in with the overall bath design, says Bill McKeone, design manager for Kallista®, a division of Kohler®. McKeone designed sinks for more than 25 years before shifting gears to work for Kohler tile brand Ann Sacks®. The change gave him some perspective about sinks and the bathrooms they live in. "I was used to putting all of my thoughts into that one product, focusing on every detail," he says, adding that later, "I came to appreciate that the sink is only one piece of the big picture—that there has to be unity in the room."

When choosing a lav, it's important to consider where and how the sink will be used, and by whom. Designers of both sinks and bathrooms agree that the powder room is the best place to be creative. Wow and bling belong in the room to which guests are directed, says Ann Morris, a kitchen and bath designer from Fort Lauderdale, Fla. "The sink you choose depends on the theme of your bathroom," says Morris. "With so many materials out there, you can make your sink the focal point of your powder room."

To be clear, we're talking about a little-used powder room, not the one the family runs in and out of on a daily basis. "You can be really playful in the powder room, as long as it's used for just a little bit of hand-washing," says North Carolina architect Sophie Piesse. "In my house, the first-floor powder room is used by my kids all the time." Clearly, that's not the best place for a pricey vessel sink.

Master bathrooms offer opportunities for beauty and drama, but once again, it's important to consider purpose. Do you wash your face, shave, and brush your teeth there? Or do you also blow-dry your hair and apply makeup? If so, how much counter space do you need? Do you wash your hair at your sink? If so, depth may be a concern.

Budget comes into play here as well. While twin sinks have been in vogue for some time now, ask yourself if you really need them. Two sinks mean two faucets and twice the plumbing, which can be costly. Twin sinks also cut down on counter space.

What does all this variety mean for homeowners? Today's sink options are so exciting that it's hard not to have some fun when choosing them. "It's important to do what you like. Remember, you're the one who has to use the sink," says Travis Rotelli, an interior designer for Kohler. "I understand that people think about resale, but I believe that done properly, a bath sink can be beautiful and functional—and be something that the next guy will like."

Color? Keep it controlled

It's official: Coordinated bath fixtures in shades of pink and aqua have gone the way of crocheted toilet-roll cozies and seahorse wallpaper. While American Standard once offered china sinks in 11 colors, its go-to palette today numbers a mere three or four—all neutrals, depending on the model. "It used to be that color in the bath was driven by fixtures and tiles," says Gray Uhl, the company's design director, "but since there has been such an explosion of color in

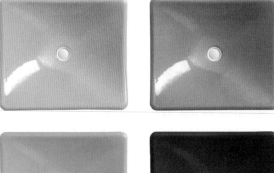

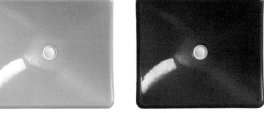

NOT COY ON COLOR. Kohler's Jonathan Adler collection turns up the color volume, but most designers suggest keeping lavatories low key.

materials and accessories, including fabrics, fixtures are now the basics around which colors are chosen."

These days, it doesn't get any better than white. "I think white is nice and simple, and it's generally cheaper," says architect Sophie Piesse. "It's contemporary and modern, and gives a bath a clean and fresh look." Likewise, Paul DeGroot, an architect in Austin, Texas, is in no hurry to specify colorful sinks. They're a throwback to the past, he says. "I remember a green cultured-marble sink that matched a green 1980s tub, and a brown lav that matched a brown toilet—yes, brown—from a 1950s home." He adds, "Hopefully, this trend won't come full circle any time soon."

Still, some manufacturers are embracing color. Kohler's Jonathan Adler collection offers three low-profile lavs in four head-turning hues, including Palermo Blue and Piccadilly Yellow. "We're getting back to more fun and exciting statement colors," says Travis Rotelli. "But even our neutrals have a fresh look. They used to be white and biscuit. Now they're more dimensional. They have almost a textured look. We call them Sea Salt, Cane Sugar, and Basalt."

Material choices

The design process really gets going once materials come into play," says Bill McKeone, design manager for Kohler's Kallista brand. Familiar, tried-and-true sink materials such as vitreous china and enameled cast iron will always have an important place in the market. Newer composites, such as high-end solid-surface materials, are often specified today because they allow for relatively fuss-free care. Material options are a major way by which the lavatory has crossed over from utility into art. Vessels made of glass, carved from stone, cast in bronze, or hammered in copper all reflect materials that have contributed to a veritable design revolution in bathroom sinks. Here are some common materials used in lavatories today.

VITREOUS CHINA

Made from a clay-and-mineral mixture that is glazed and then fired at high temperatures, vitreous china is the oldest, most common sink material. These high-gloss sinks are scratch- and stain-resistant, and require only minimal maintenance. "It's hard to beat the cleanability and decades of durability that come with vitreous china," says architect Paul DeGroot. If that's not enough, brands such as Porcher (from American Standard) boast an antimicrobial surface glaze on some china sinks that makes it even harder for stains and other nasties to gain a foothold. Although featured more often on toilets and tubs, the glaze, called EverClean®, is also available on some sinks.

PROS: When glazed and fired properly, vitreous china absorbs no water at all, making it long-lasting and sanitary. The material is also popular in basic, entry-level sinks, making it an economical choice.

CONS: Although less likely to chip or crack than other sinks, vitreous-china lavs are susceptible to damage from heavy impact.

Vitreous china

GLASS

Colored, textured, flecked, studded, or otherwise adorned, glass sinks are an artful addition to any bathroom. Tempered handmade glass is most often used to create vessel sinks, but some undercounter styles (with clear, colored, or frosted finishes) are becoming popular options. Glass sinks are elegant, versatile, and surprisingly durable. "The best glass sink is one that has texture," says Ann Morris, kitchen and bath designer. "It's much more forgiving; you don't see the drips and every splash. You're not wiping it down 24/7."

PROS: Most glass is stain-resistant and can be cleaned with any household cleanser.

CONS: Glass sinks can be pricey, and they show soap and water spots easily.

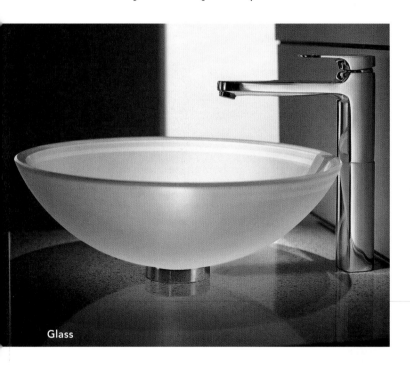

Glass

FIRECLAY

In use since the 19th century, fireclay, like vitreous china, is made from a clay-and-mineral mixture, but is fired at a higher temperature, making it even more resistant to extreme heat. The difference between the two lies primarily in the manufacturing process rather than the material itself. Fireclay is smooth and nonporous, and it won't fade or discolor. Its strength makes it the material of choice for many pedestals and console-style vanities. "Thicker and more dense than those made from vitreous china," says Travis Rotelli of Kohler, "fireclay sinks are found more often in the kitchen than in the bath."

PROS: Fireclay sinks are lead-free and highly resistant to chips, stains, and scratches.

CONS: Sometimes heavy, they often require additional structural support.

Fireclay

STAINLESS STEEL

Stainless-steel sinks come in several gauges, or thicknesses. Thicker metals are naturally more durable—and expensive. Stainless-steel lavs are available in high-end mirrorlike finishes, but it's just extra buffing that gives them that brilliant shine. Brushed finishes don't compromise durability. "Stainless-steel sinks are very trendy, but they can be noisy and appear commercial and cold-feeling," says Gray Uhl of American Standard.

PROS: Stainless-steel sinks are tough and can withstand extreme temperatures.

CONS: Stainless steel scratches and dulls over time, and it comes in only one color.

Stainless steel

STONE

Bath sinks can be carved from an extraordinary array of natural stones—from granite and marble to onyx, limestone, and even petrified wood. Stone sinks are typically available in vessel (countertop) styles and in a variety of colors. Because stone is so porous, these sinks are often sealed before shipping. It's recommended that they be resealed every year; nevertheless, some designers advise against heavy daily use. "I did a half-granite rock with the middle scooped out. It was sculptural, but it weighed 150 lb." says architect Sophie Piesse. "Reinforcing it required a structural engineer and thousands of dollars."

ENAMELED CAST IRON

One of the oldest fixture materials, cast iron is also one of the most durable. When porcelain enamel (in a wide range of colors) is applied over cast iron, the result is a workhorse of a sink with incomparable gloss and shine. Because these sinks are made from such a trusted, long-lasting material, Kohler's come with a lifetime guarantee against cracks, chips, or burns. "Recycled iron (as much as 80%) is used in the manufacturing process, so these sinks are considered by many to be green products," says Travis Rotelli of Kohler.

PROS: Enameled cast-iron sinks are solid, affordable, and easy to clean.

CONS: Installation may require extra support—and helping hands.

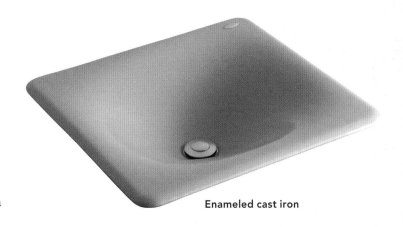

Enameled cast iron

Stone (marble)

PROS: Few fixtures steal the show like hand-carved stone sinks.

CONS: It's not uncommon for stone sinks to chip, break, or stain.

SYNTHETIC

Synthetic lavatories represent a broad range of price, quality, and appearance, from budget-friendly "cultured stone" to proprietary (and pricey) solid-surface materials. At the lower end, ground stone is mixed with synthetic resins, molded, and finished with a gel coating. Pricier solid-surface sinks are made from a blend of natural minerals and high-performance acrylics. Consistent colors and patterns run all the way through, allowing solid-surface materials to be cut, carved, routed, and inlaid to create a variety of designs. Because of the wide disparity in the quality of synthetic materials, it's important to do research.

PROS: Synthetic-sink options are endless and available at all price points. Expensive ones are durable and can be repaired and renewed by sanding.

CONS: Heat may discolor some of these sinks, and coatings may crack over time. Appearance varies greatly with price.

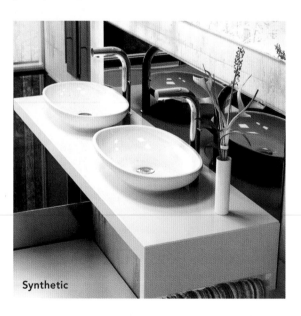

Synthetic

OTHER MATERIALS

A sink made of brass, bronze, copper, hammered copper, or nickel is a true statement piece. Most are found at the higher end of the price scale, with hand-crafted bronze among the most expensive. Brushed nickel has a warm, brown-tone appearance and a vintage feel. Copper has natural antibacterial properties.

PROS: Most metal sinks age gracefully, developing a soft patina.

CONS: Constant cleaning and care are required.

Cast-bronze

Sorting through shapes

Choosing the shape of your lavatory can feel like sitting down to a geometry lesson in which you measure every angle and carefully calculate the area inside and out of the sinks on your short list. It also can come down to an immediate response: the conviction that the flat, minimalist pool you saw online is a must-have for your new powder room. Designers see it both ways. While scale and proportion make certain shapes more suitable for a particular space, the choice often comes down to aesthetics. Although certain shapes inherently offer a more modern vibe (rectangles fall into this category) and others read as more traditional (ovals), almost any shape can work in any bath, depending on its material and general style. Given the imagination of today's sink designers, though, there's no question that shape has become one more critical consideration in choosing the perfect lav, and not always an easy one. "Let's say you come upon a really cool octagonal shape, and everyone agrees it's really cool," says Kallista's McKeone. "If it conflicts with everything else that's going on in the bath, is it really that cool?"

BOWLS

Hands down, the bowl-shaped vessel sink is the most artful option for any bath. Vessels get an A+ for the vast array of materials, sizes, and styles they reflect. While we're speaking here primarily of round, deep bowls with sloping sides, the term vessel has been used to describe a wide array of top-mounted sinks of various shapes, all designed to mimic a portable basin that's been set artfully on the flat surface of a countertop. Although vessel sinks are dismissed by some as trendy, most designers are convinced they are here to stay. "Vessel sinks are beautiful," says architect Sophie Piesse. "They can be very sculptural, but an inescapable truth is you've got to keep the inside and outside clean. More surface means room for fingerprints."

PROS: Our sources were unanimous: No sink makes a design statement better than a vessel.

CONS: Because of their height, vessel sinks often require wall-mounted faucets, of which there are fewer choices available; it also takes care to get the location and alignment right.

Vessel

ROUND

Today's round sinks edge a bit toward contemporary styling, but they've fallen out of favor with many designers, who see drop-in rounds as dated. Under-mount and vessel models, however, still retain something of a modern cachet. The most common size for round sinks is 15 in. dia. "Consumer feedback is showing that round sinks, although versatile, are not on as many homeowners' wish lists as you might think," Travis Rotelli of Kohler.

PROS: Round sinks tend to be smaller, so they can fit into tighter spaces.

CONS: Smaller round sinks can make it more difficult to keep splashing under control.

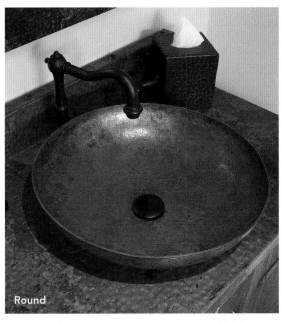

Round

WADING POOLS

The average, practical depth for a lavatory is 6 in. to 8 in., but some of the newer wading-pool sinks measure no more than 2 in. from lip to drain. "The trend over the past 10 years has been toward shallow sinks," says McKeone from Kallista. While these sinks play to drama, their shape owes its functionality to the trend toward sustainability. "It's really about water conservation," McKeone says. "We have flow restrictors now, so water is coming through at a lower pressure than in the past. Plus, it's a cool look." "As to practicality, there's a misconception that these sinks splash water everywhere. Not true. You just have to get used to how the sink and faucet work together," says Travis Rotelli of Kohler.

PROS: They're the sleekest, most provocative sinks on the market.

CONS: Detractors maintain that these edgy sinks create a splashfest and are nothing more than a passing fancy.

Wading pool

RECTANGULAR

The darling of many designers, the rectangular sink is both attractive and practical. Think about stretching your arms out and washing up, says Kohler's Rotelli: "A rectangular sink gives you plenty of room. It's far better than a square sink." The horizontal aspect of a rectangle also allows plenty of room for faucets while keeping splashes in check.

PROS: The rectangle is a great look that works for drop-ins as well as undermounts.

CONS: This sink's severe angles can seem out of sync in some more curvaceous baths.

Rectangular

SQUARE

Appealing in its simplicity, the square sink with vertical sidewalls and a flat bottom is a popular choice. That said, a square sink that's wide enough for washing is also going to be quite deep front to back, which may be problematic depending on the depth of the vanity. Designer Morris doesn't think square sinks need to be so severe. "I prefer square shapes, but not square bottoms. I like a scooped bottom because it softens the look and also drains better," she says.

PROS: Smaller squares work well in compact baths where twin sinks are a must.

CONS: A larger square sink on a conventional vanity top limits faucet selection.

Square

Consider size and scale

In the bath, as in any room, proportion can make the difference between a serviceable design and a great one. In finding a sink to fit your bath space, it's not just about the sink itself, but the surrounding area as well. Bath designer Ann Morris notes that with so many fixtures available, it's easy to create an illusion of comfort in less-than-ideal spaces. A tiny powder room, for example, feels more spacious with a sink that fits well, a faucet that suits it, and companion pieces (mirrors, lighting, etc.) that complement them both. The thinking among sink designers at American Standard, says Gray Uhl, is that counter space is as important to consumers as the sink they choose. He adds that accessibility—for children as well as homeowners who are aging in place—has never been as critical as it is today.

TROUGH

Trough-style sinks—those seriously oversize basins evocative of swimming pools—have been showing up in baths everywhere of late. Sleek and incomparably contemporary in style, most tend to be as shallow as they are wide. "A trough doesn't really satisfy the need for 'your sink, my sink.' Although it's a good look, it's one that risks looking institutional if not done right," says Gray Uhl of American Standard.

PROS: The wide scale of a trough sink suits large baths with expansive counters.

CONS: Most are at the high end of the price scale.

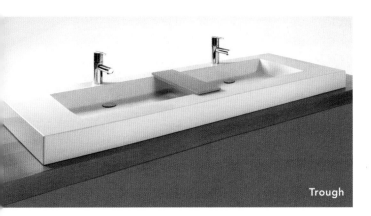

Trough

COMPACT

There's a clear need for small sinks that look good—especially in powder rooms used exclusively by guests. Most manufacturers recognize that and have added compact lavatories (in pedestal, wall-mount, and vanity styles) to their collections. Porcher offers its popular Solutions line, while Kohler's Tresham integrated vanity-top sink measures only 19½ in. from front to back. "Nixing the vanity frees up floor space, making wall mounts a good choice for a small bath, both physically and psychologically," says architect Paul DeGroot.

PROS: New compact designs can add style to even the tightest baths.

CONS: Smaller sinks don't typically offer much in the way of counter space.

Petit pedestal

Style at any price

With such a wide variety in materials, manufacturers, and designs, prices for bath sinks vary widely—even within the confines of a single type. Here's just a small sample of what's available at various price points in the vessel category.

Clear glass vessel. $115

Sandstone vessel. $350

Rectangular oil-rubbed bronze vessel. $1,007

Wavelet decorative vessel in copper. $4,995

Seven Basic Styles of Bathroom Sink

BY DON BURGARD

Kitchen sinks not only have to accommodate pots and pans but also have to withstand the beating that these items regularly inflict on sink basins. By contrast, bathroom sinks only have to be big enough to fit a pair of hands comfortably and durable enough to withstand hot tap water.

Because of this limited purpose, manufacturers have been free to develop a dizzying array of designs, which can make choosing a bathroom sink as much an aesthetic decision as a practical one. Even so, most bathroom sinks come in a handful of basic styles, each of which has pros and cons.

Pedestal

Pedestal sinks look like birdbaths. They come in two parts, with a wall-mounted sink sitting atop a pedestal secured to the floor. The pedestal is open in the back to provide access for the drainpipe and supply lines.

PROS:

- This can be a practical, attractive choice for a small space where there isn't room for cabinetry.
- If adequate storage exists elsewhere, a pedestal sink's unique design can enhance the look of a small or medium-size bathroom.

CONS:

- The sink attaches to the wall, which means you'll have to install blocking behind the finished wall if it's not there already.
- Having no cabinet, shelves, or counter, a pedestal sink provides no storage space.

Pedestal

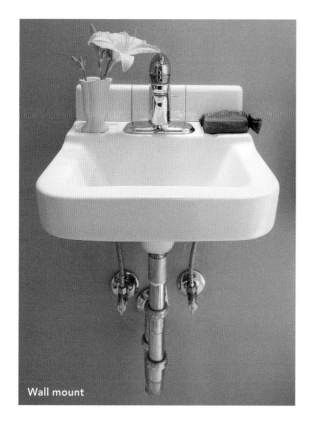

Wall mount

Integral

Wall mount

These sinks attach to the wall only and are open underneath. Some, called semipedestal sinks, come with shrouds that cover the plumbing all the way to the wall.

PROS:

- Most units can fit into small or even tiny spaces.
- A wall-mount sink is the only type that doesn't take up any floor space.
- The open space underneath a wall-mount sink usually provides easy wheelchair access.

CONS:

- As with a pedestal sink, you may need to install blocking in the wall.
- This sink provides no storage space.

Integral

An integral sink is of one piece with the surrounding counter and can be made from a wide variety of materials.

PROS:

- Installation is simple: Sink and countertop are installed at the same time.
- One-piece construction means no crevices for capturing dirt, hair, or other debris.

CONS:

- Replacing a sink means replacing a countertop as well, and vice versa.
- There's no opportunity for creatively matching a counter with a sink.

Drop in

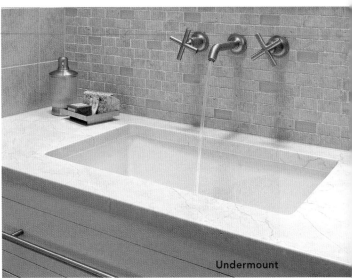

Undermount

Drop in

Drop-in sinks, also called self-rimming sinks, fit inside a hole cut in the countertop. The rim rests on the edge of the hole and is secured to the countertop with a waterproof sealant, such as silicone caulk. Fixtures are usually installed through the back of the rim, so these sinks can be purchased with the necessary holes already drilled.

PROS:

- The cutout in the counter doesn't need to be finished; it can remain rough because it will be covered by the sink and won't be seen.
- The vanity cabinet hides the drainpipe and water supplies.

CONS:

- The sink rim makes it impossible to wipe water from the counter into the sink.
- These sinks tend more toward the practical than the beautiful.

Undermount

Unlike a drop-in sink, an undermount sink is attached to the counter from below. This means that the counter edges must be finished rather than remaining rough cut. A support structure generally isn't necessary with cast-iron bathroom sinks, which are smaller and lighter than their kitchen counterparts.

PROS:

- Has a sleeker appearance than drop-in sinks.
- With no rim in the way, you can wipe water from the counter directly into the sink.

CONS:

- Unless you remove the vanity top, you can't install an undermount sink as a retrofit.
- An undermount installation leaves the edges of the cutout exposed, so these sinks can be used only with waterproof countertop materials, such as granite, marble, or a solid-surface synthetic.

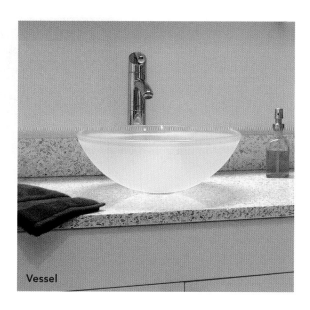

Vessel

Console

Vessel

Vessel sinks sit atop the vanity and are exposed on all sides. As a result, they often are as much pieces of sculpture as functional sinks. They come in the largest range of materials, including glass, marble, and cast bronze, as well as more common materials, such as vitreous china and fireclay. Vessel sinks have no faucet holes, so fixtures need to be mounted on the wall or on the counter. They also don't have overflow holes, so if you have children and/or are absentminded, you'll probably want to install a grid drain rather than a stopper drain.

PROS:
- No matter what they're made of, vessel sinks are visually striking.
- Because the hole cut in the countertop is very small, much more material remains, allowing the counter to complement the sink visually rather than just providing a place for it to rest.

CONS:
- Although vessel sinks made from vitreous china can cost $200 or less, vessels made from other materials can cost thousands of dollars.
- Because it sits atop the vanity rather than inside it, a vessel sink may need to be coupled with a vanity that is less than standard height.

Console

Console sinks share some characteristics with pedestal and wall-mount sinks. Like those styles, they don't sit atop cabinets, although some have drawers or a shelf for a limited amount of storage. Console sinks can either be freestanding, in which case they are supported by four legs, or mounted to the wall and supported by two or four legs. These legs can be anything from simple steel tubes to decorative posts made from the same material as the sink, such as vitreous china or fireclay.

PROS:
- If the legs are far enough apart, a console sink can accommodate a person in a wheelchair.
- The extra width usually allows for some space on each side of the basin for toiletries.
- With some designs, towel bars can be added to the sides.

CONS:
- Its extra width makes a console sink too big for a small bathroom.
- Plumbing is usually exposed, so PVC or ABS drainpipes are probably out of the question.
- Wall-mounted models may require blocking.

Tubs for Small Spaces

BY JEFFERSON KOLLE

A standard bathtub is 60 in. long and 30 in. to 32 in. wide. There's no such thing as a standard bathroom, though, especially because people are tucking them into smaller spaces in their homes.

To help outfit these compact spaces, several manufacturers make standard-shape tubs in small sizes. For instance, Vintage Tub & Bath® (www.vintagetub. com) sells a 4-ft.-long claw-foot tub with a 29-gal. capacity. Before you envision a lanky movie cowboy shivering uncomfortably in a galvanized basin, though, know that there are small tubs that still hold a lot of water. A corner, safety, or soaking tub could be just what you need.

Before you buy a small tub, it's a good idea to study all the literature. Most tubs are sold without fixtures, which can get quite pricey, and drains. For something as large as a tub, even a small one, shipping can be expensive—and don't forget return shipping if you make a mistake. Talk to your plumber about any reservations either of you might have; know that some soaking tubs may not have built-in overflow drains. If you're going to do your own installation, plan on a few trips to the plumbing-supply store.

Small tubs for renovations

Adding a small tub to an existing bathroom or turning a small room in your house into a bathroom can present a set of problems beyond just finding the floor space. Or maybe your home already has a small bath that needs updating.

Tub drain-line traps typically hang in the bay between floor joists. This can present problems in existing homes, especially older ones that might have joists less than 8 in. deep. In some cases, you may not be able to access a finished ceiling below where you want to install a tub, or there could be a beam or other structural member that can't be cut.

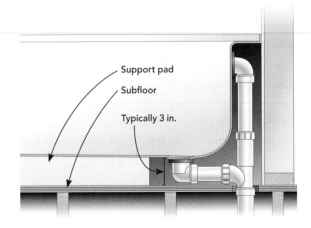

Support pad

Subfloor

Typically 3 in.

AMERICAN STANDARD'S AFR tub makes adding a tub to an existing space simpler.

Manufacturers have the perfect workaround for cases such as these. Above-floor-drain (AFD)—sometimes known as above-floor rough-in (AFR)—tubs are built on a pedestal so that drainpipes can run under the tub but above the floor joists (see drawing on the facing page). This means that you won't have to cut into the existing floor to plumb a drain. From outside the tub, AFD models appear to be deep, but if you look into the tub basin, you'll see otherwise.

American Standard's Princeton® AFR tub (see photo above) is 60 in. by 30 in. with an exterior height of 17½ in. However, the bathing depth is only 13¼ in. Kohler's Dynametric® AFR tub is 60 in. by 32 in. with a 16¼-in. height. The bathing depth is 13 in., and the tub holds 35 gal.

If ceiling-height clearances are minimal, there may not be enough headroom to stand up in an AFD tub.

Corner Tubs: A Fit for Unused Spaces

An unused corner in a small bathroom can be the perfect place to shoehorn in a corner tub. Available as either freestanding or drop-in units (which require you to build a surround), they are made in a variety of materials and colors.

Canadian-based Neptune (www.produitsneptune.com) has a corner tub called the Wind that is as sleek as it sounds (see photo below). The Wind is somewhere between a standard rectangular tub and a traditional triangular corner tub. The 60-in. by 30-in. by 20-in. tapered footprint is 21 in. deep, and holds 56 gal.

THE WIND CORNER TUB by Neptune could be the perfect shape for an unused corner of your bathroom.

WALK-IN TUBS ARE NOT JUST FOR THE IMMOBILE

AMONG OTHER THINGS, the Americans with Disabilities Act (www.ada.gov) made buildings more accessible to people in wheelchairs. It also gave rise to a whole line of walk-in bathtubs that are easy to get in and out of for people who might have trouble lifting their legs over the high wall of a standard tub.

Walk-in tubs are equipped with watertight, in-swinging hinged doors. When the tub is filled, water pressure pushes the door tighter to the jamb, securing the seal. The bathing position is more upright than in a conventional tub; you sit while bathing, rather than lie horizontally.

Consequently, while the tubs' footprints are smaller, their water capacities can be as generous as standard tubs. (Think of the difference between a bowl filled with water and a drinking glass filled with water.) It's common for these tubs to be equipped with sturdy stainless-steel handrails, but before you think that they are going to make your beautiful bathroom look like a dreary nursing home, know that they are sleek, elegant, and designed for residential use.

Walk-in tubs are more complicated, and the price reflects that added complexity. Prices range from $1600 to $5500, depending on the size, material, and amenities (faucets, whirlpool, or air jets).

Safety Tubs® (www.safetytubs.com) makes a line of walk-in tubs, the smallest of which has a footprint of 48 in. by 28 in. by 38 in. The tubs are either acrylic or gel-coated fiberglass, and they have a water capacity of 45 gal. A built-in seat is molded into the body of the tub, and you can order them with water and/or bubble jets.

Acrylic tubs are vacuum-formed over a mold and are reinforced with fiberglass, creating a continuous, nonporous waterproof membrane. Gel-coat tubs are made from colored polyester resins sprayed into a mold and reinforced with fiberglass particles. Generally, acrylic tubs cost more than gel-coat models, but they are stronger, retain their glossy, colorfast finish longer, and are easier to clean.

The Model 2645, the smallest walk-in tub made by Bathing Solutions (www.bathing solutions.com), is only 26 in. by 45 in. by 47 in., making it easy to fit through even the smallest doorway.

Walk-in tubs are made in a variety of configurations; you can specify a left- or right-swinging door, which is handy for small bathrooms. Many have more than one drain and often a pump that helps the water to evacuate quickly so that you don't have to sit too long in cooling water before you are able to swing open the door.

Soaking Tubs: Deep Bath, Small Footprint

In traditional Japanese culture, bathing is a full-immersion experience—a contemplative ritual. Similar to walk-in tubs, Japanese tubs are deep and are often equipped with a seat. Although some are large enough to accommodate the whole family at once, many single-person soaking tubs are perfect for smaller bathrooms. Available in materials from traditional coopered-wood slats to stone, composites, or metal, soaking tubs can be built into a tiled surround or mounted freestanding on the floor.

If you're considering a freestanding tub, talk to your plumber about installing a floor drain in your bathroom. It can be relatively cheap insurance against wayward splashes, especially when exuberant children are involved.

Premier Copper Products (www.premiercopper products.com) makes a cylindrical, hammered-copper Japanese-style tub with an inner diameter of 39 in. and a height of 36 in. (see photo right). Pricey and beautiful, the tub includes a built-in seat. If stone is your particular extravagance, check out the Oval Soaking Tub (see photo below) made by Stone Forest® (www.stoneforest.com). You also should consult a structural engineer for this one; the dry weight of the 48-in. by 39-in. by 42-in. tub, which has a 100-gal. capacity, is 2,400 lb.

If you want to save some of your bathing-experience funds for new rubber duckies, there are a few soaking tubs that will cost you a lot less. The freestanding Ofulo 1—from At House (www.at-house.com)—has inside dimensions of 31½ in. by 23½ in. by 23½ in. and a 66-gal. capacity (see photo below right). The fiberglass tub, made in Japan, is primarily meant to be installed in an existing shower and drains into the shower's drain. It's available in either a left- or right-hand drain and has an integral cover.

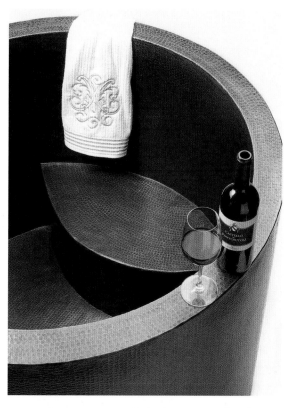

PREMIER COPPER PRODUCT'S Japanese-style tub

STONE FOREST'S oval soaking tub

AT HOUSE'S freestanding Ofulo 1

Freestanding Tubs

BY MARIA LAPIANA

In many ways, the shower—in all its walk-in, double-wide, steam-powered, glass-tiled glory—has eclipsed the tub in today's upscale bath. There's no doubt that showers are more practical than tubs if all you want to do is get really clean really fast (they call it performance showering in the industry). But what if you'd prefer to wash the day away with immersion in a deep, soothing bath—and make a design statement in the process? Consider the current darling of bath designers: the freestanding tub.

STONE FOREST OVAL SOAKING TUBE Marble

STONE FOREST NATURAL Granite

AMERICAN STANDARD CADET Acrylic

BARTOK DESIGNS
Hinoki wood

WETSTYLE BBE01-SHELF
Composite and wood

NATIVE TRAILS
AURORA Nickel

BISAZZA BAGNO SOAPBATH
Fiberglass

MAAX SAX Fiberglass

Freestanding bathtubs have been around since ancient times. In the 19th century, the classic claw-foot was considered a symbol of affluence. It eventually became mainstream, but its dominance was soon challenged. Thanks to advances in plumbing (and Kohler), the first built-in tub was introduced in 1911 and went on to replace the stand-alone claw-foot as the bathroom mainstay for 50 years. In the 1960s, wall-hugging tubs laid claim to the luxury market as well, with the introduction by Jacuzzi® of the jetted spa tub.

But the freestanding tub is enjoying renewed popularity. That may be due to the many features and design options freestanding tubs offer. They're available in a wide array of sizes and shapes, and in materials ranging from acrylic to cast iron, natural stone, copper, and even wood. Although purists scoff, those who seek a massage or light show along with their soak will find in many freestanding models a plethora of features more commonly associated with spa tubs: air jets, hydrotherapy systems, chromotherapy, aromatherapy, and sound systems.

These days, there's a tub out there to suit every style, including minimalist bath designs that intentionally frame the tub as a sculptural work—which many of today's tubs are. (The Soapbath, designed by Marcel Wanders for Italian maker Bisazza Bagno and shown on p. 63, takes creativity to a whole new level.) "The freestanding tub has really become the focal point or centerpiece of a room," says Rebecca Seiler, bathing product manager for Kohler. "They're doubling as works of art. It's the perfect blend of design and function."

Another reason freestanding tubs are so popular is that they're flexible. Equipped with a floor-mounted filler, the typical tub—at 60 in. to 66 in. long and 30 in. to 40 in. wide—can be placed practically anywhere. Even in tight places, the air around and under them gives the impression of spaciousness. "People are moving into smaller homes, and while the definition of luxury is now an en suite bath for every bedroom, we're having to scale down those spaces," says Gray Uhl, brand education director at American Standard Brands. In luxury baths, gracious stand-alones have taken the place of the once-popular whirlpool tub, possibly due to environmental concerns. "The beauty of most freestanding tubs is that they don't have pumps or motors," Uhl says. "In general, they are only large enough to fit one person, so they use less water, too." Add to that the trend toward simpler baths—rooms that evoke a Zen-like calm—and you have a serious demand for beautiful, freestanding fonts of relaxation.

When Maria Stapperfenne reviewed the entries to the bath category for the 2014 National Kitchen and Bath Association Design Competition, she was overwhelmed by the number of freestanding tubs she saw. "We looked at literally hundreds of entries," says Stapperfenne, president of the NKBA. "Virtually every full bath had a freestanding tub in it. No kidding. No more built-ins. We're done with them."

Designed to catch the eye

That said, Stapperfenne acknowledges that freestanding tubs are not for everyone, particularly if there are young children to bathe or if a family member would have difficulty climbing into a freestanding tub. "Let's just say this is not the kind of tub you'd see in universal design," she says.

There are essentially three styles of freestanding tubs: floor-set models, which sit directly on the floor; footed tubs (the iconic claw-foot remains a popular choice); and pedestals, which have a plinth or frame that raises the basin off the floor. In terms of shape, today's models run the gamut, from rectangular tubs to oblong tubs to graceful slipper tubs, which have a sloped end that is higher than the other end. Then there are soaking tubs—deep basins with strong vertical sides. In traditional Japanese culture, these ritual-specific tubs, known as ofuro, are designed for leisurely, restorative immersion—but only after a shower. Made of aromatic woods such as hinoki, a type of cypress with antibacterial qualities, the tubs release a soothing, wood-and-citrus scent when filled.

Just as they can satisfy any design style, freestanding tubs are available in a wide range of prices—from no-frills models just under $1000 to such products as American Standard's Cadet®, a retro design equipped with a tub filler and hand spray that sells for around $1800 to the Clothilde, an elegant, tin-lined copper tub from Waterworks® that can be yours for a little over $46,000. What you typically get at the higher end is an emphasis on quality and design, says Kohler's Seiler. In addition to some of the more glamorous material choices like marble or copper, she says, "you get thoughtfully placed curves, more comfort in integral lumbar supports, and depth, which delivers a more luxurious experience."

Whatever your budget, be sure you are the one to choose your tub. "Take a test drive," says Stapperfenne. "It may seem silly, but you should get in, with your clothes on, and see how it feels." Consider length: Can you stretch your legs out to a relaxed position? Consider the backrest: How tall is it? Does the slope feel good? Consider ease of entry: Can you step over the sides easily? Even the most beautiful tub won't enhance your bath if you find that you don't use it.

Russell Adams, president and chief of design for MTI®, has a different take. "We think of our tubs as art for the bath," he says. "You may not be using it every day, but you are walking by it. We make sure our tubs are relaxing, even just to look at."

Tub materials: Design flexibility meets everyday durability

ACRYLIC

Common and available in many styles, acrylic tubs are made from vacuum-formed acrylic sheets reinforced with fiberglass.

PROS: Durable; lightweight; easy to install; available in many colors, shapes, and sizes

CONS: Easily scratched if cleaned with abrasive products

ACRYLIC Acri-Tec VT180B

ENAMELED CAST IRON

These "old school" tubs are made by pouring molten iron into a mold, then smoothing it and coating it with a heavy layer of enamel.

PROS: Strong and durable; resistant to scratches, cracks, and chips

CONS: Very heavy; may require extra labor and floor reinforcement to install

ENAMELED CAST IRON Kohler Iron Works Historic Bath

ENGINEERED STONE/COMPOSITE

To make these tubs, a mixture of ground minerals and resin or other binding agents is liquefied, poured into a mold, and hardened. Because these mixtures are proprietary, characteristics and quality vary widely.

PROS: Durable; heat and stain resistant; less porous than natural stone

CONS: Can be prone to hairline cracks if surface coating wears away

ENGINEERED STONE MTI Elise 2

NATURAL STONE

Many natural stones—such as granite, onyx, sandstone, travertine, and marble—can be carved into freestanding tubs.

PROS: Very elegant; organic in appearance

CONS: Extremely heavy and, in most cases, requires reinforcement of the floor; very expensive

NATURAL STONE Stone Forest Oval

METAL

Often hammered and sometimes coated on the inside, genuine copper tubs are warm and natural looking. By contrast, tubs made of nickel or stainless steel exude a more contemporary vibe.

PROS: Elegant; durable; requires minimal maintenance; develops a natural patina over time (copper)

CONS: Usually must be custom-made; very expensive

METAL Native Trails Aspen in copper

WOOD

Often made of teak, but available in other woods, these tubs are harder to find than most. They may or may not be sealed.

PROS: Can be customized and finished

CONS: Best used as a dedicated soaking tub; expensive

WOOD Zen Bathworks®

FIBERGLASS

These tubs are made by forming layers of fiberglass into a desired shape, then coating it with gel-coat resin. (It's also known as FRP, or fiberglass-reinforced plastic.) Cost and quality vary greatly.

PROS: Lightweight; easy to install; finish can be repaired

CONS: Cheap fiberglass tubs are prone to flexing and are not very durable

FIBERGLASS Maax Sax

ISSUES WITH BIG TUBS: WEIGHT AND FLOW

Freestanding tubs are generally deeper and hold more water than the average built-in, which raises two issues worth thinking about: getting the tub filled fast, and making sure your bathroom floor is strong enough to support it once it's filled. While an average built-in tub holds 30 gal. of water, deep stand-alone models can hold twice that.

EPA standards limit the flow of water from showerheads and bath faucets to 2.5 gpm (gal. per minute) and 2.2 gpm, respectively, but when it comes to filling a bathtub, slowing down the rate of flow is the last thing you want to do. Say you have a 60-gal. tub. A filler rated at 16 gpm will fill the tub in just under 4 minutes. Slow the flow down to 7 gpm, and the tub will take nearly 9 minutes to fill. That not only means waiting longer for your splash; it also means more time for the hot water in the tub to cool off.

To ensure a good flow rate, your tub filler—whether it's mounted on the deck, the wall, or the floor—should be connected to a ¾-in. supply line. If you're considering a really big tub, make sure your water heater has the capacity to deliver that much hot water at once. A final consideration, notes Danbury, Conn., plumber Mike Lombardi, is that your tub's drain and vent need to be sized to remove large amounts of water without siphoning. Most large-capacity tubs can be connected with a 1½-in.-dia. trap and drain, but the waste arm shouldn't exceed 6 ft. If your stand-alone tub is out in the middle of a large bathroom, a 2-in.-dia. drainpipe will allow you to increase this distance to 8 ft.

Unless they're made of stone or another inherently heavy material, freestanding tubs are themselves no heavier than most built-ins; however, the large number of gallons they hold (at just over 8 lb. per gal.) can put a lot of strain on a floor system. Despite this, freestanding tubs usually do not require additional floor support in new homes built to code, Lombardi says. Still, most manufacturers' installation instructions recommend that you confirm the floor's load rating before installation. If support appears to be an issue (in older homes, for example, or where joists are notched or damaged), it may pay to consult an engineer. When the feet on a footed tub land in the middle of a joist bay, installing solid blocking below can prevent subfloor deflection and cracked tiles.

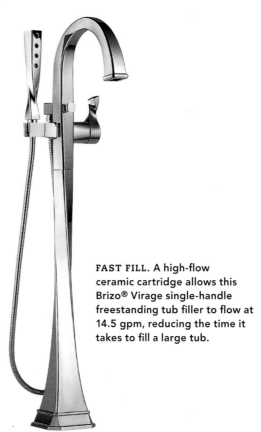

FAST FILL. A high-flow ceramic cartridge allows this Brizo® Virage single-handle freestanding tub filler to flow at 14.5 gpm, reducing the time it takes to fill a large tub.

The Basics of Bath Fans

BY MARTIN HOLLADAY

In the old days, if your bathroom was smelly or humid, you opened a window to air it out. Doing so in the dead of winter or the dog days of summer, however, came with an energy and comfort penalty.

Surprisingly, modern building codes still support the use of windows for bath ventilation. According to the 2009 and 2012 International Residential Code (sections R303.3 and M1507.3), bathrooms with an operable window don't need a fan.

Bath fans are great at exhausting humid or smelly air, so (in spite of the code loophole) every bathroom should have one.

How much ventilation do I need?

According to code, a bathroom without a window must have an exhaust fan with a ventilation rate of 50 cfm for intermittent operation or 20 cfm for continuous operation. In the past, many builders and code officials interpreted this to mean that the fan should be rated at 50 cfm. Yet once a 50-cfm fan is connected to ductwork, it may move only 25 cfm because of the duct's static pressure.

That's why conscientious builders and most green-building programs call for bath-fan airflow to be verified. The old trick of putting a single square of toilet paper on the grille won't cut it. Instead, you need a device such as the Exhaust Fan Flow Meter from Energy Conservatory® (energyconservatory.com).

A SMARTER FAN. With an electronically commutated motor, the Panasonic® WhisperGreen Select™ boosts fan speed automatically to compensate for static pressure within the ductwork. It also can be equipped with a time-delay feature, humidistats, and occupancy sensors for more precise ventilation control.

CHECK THE FLOW. Check the exact cfm with a digital manometer and a device such as the Exhaust-Fan Flow Meter to confirm that the fan is delivering the ventilation required by code and by green-building programs.

Where does the makeup air come from?

If the door is closed and the bathroom fan is exhausting 50 cfm, then an equivalent volume of makeup air is coming into the bathroom.

If the bathroom has an exterior wall, some of the makeup air is coming from the exterior—through leaks around the window, for example. Many bath fans also pull some makeup air from the crack between the fan housing and the ceiling drywall. You don't really want unconditioned air to be entering the bathroom through this route, so you should seal that crack when installing a fan. You should also make sure that the crack between the bottom of the bathroom door and the bathroom floor is wide enough to allow makeup air into the bathroom. When makeup air comes from under the door, an equivalent amount of exterior air is entering the house through holes in the home's building

envelope. The exhausting of conditioned interior air and the replacement of it with unconditioned air from the outside is an energy penalty associated with running a bath fan, so you don't want to use it more than necessary.

Let's say your fan is only pulling 35 cfm—not enough to satisfy code or green-building program requirements. You could swap it for a more powerful model, or you could fix the ductwork by increasing its diameter, by using smooth-walled pipe instead of flex duct, or by reducing the number of elbows. Any of these approaches will work, but the last one will result in quieter operation, likely will be less expensive, and will use less energy.

Why does a bath fan have two cfm and noise ratings?

Most fan manufacturers rate fan performance at two static pressures: 0.1 inches of water column (i.w.c.) and 0.25 i.w.c. Because the installed duct system for a bath fan is likely to have at least 0.25 i.w.c. of static pressure, you should use this figure when comparing fan ratings.

More sophisticated fans—those with electronically commutated motors—adjust fan speed in response to the duct system's static pressure. At higher static pressures, these fans ventilate better, but they use more power (in watts) to achieve full airflow. Fan noisiness is measured in sones. The lower the sone rating, the quieter the fan. Manufacturers list sone ratings at 0.1 i.w.c. and 0.25 i.w.c. Use the rating at 0.25 i.w.c. for the most accurate estimate of noise. You should choose a fan rated at less than 1 sone at 0.25 i.w.c.

What makes a fan efficient?

If you want an efficient fan, look for an Energy Star model. Energy Star fans rated at 89 cfm or less must have a minimum efficiency of 1.4 cfm per watt. Fans rated at 90 cfm or more have a minimum efficiency of 2.8 cfm per watt. The Energy Star program also establishes maximum sone ratings. Fans rated at

139 cfm or less must have a maximum sone rating of 2.0. Fans rated at 140 cfm or more must have a maximum sone rating of 3.0 sones.

Because fans use electricity and remove conditioned air from a building, they should be sized appropriately and should be operated only as long as required.

The simplest way to control a bath fan is to wire the fan to come on with the bathroom light, but it's better to install a time-delay switch to operate the fan for five or 10 minutes after the switch is turned off.

Humidity-sensing switches are also available. This type of switch usually includes an override that allows the fan to be turned on regardless of the humidity level. These switches often have to be adjusted seasonally because humidity levels are generally higher in the summer than in the winter.

Some fans—for example, Panasonic's WhisperSense™ fan—include motion sensors, time-delay features, and humidity controls, eliminating the need for a special switch. If your bathroom seems damp, you should run the fan more often or longer after showers. If your bathroom always seems overly dry, you may be wasting energy by running your fan too much.

TIPS FOR INSTALLING A BATH FAN

IN ADDITION TO FOLLOWING THE MANUFACTURER'S INSTRUCTIONS, be sure to do the following:

- Verify that there is a ¾-in. to 1-in. gap between the bottom of the bathroom door and the finished flooring for makeup air.
- Seal the crack between the fan housing and the ceiling drywall with caulk.
- Check the backdraft damper inside the fan to ensure that it operates smoothly and that it wasn't taped shut at the factory.
- Use 6-in. duct rather than 4-in. duct for long or complicated runs. For all runs, choose smooth-wall galvanized duct or thin-wall PVC pipe over flex duct. However, you can use a 2-ft. length of flex duct between the fan and the rigid ductwork to reduce noise.
- In cold climates, install any attic duct so that there's a rise above the fan and then a long, gently sloping horizontal run toward the termination. This moves condensation outside.
- Make duct runs as short and straight as possible, and install the fan's

duct connection so that it's aimed toward the termination to minimize the need for elbows.

- Support ducts every 3 ft. with hangers or strapping to prevent sagging.
- Verify that the louvers or flapper at the termination are operating smoothly.
- Terminate attic ductwork at a gable wall (first choice) or roof (second choice)—never in attics or soffits. In heating climates, insulate the ducts to minimize condensation within the ductwork.

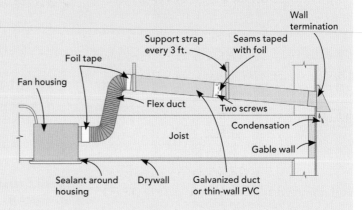

Wall termination

Support strap every 3 ft.

Seams taped with foil

Foil tape

Fan housing

Flex duct

Two screws

Condensation

Joist

Gable wall

Sealant around housing

Drywall

Galvanized duct or thin-wall PVC

Tile Backerboard Options

BY MARTIN HOLLADAY

Forty years ago, ceramic floor and wall tiles were always set in a mortar bed. Then a few builders experimented with gluing wall tiles to water-resistant drywall (aka greenboard), a method that later was outlawed because it led to mushy drywall and moldy studs.

A better solution hit the market in the early 1970s when manufacturers introduced cement backerboard. These panels are impervious to water, so they proved to be an excellent substrate for tiled tub surrounds, shower walls, countertops, and floors.

Since then, several newer types of tile backerboard—made from materials including fiber cement, gypsum, and polystyrene—have been introduced. Most of them cost about the same, except for polystyrene backerboard, which tends to be more expensive.

There is no consensus among tile contractors about which type of backerboard is best. Each material has its strengths; while one material might be more water resistant, a competing material might weigh less or be easier to cut. Adam Bey-Wagner, a tile contractor in New Fairfield, Conn., is a fan of HardieBacker®. "HardieBacker is more fibrous than regular cementboards. There's not as much aggregate. If you stand up a 3-ft. by 5-ft. piece of Durock® or cement backerboard and shake it back and forth,

it starts to lose its rigidity. HardieBacker stays stiff. It doesn't fall apart in water, and it's mold resistant."

Tom Meehan, a tile contractor in Harwich, Mass., has a different opinion. "My preferred backerboard, hands down, is Durock," he says. "It's lighter than other backerboards, and it cuts beautifully. Durock is as close to Sheetrock® as you are going to get. HardieBacker tends to break at the corners, and it's

AN ALL-TIME FAVORITE. Faster and easier than an old-fashioned mud job, cement backerboards are still a popular choice for their low cost and indifference to water.

WHEN TO BACK UP YOUR BACKERBOARD

When backerboard is installed on an exterior wall, should a vapor retarder or vapor barrier be installed between the backerboard and the studs? There is no simple answer.

Building codes requiring a vapor retarder—often interpreted to mean a layer of plastic—on the warm-in-winter side of a wall have been changing, and the use of plastic has fallen out of favor.

It's also important to remember that when a shower is located on an exterior wall, there are at least two potential moisture worries: vapor diffusion and bulk-water leaks.

Some backerboards, including polystyrene backerboards and gypsum-core backerboards such as Dens-Shield® and GreenGlass®, are already vapor retarders. In these cases, no additional vapor retarder is necessary or recommended, even when it is installed on an exterior wall.

Other types of backerboard, including cement backerboard and fiber-cement backerboard, are vapor permeable. The permeance of HardieBacker ranges from 1.75 perms to 2.84 perms, depending on thickness, making it fairly permeable to water vapor. Although manufacturers of cement backerboard have not had their products tested for vapor permeance, it's safe to say that cement backerboard is highly permeable.

Manufacturers of cement backerboard generally recommend that a moisture barrier of some sort (WonderBoard calls for #15 felt or 4-mil polyethylene sheeting) be installed behind the backerboard when used in a wet location.

According to some tile contractors, however, this is bad advice. "Plastic is a bad idea because you are nailing it on and putting holes in it," says Tom Meehan. "When there is plastic, I've found mold behind the plastic. It locks any moisture behind it, and the moisture can't dry." If you want to waterproof the wall, Meehan recommends the use of a liquid-applied membrane such as Laticrete™ Hydro Ban® or Mapei® Mapelastic™ AquaDefense on top of the backerboard. For a steam shower, he prefers a sheet membrane from Schlüter® or Noble.

hard to get an even cut without the $180 shears. Plus, it can't be installed outdoors or in steam showers."

Jane Aeon, a tile contractor in Berkeley, Calif., agrees. "I like Durock," she says. "HardieBacker sucks up thinset, and the thinset sets up too quickly. When you are trying to adjust tiles, you have more time with Durock or WonderBoard®."

As long as you choose a material recommended for the type of location where you intend to install it, any of the materials mentioned here should work well.

Cement

The first ½-in.-thick cement backerboard products on the market weighed between 3.75 lb. and 4 lb. per sq. ft. (WonderBoard still has a weight in that range.) Later, backerboards made with lightweight aggregate were introduced. These ½-in.-thick products weigh only 3 lb. per sq. ft.

Each brand of cement backerboard feels different. WonderBoard looks like the cement backerboard of the 1970s: very dense. Durock and Util-a-Crete® have more air bubbles and a lighter aggregate than WonderBoard. As Jane Aeon says, "WonderBoard is more crunchy than Durock."

Different aggregates produce backerboards with different qualities. PermaBase®, for example, includes small spheres of polystyrene that reduce the material's density. "Once I wanted to put in a soap dish the day after I had set some tiles," says Aeon. "When I took off the tiles, the PermaBase backerboard just disintegrated. Removing the tiles destroyed the backerboard. That wouldn't happen with any other type of backerboard."

Like concrete, cement backerboard is unaffected by water, so it can be installed indoors or outdoors, on floors, walls, ceilings, and countertops. While not susceptible to water damage, cement backerboard is not a moisture barrier, and it tends to wick water. In a wet environment (a shower, for example), it is important to install a waterproof membrane—either on top of the backerboard (when using a liquid-applied membrane) or behind the backerboard to stop water from reaching the wall studs or subfloor.

Cement backerboard is available in a variety of thicknesses. Thin products (¼-in.- and ⅜-in.-thick panels) are reserved for use over plywood or oriented strand board (OSB) and for tiled countertops or floors. For walls, most installers choose ½-in. or ⅝-in. backerboard. While ½-in. backerboard is suitable for most jobs, ⅝-in. backerboard might be specified for heavy tile or to match the thickness of adjacent drywall. The most common panel size is 3 ft. by 5 ft., sized to make quick work of preparing standard tub surrounds.

Some types of cement backerboard, including PermaBase Flex Cement Board, are flexible enough to be installed on curved substrates. Be careful, though; bend them too far, and they will crack.

INSTALLATION

To cut cement backerboard, score it with a utility knife, and snap it like drywall. To cut holes for showerheads, toilet flanges, or other penetrations, carbide-tipped hole saws are an excellent choice. You can also score the circumference of the hole with a utility knife or by drilling a series of small holes, then knock out the center with a hammer.

When installed on walls, cement backerboard requires a maximum stud spacing of 16 in. on center. It is fastened to studs with 1¼-in. backerboard screws or 1½-in. galvanized roofing nails spaced 8 in. on center (or 6 in. on center for ceilings). Backerboard screws are available from both U.S. Gypsum and Custom Building Products.

Most manufacturers require installers to leave a ⅛-in. gap between adjacent panels; the gap acts as a key for the thinset used to tape the seam. Seams should be taped with alkali-resistant fiberglass mesh tape. Don't use fiberglass drywall tape, which may not be able to resist the alkali corrosion associated with cement-based mortars.

When installed on a floor, cement backerboard must be set in a ¼-in.-thick support bed of thinset mortar. This leveling bed ensures that no voids under the backerboard can cause deflection.

When setting tile over cement backerboard, use modified latex thinset or unmodified dry-set mortar.

STRENGTHS

Cement backerboard has unsurpassed water resistance.

DRAWBACKS

Cement weighs more than other types of backerboard. Because cement backerboard is brittle, some tile contractors don't like to use it on floors. According to Tom Meehan, "If you use cement backerboard on a floor, the tiles will have a tenacious bond, but if there is a little bit of give, you will get cracking of the tiles or grout."

MATERIALS AT A GLANCE

1. **Product:** Durock Next Gen (USG™) **Thicknesses:** ⁵⁄₁₆ in., ½ in., and ⅝ in. **Sizes:** 32 in. by 5 ft. or 8 ft.; 3 ft. by 4 ft., 5 ft., or 6 ft.; 4 ft. by 4 ft. or 8 ft.

2. **Product:** PermaBase (National Gypsum®) **Thicknesses:** From ¼ in. to 1 in. **Sizes:** Vary depending on thickness; 32 in., 36 in., or 48 in. wide by 4 ft., 5 ft., 6 ft., or 8 ft. long

3. **Product:** WonderBoard (Custom Building Products®) **Thicknesses:** ¼ in. and ½ in. **Sizes:** 3 ft. by 4 ft. (¼ in. only), 3 ft. by 5 ft., and 3 ft. by 8 ft. (½ in. only).

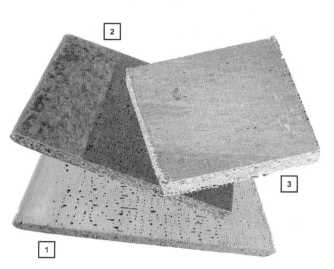

Polystyrene

Polystyrene backerboard consists of panels of either expanded (EPS) or extruded (XPS) polystyrene protected by facings made of fiberglass and polymer resin. Brands include FinPan ProPanel®, Schlüter Kerdi-Board, and Wedi® Building Panel. While the Wedi and Schlüter products have XPS cores, the FinPan product has a core of EPS.

Polystyrene backerboard is offered in a wide range of thicknesses and is suitable for use on walls, floors, ceilings, and countertops. Surprisingly stiff, it is strong enough to be used to build shower benches, curbs, or bathroom furniture, as long as panels of the material are used as "studs" for structural support where necessary.

BEYOND BACKING. Polystyrene backerboards are lightweight, waterproof, and easy to cut. Schlüter's thicker panels can be used in place of framing for structural applications, such as a shower bench.

INSTALLATION

Polystyrene backerboard can be cut with a utility knife. Most manufacturers advise using screws and washers to fasten the panels to walls or floors. For a waterproof installation, treat seams with sealant and waterproof sealing tapes (available from panel manufacturers).

STRENGTHS

It weighs less than any other type of backerboard. It is waterproof and will not wick water, and once the seams are sealed, the panels provide a water barrier. Sheets are also available in more sizes and thicknesses than other backerboards.

DRAWBACKS

Polystyrene costs more than other types of backerboard.

MATERIALS AT A GLANCE

1. **Product:** ProPanel (FinPan) **Thicknesses:** ¼ in. and ½ in. **Sizes:** 3 ft. by 5 ft.

2. **Product:** Wedi Building Panel (Wedi) **Thicknesses:** From ⅛ in. to 2 in. **Sizes:** 2 ft. by 4 ft. (⅛ in. only) or 8 ft.; 3 ft. by 5 ft. (¼ in. and ½ in. only) or 8 ft.

3. **Product:** Kerdi-Board (Schlüter) **Thicknesses:** From ³⁄₁₆ in. to 2 in. **Sizes:** 48 in. by 64 in. (³⁄₁₆ in. to ½ in.), 4 ft. by 8 ft. (³⁄₁₆ in. to ½ in.), and 24½ in. by 96 in. (¾ in. to 2 in.)

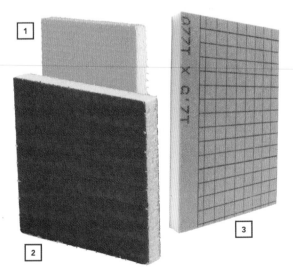

Fiber cement

The same ingredients used to make cement backerboard are present in fiber-cement backerboard; the difference is that fiber cement also includes cellulose fiber. The main brands of fiber-cement backerboard are HardieBacker and CertainTeed® Fiber Cement BackerBoard. HardieBacker comes in two thicknesses: ¼ in. for floors or countertops and 0.42 in. for walls. At about ⁷⁄₁₆ in., 0.42-in.-thick HardieBacker is a little thinner than ½-in. cement backerboard, which is one reason why it is lighter (2.6 lb. per sq. ft.).

INSTALLATION

Fiber cement can be scored with a knife and snapped like drywall—although noncarbide utility-knife blades tend to dull quickly—or be cut using electric shears developed for cutting fiber-cement siding. Manufacturers recommend that fiber-cement not be cut with a power saw or grinder because such power tools create silica dust, a health hazard.

Fastening requirements for fiber-cement backerboard are the same as for cement backerboard: Use 1¼-in. backerboard screws or 1½-in. galvanized roofing nails spaced 8 in. on center. It is sometimes difficult to get screws to sit flush with the dense surface of fiber cement. If you're having this problem, use nails. Seams should be finished with thinset mortar and alkali-resistant fiberglass mesh tape.

Use only latex-modified thinset when installing tiles on fiber-cement backerboard.

STRENGTHS

Fiber cement is less brittle and weighs less than traditional cement backerboard. Because fiber-cement backerboard has a smoother surface than cement backerboard, it can be finished with paint or wallpaper. That makes it a good choice for finishing walls in damp areas like basements.

DRAWBACKS

Some traditionalists are reluctant to use products that contain cellulose in a wet environment. However, fiber-cement backerboard manufacturers warrant their products for use in showers and other wet areas.

MATERIALS AT A GLANCE

1 **Product:** BackerBoard (CertainTeed)
Thicknesses: ¼ in. and ½ in. **Sizes:** 3 ft. by 5 ft. (only available size for ½-in. thickness), 4 ft. by 4 ft., and 4 ft. by 8 ft. (½ in. only).

2 **Product:** HardieBacker (James Hardie)
Thicknesses: ¼ in. and ½ in. **Sizes:** 3 ft. by 5 ft. and 4 ft. by 8 ft.

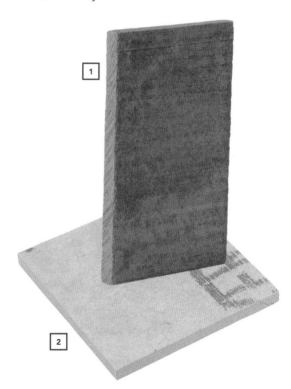

Gypsum core

While ordinary drywall has a paper facing, most brands of gypsum-core backerboard include a waterproof facing (usually a fiberglass mat). Brands include CertainTeed Diamondback® Tile Backer and Georgia-Pacific Dens-Shield.

Gypsum-core backerboard is available in the usual range of thicknesses: ¼ in., ½ in., and ⅝ in. The ½-in. product weighs 2 lb. per sq. ft., making it lighter than cement backerboard or fiber-cement backerboard. It can be used for walls, ceilings, and countertops, but it is not suitable for use on most floors or for any outdoor application.

USG's Fiberock® is a gypsum-based backerboard that isn't really comparable to other gypsum-based products. Unlike Dens-Shield, Fiberock has no fiberglass-mat facing. According to the manufacturer, it is made of a "gypsum/cellulose-fiber combination" and is "water resistant to the core." The manufacturer warrants the use of Fiberock in wet areas like showers.

INSTALLATION

Gypsum-core backerboard can be scored and snapped like regular drywall. Fastening requirements are similar to those for other types of drywall: It can be fastened with 1¼-in. backerboard screws or 1½-in. galvanized roofing nails.

As with HardieBacker, latex-modified thinset should be used to set tile on gypsum-core backer-board.

STRENGTHS

This type of backerboard is relatively light and easy to install; handles much like drywall.

DRAWBACKS

Gypsum-core backerboard is best used in areas that are usually dry. It cannot be used outdoors, and most experts advise against its use in areas that experience daily wetting. Gypsum-core backerboard should never be used for a shower floor or shower curb, or in a sauna or steam room. Gypsum-core backerboard can't be used on floors with tiles that are smaller than 2 in. by 2 in.

MATERIALS AT A GLANCE

1. **Product:** Fiberock Aqua-Tough (USG) **Thicknesses:** ¼ in., ⅜ in., ½ in., and ⅝ in. **Sizes:** 3 ft. by 5 ft., 4 ft. by 4 ft. or 8 ft.

2. **Product:** Diamondback (CertainTeed) **Thicknesses:** ½ in. and ⅝ in. **Sizes:** 4 ft. by 5 ft. or 8 ft.

3. **Product:** DensShield (Georgia-Pacific) **Thicknesses:** ¼ in., ½ in., ⅝ in. **Sizes:** 4 ft. by 4 ft. (only available size for the ¼-in. thickness), 32 in. by 5 ft. or 8 ft., 4 ft. by 8 ft.

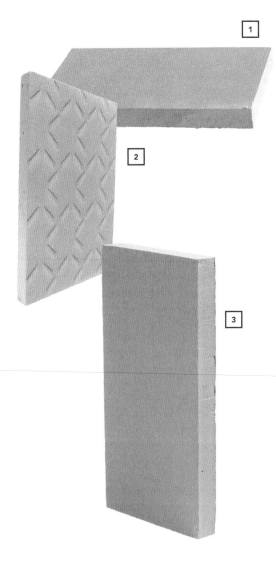

Miles of Tiles

BY DEBRA JUDGE SILBER

The tile you choose not only has a substantial impact on the cost of a bathroom project, but it also affects how the new bath functions, ages, and impresses those who peek inside. If that's not daunting enough, consider the sheer volume of choices available inside the local tile showroom.

Designer-builder Patrick Sutton of Austin, Texas, suggests that clients avoid the tile store until they know what they're looking for. "I always tell people, 'I can't forbid you from going to a tile showroom, but I wish you wouldn't. Sit down first and make a list of what you're trying to do. Then go to the tile store.'" Lexington, Mass., architect Lynn Hopkins encourages clients to consider the style of the whole house before choosing one feature—which could be tile—to set the design tone for the bath. "Ask: What is this tile saying about the character of the room in which it wants to be? It gives you a context in which to make all those other decisions."

Aesthetics aside, there are other qualities you'll want to look for. One is strength, which will determine whether the tile is suitable for wall or floor applications (or both). Another is slip resistance. You can judge slip resistance based on the coefficient of friction (a COF of 0.5 or above is OK for floors), or you can do what many builders do: Run your hand over the surface. A third feature to consider is shade

variation, or the degree of difference in color and pattern from one tile to the next. Shade variation is designated by a V followed by a number from 1 to 4, with 1 having the least variation (minimal to no difference) and 4 having substantial, sometimes dramatic, variation in color or pattern between tiles.

Tile isn't forever, but try to choose one you can love for the long haul. "Find something you know you can be happy with for the next 10 to 20 years," advises Tom Meehan, a master tilesetter in Harwich, Mass. He adds that it's not just the tile, but also the complete design that matters. "When guests look in, you want them to say, 'What an incredible bathroom!' not 'What incredible tile!'"

CERAMIC

Made of clay mixed with minerals and water, ceramic tile, like that used on the floor on p. 77, comes in a broad array of shapes, sizes, and colors. Initially fired to create bisque ware (unglazed ceramic), it can be fired a second time with a ceramic glaze to produce a surface that is stain and scratch resistant. The tile body itself, however, is porous. Depending on its hardness rating, ceramic tile can be used on either walls or floors. For the most part, ceramic tile is easy to work with snap cutters and nippers, making it DIY-friendly. Although ceramic tile traditionally has been the most economical choice, the availability of porcelain tile in recent years has lessened ceramic's dominance in the market.

PORCELAIN

In the past decade, the price of porcelain tile has dropped; this and its many favorable attributes have led it to overtake ceramic in popularity. At the same time, new glazing techniques that closely mimic the look of natural stone have made it a durable, less expensive alternative to marble and limestone. "You get the look of old stone with zero maintenance," explains tilesetter Tom Meehan. Made of clay and finely ground sand, and fired once

under high heat and pressure, porcelain is denser and stronger than typical ceramic tile. It is also less porous; with a water-absorption rate less than that of ceramic, porcelain tiles are often frostproof. Like ceramic tile, porcelain tile may be glazed or unglazed. Unglazed porcelain tile is sometimes called through-body, because the composition of the tile is uniform throughout. Much of the floor tile sold today is glazed porcelain, says Joshua Levinson, president of Artistic Tile, a distributor. "Porcelain production involves the use of fine-grained clays, which can be pressed more densely and fired at a higher temperature than traditional red-clay-body double-fire tile, making the product more resistant to wear," he says.

A NEW FAVORITE. Porcelain tile is denser and stronger than ceramic making it an increasingly popular tile choice.

A RANGE OF OPTIONS. There are a vast array of stone options for your bathroom ranging from large stone slabs to small rock-size tiles.

NATURAL STONE

Appearing in many forms in today's baths, natural stone shows up in formats that range from large slabs to tiny pebbles to uniform, cut tile. Add to that the many types of stone available—marble, granite, limestone, and slate among the most popular—and you have a wide variety of options. This variety also presents differences in qualities among stone types—such as stain resistance, durability, and porosity—so it's important to choose a type of stone that you can live with and that your tilesetter is confident installing. Limestone, for example, is popular, is fairly easy to work with, and comes in a variety of types; Jerusalem limestone is among the most dense and durable. Green marble, on the other hand, is more fussy: Contact with cement-based thinset will cause it to cup, requiring the use of resin-based thinsets.

Cutting stone tile requires the use of a wet saw, another reason why it's worth considering a professional installation. All stone tile should be sealed, but some tiles need more upkeep than others. Because much of the appeal of natural stone derives from surface variations from piece to piece, careful blending of shades—often by working from different boxes—is important for an attractive, "soft-slab" effect.

METAL

This material came on the scene with a splash some 10 to 15 years ago, and it remains popular primarily for accents. Not all metal-looking tiles are metal, however. Some are ceramic with a metal cap; still others are cast in resin and coated with a metallic finish. Stainless steel, nickel, and bronze are among the most popular. Generally, metal tiles install like ceramic tiles, although they are far more difficult to cut.

A TOUCH OF METAL. Accent tiles either of metal or that just look like metal are sure to make a statement.

GLASS

Often transparent and more brittle than ceramic or stone, glass tile requires careful installation, but the shimmer it adds to a bathroom can't be denied. Because glass is nonporous, sealing is not a concern, but glass can scratch and can be slippery, which is something to think about if you're considering a glass-tile floor. Available in luminous colors and often enhanced with texture or metal highlights, glass tile can be pricey—an argument for using it in small doses as a border accent, sink backsplash, or singular wall. Glass tiles are available with a percentage of recycled material.

"Glass is very big, and it's going to stay that way for a while," says Meehan. Its steady popularity has resulted in a large supply of glass tile of varying quality and individual characteristics that can complicate installation. This, Meehan says, makes it especially important to follow the installation

SMOOTH MOVES AND ROUGH CUTS: TRENDS IN BATHROOM TILE

ARTISAN AND HANDMADE TILE

When you buy an artisan tile, you get a handmade product for which irregularity is the desired effect. They're more expensive, too—as much as four times the cost of mass-produced, machine-made tile. In addition, shape variations may require larger grout joints and more painstaking installation. That said, the look is one of a kind. "There is a humanizing effect that results from the irregularities of handmade tile," says Joe Taylor, president of the Tile Heritage Foundation in Healdsburg, Calif. "You walk into a bathroom with handmade tile, and it's noticed. It makes a statement: It says, 'This is artistic; it's beautiful.'" The foundation offers a directory of artisan-tile sources at tileheritage.org.

INK-JET PORCELAIN

Recent years have seen an explosion in porcelain tile digitally printed with a surface image that makes it appear like a different material—most often stone, but also wood, leather, and even fabric. The reasons are obvious: Stone is pricey, and neither fabric nor wood fares well in a damp bathroom environment. These tiles are found in big-box stores as well as high-end showrooms, with the expected difference in both cost and image quality. The detail of the ink-jet printing is the best measure of quality, says Artistic Tile's Joshua Levinson.

"Are many dots visible, or is the printing detail so fine that dots are not visible at a normal viewing distance?" Printed tiles may be embossed and often have precise, rectified edges so that they can butt tightly together.

SUSTAINABLE TILE

The availability of tile made from recycled materials keeps expanding, particularly in the area of glass tile, and manufacturers of all types are promoting their environmental friendliness. Oceanside Glasstile® takes environmental responsibility to the next level with its Blue™ brand tiles, which combine up to 82% postconsumer recycled content with a new melting technology that reduces energy use by 30%. Crossville® has developed a system of processing its own scrap tile back into powder, which then is used in manufacturing new tile. Many artisan tile makers practice good environmental stewardship as well, so it pays to seek them out. The Tile Council of North America's Green Squared® Certified mark identifies tiles that meet certain criteria in the use of sustainable materials and eco-friendly manufacturing and corporate practices. So far, several hundred tile lines from eight manufacturers have been certified (greensquaredcertified.com).

MOSAIC TILE

It's hard to beat the variety available today in mosaic tile. Mosaics can come in many shapes and patterns—from Roman-style tesserae to sleek linear glass. Many combine several materials—including glass, natural stone, and metal—into one color-coordinated pattern. Several manufacturers provide custom mosaics, with some offering online tools that allow you to create your own color blend or gradient in mosaic that the company then will produce for you. Tilesetter Tom Meehan acknowledges that mosaic tiles make a good DIY project, but he cautions that it's important to take your time. Solid or opaque mosaics come mounted on a fiber mesh that makes installation easy; transparent glass mosaic tile comes face-mounted on paper.

in place," says designer-builder Patrick Sutton. Tilesetter Meehan is less harsh, but still cautious. "As a border or an accent, they're great," says Meehan, who nonetheless recommends grout release and professional installation.

LARGE-FORMAT TILE

Defined as porcelain tiles with one edge measuring 15 in. or more and glass tiles with an edge measuring 3 in. or more, large tiles are, well, big. Popular sizes include 12-in. by 24-in. rectangles and 6-in. by 18-in. planks. They're not the right choice for every bathroom, though, particularly if you're going for an antique or vintage look. Also, the bigger the tile, the more stable the substrate needs to be to prevent cracking. Installation of large tiles can be tricky; particularly in the case of glass, large tile is best installed by a professional.

SPLIT-FACE TILE

Tiles that pop from the wall literally add a new dimension to your bath design, but if you ask whether they're a good idea, get ready for a protracted conversation. The uneven surfaces referred to as split face that appeared a few years ago have found a limited audience. Installation challenges are one reason. "You can't grout the stuff, so you're relying on the backer to hold it

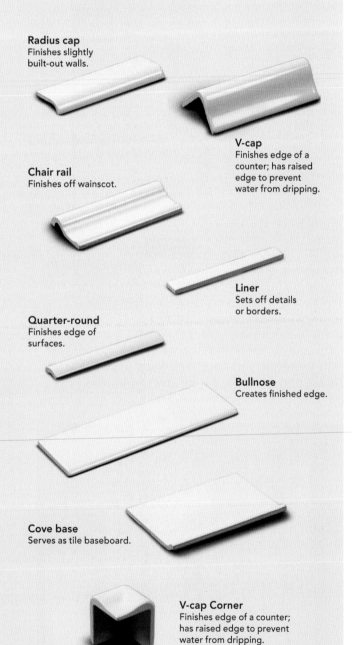

Field
Fills wide areas.

Radius cap
Finishes slightly
built-out walls.

V-cap
Finishes edge of a
counter; has raised
edge to prevent
water from dripping.

Chair rail
Finishes off wainscot.

Liner
Sets off details
or borders.

Quarter-round
Finishes edge of
surfaces.

Bullnose
Creates finished edge.

Cove base
Serves as tile baseboard.

V-cap Corner
Finishes edge of a counter;
has raised edge to prevent
water from dripping.

A SHOWSTOPPER. Glass is so popular because it makes such a statement. But proper installation is important.

instructions from the manufacturer of your particular tile. Artistic Tile's Levinson echoes that opinion, adding that anyone considering working with glass tile should consult the glass-tile selection and installation guide in the Tile Council of North America's Handbook for Ceramic, Glass, and Stone Tile Installation, available at tcnatile.com.

Which tile where?

SHOWER WALLS

Tile on shower walls should extend at least 72 in. high for complete protection from water, although there's also the option of wrapping the ceiling for a complete enclosure. Large rectified tile allows for fewer and smaller grout joints, discouraging mold. Using the same tile in the shower as on the walls can help a small bath to appear larger. On the other hand, if the bathroom is large enough, a different tile can define the shower as its own space.

SHOWER FLOORS

It's important that tile used on shower floors be slip resistant. Small tiles (1 in. to 3 in.) provide a secure grip and also accommodate the slope needed for drainage. Manufacturers typically match their larger-format floor tiles with smaller tiles specifically for shower floors. Stone pebbles are popular, but beware: Less expensive products can have irregular surfaces that are less than therapeutic.

BATHROOM FLOORS

Strength and slip resistance are key here. Tile manufacturers use coefficient of friction (COF) to rate slip resistance. A COF of 0.5 is acceptable; higher numbers offer more traction. Keep in mind that grout lines around smaller tiles improve traction. Floor tiles also need to be durable. The Porcelain Enamel Institute (PEI) rates tile durability on a scale of 0 to 5, with 5 being the toughest commercial-grade tiles. For residential floors, a PEI rating of 3 is fine.

BATHROOM WALLS

You don't have to tile every wall in your bath, but it is a good idea to protect areas prone to splashes, including those behind the sink and toilet. Tile wainscot traditionally fulfilled this function, but it has started to fall out of favor. Wainscots typically range from 36 in. to 48 in., although taller, European-style wainscots of 54 in. are an option. How the wainscot meets the wall—with a decorative border, crown, or cap—can add to the bathroom's character.

MAKE THE RIGHT CHOICE. It's important to consider where you will be installing tile when picking out materials.

SOURCES

CERAMIC
American Olean® Satinglo™ hexagon, americanolean.com

PORCELAIN
Daltile® Spark™ Colorbody™ Porcelain, daltile.com

ARTISAN
Universal Tile & Marble, universaltilemarble.com

INKJET PORCELAIN
American Olean Kendal Slate™, americanolean.com

NATURAL STONE
Island Stone® marble and quartz mix, islandstone.com

MOSAIC
Oceanside Glasstile Tessera mosaic blend, glasstile.com

METAL
Crossville Mixology, crossvilleinc.com

METAL SAMPLE
Universal Tile & Marble, universaltilemarble.com

GLASS
Oceanside Glasstile Tessera mosaic with Haiku field, glasstile.com

GLASS SAMPLES
Tile America®, tileamerica. com; Universal Tile & Marble, universaltilemarble.com

SPLIT FACE
Island Stone Rustic Cladding, islandstone.com

TRIM SAMPLES
The Home Depot®, homedepot.com; Tile America, tileamerica.com

Smart Choices in Bathroom Flooring

BY MATTHEW TEAGUE

Wood

Tile

Vinyl

Linoleum

Cork

Rubber

Concrete

Bathroom floors come with their own particular set of requirements. Like any floor, they should be chosen with style, durability, and comfort in mind. But a bathroom floor also must be able to handle moisture and humidity from daily use as well as any possible leaks that could occur in the future.

That said, not all bathrooms are created equal. While the family bath may have to endure splashing toddlers in the tub, you can use a master bath more responsibly, wiping up small spills as they occur. A guest bath or half-bath may be even less threatened by water. The less use your bathroom sees and the fewer fixtures it houses, the more options you have for bathroom flooring.

Choosing a bathroom floor that can handle the required amount of water is the first hurdle. You can expect a certain amount of water all the time— drips as you get out of the shower or puddles from the occasional overspray, for instance. Those minor mishaps are easily wiped up, but it's the months or years of that small bead of water dripping around a shower door or condensation running down the side of the toilet that is more likely to cause trouble. Also, because the bathroom has more plumbing than any other room in the house, it's the place most likely to spring a leak. Just hope it doesn't happen while you're on vacation.

In addition to the water you see, there's also the water you can't see: humidity, which affects some floors more than others. While a vent fan helps, you have to make sure that everyone turns it on. You also can wire it through a timer to run for a while after you leave the room.

Remember that all bathroom floors should be well-sealed and maintained, but that some require more work than others. Also, it's entirely possible that those splashing toddlers will turn into sloppy teenagers.

Despite arguments, wood can work

The arguments against solid- and engineered-wood floors in a bathroom are obvious: Wood not only absorbs water pretty easily, but it also swells in the process. The everyday humidity of a bathroom may test the limits of expansion joints where the floor meets the walls. In cases of prolonged leaks, it's almost a given that any species of wood floor, and probably the subfloor, will have to be torn out.

Still, wood floors are beautiful and feel good underfoot, often providing a smooth transition from bedroom to bath. Although it is hard to find a designer who claims that putting wood flooring in the bathroom is a good idea, when pressed, almost all of them will admit to doing it regularly. It's really a case of risk assessment.

In a family bath that sees heavy use from kids, wood flooring just doesn't make sense. But in a master bath where the residents understand that standing water has to be wiped away, or don't mind the character and patina of water-stained floors, wood flooring will last as long as it will in any other room of the house.

Consider sectioning off the bathroom so that wetter areas are floored using a more moisture-friendly material. Architect David Edrington uses solid surfaces like stone or marble—often offcuts from countertops—to prevent condensation on the toilet from reaching wood floors. Because hardwoods exposed

WOOD SOURCES

ADVANTAGE TRIM & LUMBER
www.advantagelumber.com

BRUCE HARDWOOD FLOORING
www.bruce.com

CARLISLE WIDE PLANK FLOORS®
www.wideplankflooring.com

GOODWIN HEART PINE
www.heartpine.com

HEARTWOOD PINE FLOORS
www.heartwoodpine.com

MOUNTAIN LUMBER CO.®
www.mountainlumber.com

PERMAGRAIN®
www.nydreeflooring.com

TARKETT®
www.tarkett.com

WHAT IT'S WORTH
www.wiwpine.com

to humidity will expand and contract, high-quality vent fans are a must.

The maintenance for wood in the bathroom is the same as for any other room: Sweep and mop. But you should expect to refinish the floors at the first signs of a worn finish. Penetrating water not only expands the wood, but also bleeds down toward the subfloor. To assess the finish, perform the same water-droplet test used on tile (p. 86).

The best chance at success is probably engineered-wood flooring. Not to be confused with laminates (p. 86), engineered flooring is a layer of real wood backed by layers of plywood, which minimizes movement caused by humidity. Because it's less likely to cup or warp, there is less chance that gaps will open between planks, allowing water to penetrate. Factory finishes are often top quality, and they cer-

Engineered-wood flooring

Solid-wood flooring

tainly ease installation, but to seal the joints between planks completely, opt for unfinished engineered hardwoods and lay on the finish yourself.

Tile offers sensible style

Tile is likely the first option that comes to mind when you think of bathroom flooring, and for good reason—it's the most popular. Made of clay and other nonmetallic minerals shaped, pressed, and fired at high temperatures to create a hard surface, tile can handle water and comes in an almost endless variety of styles. You can choose from ceramic, porcelain, natural stone, or, in small doses, even glass. On the downside, tile is tough on your legs and back. In a room where you're often barefoot, it's also cold. It might feel nice on the Texas coast, but it is less than ideal for Maine winters. That said, adding radiant in-floor heat to a bathroom floor—tile or otherwise—is now easier than ever.

The important factors to consider when shopping for bathroom floor tile are water porosity and slip resistance.

SOME TILE IS ABSORBENT

The higher the tile's porosity, the more water it will absorb. The determining factors are the body of the tile and, if any is used, the surface glaze. Porcelain, for instance, has a dense body and a durable glaze, so its absorption rate is about 0.5%. On the other hand, a Sausalito ceramic tile left unsealed can be up around 25%—basically a sponge. Your best bet for a bathroom floor is to use unglazed tiles with an absorption rate of no more than 0.5%, or glazed tiles with an absorption rate of 3% or less.

A higher porosity rate doesn't mean you can't use the tile, but it does mean that you'll have to seal it after installation and reapply the sealer every year or so to prevent standing water from reaching the vulnerable subfloor. Check the absorption of stone or porous tiles by placing a small amount of water on them. If the drops of water bead up and stand on top of the surface, it's sealed; if they absorb into the surface, it's time to reseal. The photo on p. 88

THINK TWICE BEFORE CHOOSING LAMINATE FLOORING

BECAUSE OF THEIR RELATIVELY LOW COST, laminates have become a popular choice in flooring. Most modern laminates—whether in planks or tiles— click together to form a floating floor with dry mechanical joints. While these joints are touted as being water-resistant, they aren't waterproof. Water may eventually reach the fiberboard core of the flooring, or the subfloor below. If you insist on laminate, opt for a style that installs with a one-piece continuous vapor barrier that covers the entire subfloor instead of having it attached to the bottoms of individual tiles or planks.

illustrates the difference in absorption between a sealed and an unsealed terracotta tile.

SLIPPERY WHEN WET

Slip resistance is rated with what's known as a coefficient of friction. Ideally, tile floors in showers should have a coefficient of "0.60 wet" or greater. It's not a bad idea to follow this same rule for the entire bathroom, which, at some point, is likely to be wet underfoot. These numbers, however, rule out heavily polished tiles or stones like granite, marble, or travertine, which have a much lower slip resistance. A lower rating doesn't mean that you can't use smooth tile, but if you push the limits, it's a good idea to supplement the area with some type of rug or bath mat outside the shower and tub. Choosing a textured tile is a bit of a trade-off: More texture creates greater slip resistance and hides a little dirt, but it also makes the tile tougher to clean. Remember that floor tiles can be used on walls, but not all wall tiles can be used on floors.

GROUT CHOICE MATTERS

Modern tastes lean toward thin grout lines because no matter how nonporous the surface or how well

TILE SOURCES

CERAMIC TILES OF ITALY
www.italytile.com

CROSSVILLE
www.crossvilleinc.com

DALTILE
www.daltile.com

FIRECLAY TILE
www.fireclaytile.com

GREEN MOUNTAIN SOAPSTONE
www.greenmountainsoapstone.com

MANNINGTON
www.mannington.com

MARBLE GRANITE DEPOT
www.marblegranitedepot.com

MOSAIC TILE COMPANY
www.mosaictileco.com

TILE COUNCIL OF NORTH AMERICA
www.tileusa.com

IMMUNE TO STAINING. Epoxy grout, while more difficult to use, resists stains and provides a strong bond.

you seal it, grout lines catch dirt. To reduce the dirty look as much as possible, choose a grout with a low absorption rate. The lower the absorption rate, the more resistant the grout is to staining and discoloration. Regular, nonmodified grouts run about 10%; modified grouts average about 5%; and epoxy grouts have an absorption rate of no more than 0.5%.

Most of the grouts on store shelves are latex- or polymer-modified; both are fine for most bathrooms. These products are just as easy to work with and offer the grout a little flexibility (about $\frac{1}{64}$ in.) to combat cracking. Epoxy grouts (p. 87) have the reputation of being difficult to work with, but modern products are much easier to use than those of 10 or 15 years ago. Epoxy grout is dense and provides a tenacious bond. And while you can't leave coffee sitting on it for days, it's otherwise immune to staining, which is a welcome treat in the bathroom, where one of your major tasks is to wash away dirt.

The newest entrants to the market are glass grouts, such as Prism® from Custom Building Products, which use crushed glass (usually recycled) instead of sand. Glass grout is easy to work with and is less prone to shade differences because it has a lower absorption rate, somewhere between modified and epoxy grouts. And unlike the sand found in traditional sanded grouts, glass doesn't absorb water, which means that it cures to a more uniform color.

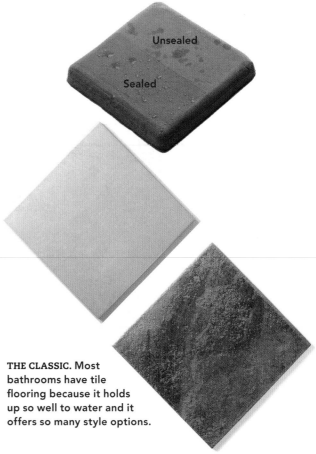

THE CLASSIC. Most bathrooms have tile flooring because it holds up so well to water and it offers so many style options.

WHERE TILE FLOORS GO BAD

WANT A LONG-LASTING TILE FLOOR? Start with a proper installation.

REINFORCE THE SUBFLOOR

Tubs, vanities, and toilets are heavy. Add tile, and it's often necessary to beef up the floor to prevent cracked tile or grout lines. Unless you're using an uncoupling membrane like Schlüter-Ditra (below), which can be installed over ¾-in.-thick floor sheathing, use layers of plywood to create a subfloor thickness of 1⅛ in.

CHOOSE THE RIGHT CEMENT

Never use mastic on the floor; tiles should always be placed in thinset cement. Choose a latex-modified thinset over a wood subfloor. Nonmodified thinset is a good choice for installing over concrete, but it will come loose from wood substrates.

DON'T OVERWATER THE GROUT

Too much water added to the grout mix washes out the portland cement and weakens the grout.

The same goes for washing off the grout after installation; keep the water to a minimum to keep the grout at its strongest.

WATCH FOR CRACKED CONCRETE

Setting tile over concrete that already shows signs of cracking is a recipe for trouble. Use a crack-isolation membrane, such as Noble Company's NobleSeal®, to separate the tile from failing concrete.

USE "SOFT" JOINTS WHERE NECESSARY

Hard grout joints where the floor meets the tub or butts up to the tile baseboard will eventually expand and crack. Instead of grouting these edges, use a noncementitious caulk—sanded and nonsanded varieties are available depending on the type of grout—that matches the grout color.

Resilient floors have come a long way

Resilient floors, which compress a bit when walked on, are a good choice because they are quiet, feel good underfoot, and in many cases are water resistant. Resilient floors are available in either sheets or tiles, but the fewer the seams, the better.

LINOLEUM

Linoleum was largely ignored from the 1960s to the 1990s, when vinyl dominated the resilient-flooring market. In the past 15 years, however, it has made a great comeback, due largely to its status as a green product. Modern linoleum, such as Forbo's® Marmoleum® or Armstrong's Marmorette, is made of all-natural products (linseed oil, wood flour, limestone, and tree resins pressed onto a natural jute backing), is biodegradable, and has few or no VOC emissions. It can be installed using a solvent-free adhesive and is naturally water resistant, antistatic, antimicrobial, and antiallergenic. Linoleum is homogenous throughout, which means the appearance suffers little with wear. It also ages well. Exposure to air hardens the linoleum, but it remains resilient.

Avoid seams by choosing sheet linoleum instead of tiles, and either run the material under the tub or seal joints with silicone to prevent water from working its way to the subfloor. Maintenance requires only sweeping and occasional damp-mopping using a pH-neutral cleaner. You also can reseal linoleum, and you should at least test the sealer every year. Linoleum pricing is comparable to wood or high-end vinyl.

LINOLEUM SOURCES

ARMSTRONG WORLD INDUSTRIES
www.armstrong.com

FORBO FLOORING SYSTEMS
www.themarmoleumstore.com

A GOOD OPTION. Resilient flooring feels good underfoot and typically stands up well in a wet environment.

Rubber

CORK

Cork flooring can be classed as both an engineered product, because it consists of a sandwich of substrates, and a resilient floor, because it compresses and springs back, making it softer underfoot and more forgiving on your joints. Most cork flooring installs with click-together joints. Some claim that it forms a gasketlike seal, making it resistant to water infiltration, but a glue-down product is preferred in bathrooms. To help seal the joints between tiles and to increase water resistance, lay on a few extra coats of sealer after installation. You also can buy cork flooring in sheet form, which may be preferred in bathrooms.

CORK SOURCES

AMCORK®
www.amcork.com

CORKDIRECT
www.corkdirect.com

LUMBER LIQUIDATORS®
www.lumberliquidators.com

USFLOORS®
www.usfloorsllc.com

RUBBER

For a more commercial look in the bathroom, consider a rubber floor. It's warmer than tile or even hardwood, and it feels good underfoot. Some consider it a green product: Expanko®'s Reztec is made of recycled rubber (often from old tires), and the company's XCR-4 is made of cork rubber. It comes in both sheets and tiles, though sheet rubber is less expensive and preferred in wet areas. While it can be laid loose, you're better off gluing it down with an adhesive that isn't water soluble. It's also a good idea to use a membrane or to paint on a waterproofing layer like Gacoflex® before installing the floor. To minimize off-gassing and the resulting odor, Expanko recommends laying on a sealer coat before adding your finish coats.

RUBBER SOURCE

EXPANKO
www.expanko.com

Cork

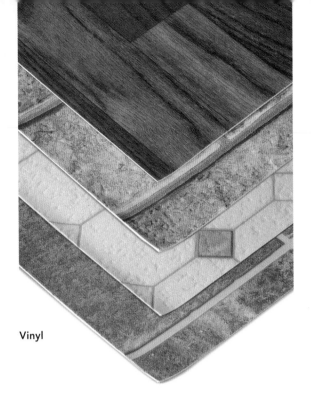
Vinyl

VINYL SOURCES

AMTICO® INTERNATIONAL
www.amtico.com

ARMSTRONG WORLD INDUSTRIES
www.armstrong.com

CONGOLEUM®
www.congoleum.com

MANNINGTON®
www.mannington.com

VINYL

Today's vinyl is made to mimic almost any flooring choice you can imagine, in both appearance and texture. The $\frac{1}{16}$-in. to $\frac{1}{4}$-in. flooring is composed of multiple layers: a wear layer, a decorative layer, a foam core, and a backing of either felt or fiberglass. Fiberglass backing is the best choice for bathrooms because felt backing doesn't react well to water. Fiberglass backing also has a layer of vinyl on the bottom, making the product itself completely waterproof.

Although it's available in tile up to 12 in. sq., 6-ft.- or 12-ft.-wide rolls are often a better choice for smaller bathrooms because they leave no unsightly, water-threatened seams. The material can be glued down, applied with a pressure-sensitive adhesive, or floated. For the ultimate peace of mind, opt for a glued-down floor. Leave a gap at the perimeter of the room, cover it with baseboard, and seal the joint with silicone. Where vinyl meets the tub, shower, or toilet, it's always best to run the flooring under the edges to eliminate that edge seam. If that's impractical, seal the joint with silicone. Maintenance of vinyl is minimal: Sweep and damp-mop, using manufacturer-recommended products.

Concrete is a durable, stylish choice

Concrete floors lend a modern, industrial look that is quickly catching on—and with good reason: They can be poured using local ingredients, making them a green choice. If you're already pouring a concrete slab, the expense of finishing and sealing is nominal. As far as handling the water present in a bathroom, well-sealed concrete shouldn't have any problem. On the downside, concrete almost always feels cold to the touch, so using heat mats or some kind of in-floor heat is a good idea.

While not a frequent choice, a concrete floor in the bathroom should, in many cases, be an obvious one. Concrete can be finished in a variety of ways using colors, stains, and aggregates of almost any kind. Concrete can be left rough or polished smooth, but before you buff it to a glasslike finish, remember that slip resistance is a major concern in the bathroom; a swept or textured finish might be better.

Maintenance for a concrete floor is minimal: Sweep and damp-mop as needed. But you should check the sealer on the floor every year or so. Again, use the water test: If a drop of water beads up, the floor is well-sealed; if it absorbs into the concrete, apply a fresh coat of sealer.

AN UNEXPECTED CHOICE. While not a common bathroom flooring option, concrete works well in a wet environment making it a good fit for a bathroom.

EASY HEAT FOR A BATHROOM FLOOR

WARMING THE BATHROOM FLOOR is much easier than it once was. There is a wide range of manufacturers offering electric, in-floor heating systems. These radiant systems feature electric coils woven through a section of matting. They are wired to a wall-mounted thermostat, or set on a timer to provide heat only when you need it. Although they won't provide enough heat to replace your main system, they'll keep your toes toasty. You can use them in conjunction with a wide range of flooring systems, including tile, stone, and engineered products.

These mats raise the floor level slightly, which means you'll have to use a floor-leveling compound to get over the wires. A few products, like those from Nuheat®, can be set into the thinset during tile installation. You can buy prefab mats or have them custom-cut to cover the entire floor, which is more economical than you might imagine. These systems typically add only a few hundred dollars to the price of the floor.

Linear Drains for Custom Showers

BY JUSTIN FINK

There are no two ways about it: A site-built shower is one of the best parts of a custom bathroom. By shedding the constraints of a factory-made tub or shower unit, you expand design options. You can get creative with the shower's size, layout, and door location, and you can include features such as niches and benches. Custom showers have always been held back, though, by the four-way fall required with a traditional, centrally located drain. Linear drains offer several design options that were previously difficult, if not impossible.

These drains may change your installation methods, though. If you're comfortable with PVC membrane, a mortar bed, and a traditional clamp-down shower drain, rest assured that several companies make linear drains that essentially sit on top of a standard clamp-style shower drain. There are also several options for more modern waterproofing methods. Many linear drains are intended for a "thin bed" installation, where the waterproofing layer is just below the finish tile rather than under a thick bed of mortar. Many times, the drain is

designed to be part of a larger system of available waterproofing components.

Along with requiring some new installation methods, linear drains also cost more, and that can be a barrier. Compared to a conventional $15 clamp-style shower drain, a 30-in. linear drain sells for about $500. The argument made by manufacturers is that the savings comes in reduced labor for the tile installer because it's faster and easier to create a one-way slope.

4 installation styles

Aside from fit and finish, the difference among drains is in how they install and how they integrate into the waterproofing used in the shower pan. The first step in choosing a drain is determining how the shower pan will be built.

FIT AND FINISH. Grate designs and finishes vary by manufacturer, from simple stamped plates to heavy-gauge wedge wire. Many also offer a "tile-in" version (left) that allows you to tile the top of the linear-drain grate so that it matches the rest of the shower floor. This often is the least expensive linear-drain option.

DOWN THE DRAIN

WITH A CONVENTIONAL SHOWER DRAIN, the surrounding shower pan has to be sloped toward the center from all directions, referred to as a four-way fall. Installers are limited to tiles that are 4 in. or smaller to cover the slope smoothly on all four sides.

Linear drains at the perimeter of the shower pan offer three big advantages over a centrally located drain: (1) The four-way fall is replaced with a much simpler one-way slope; (2) large-format tiles can be installed; and (3) a barrier-free shower is easier to build because the linear drain can be placed at the entry, where a curb would normally separate the wet area from the rest of the bathroom.

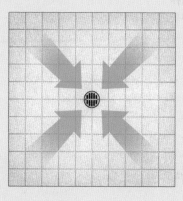

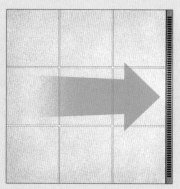

SIZE IT ON SITE

SOMETIMES PLANS CHANGE or the plumber puts the drainpipe in the wrong spot, so it's nice to have the option of a linear drain that you can size and reconfigure on site. Infinity Drain makes site-sizable kits that allow you to cut the drain body to the required length and locate the drain outlet anywhere along its length. The pieces then are either solvent-welded together (for a PVC drain body) or joined and sealed with Sikaflex® sealant (for a stainless-steel drain body).

1. EXTENSION STYLE

There is some variation in the installation process, but all the linear drains in this category are essentially an extension of the common clamp-down shower drain. Depending on the brand, the connection is made either with a threaded tailpiece attached to the linear-drain body or a rubber adapter that bridges the gap between the clamp-down drain and the linear-drain body's rigid tailpiece.

The appeal of this old-school-style installation is the reduced learning curve for tilesetters used to working with traditional mortar beds and PVC membranes. The waterproofing materials are less expensive, but don't forget that the mortar bed under the PVC membrane still needs to be pitched evenly from all directions toward the drain just as in a traditional shower. Also, these drains often require a thicker mortar bed compared to the other drain-body and connection options. Available from California Faucets®, Jaclo®, Infinity Drain®, Shower Grate Shop.

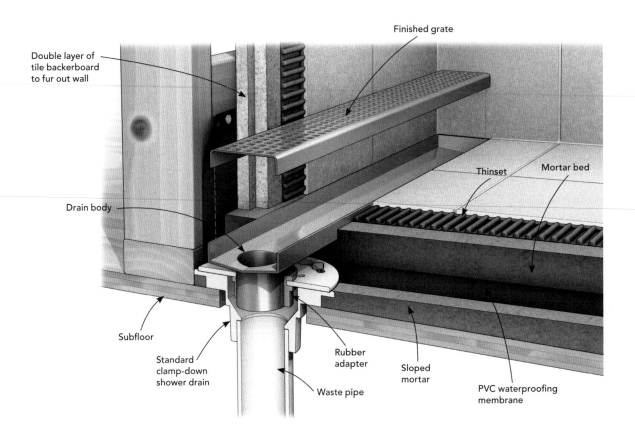

Double layer of tile backerboard to fur out wall

Finished grate

Thinset

Mortar bed

Drain body

Subfloor

Standard clamp-down shower drain

Rubber adapter

Waste pipe

Sloped mortar

PVC waterproofing membrane

2. CLAMP RING

This style of drain is a marriage of techniques both old and new. Setting the PVC or ABS drain body is a cinch: Attach it to the subfloor with screws, tying into the plumbing with a traditional solvent-weld connection. The mortar bed or factory-made pan slopes toward the drain, and the waterproofing membrane is laid on top, overlapping the drain body. With the membrane in place, a ring is clamped down with screws, creating a mechanical seal between the shower pan and the drain body just as with an old-school clamp-down shower drain.

PRECLOG CLEANOUT

EVERY LINEAR DRAIN has a decorative grate that can be removed to allow the drain body to be cleaned or unclogged. The Noble Company's FreeStyle Linear Drains™ up the ante with a pair of strainers that help to catch debris before it hits the outlet pipe and leads to a clog worthy of a plumbing snake.

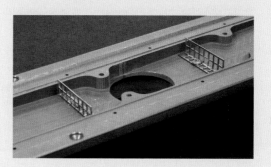

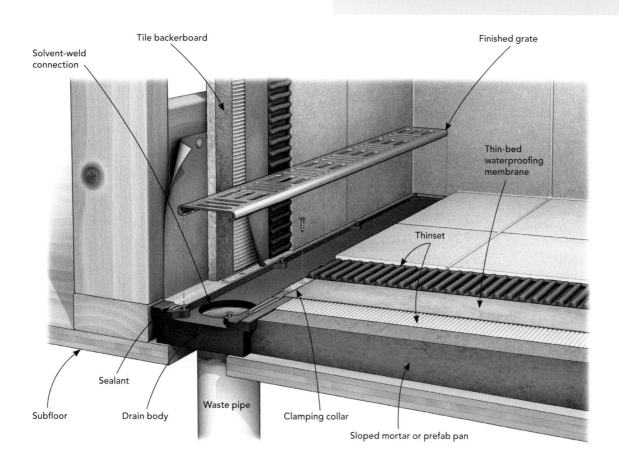

Solvent-weld connection

Tile backerboard

Finished grate

Thin-bed waterproofing membrane

Thinset

Sealant

Subfloor

Drain body

Waste pipe

Clamping collar

Sloped mortar or prefab pan

3. BONDED FLANGE

This drain is designed as part of a foolproof start-to-finish kit that takes you from a blank slate to a shower pan that's waterproof and ready for tile. These systems typically include a trim-to-fit factory-sloped pan, a fleece-backed thin-bed waterproofing membrane (such as Schlüter Kerdi-Board), and a compatible drain with a skirt of membrane factory-sealed to the top edges of the drain body. Waterproofing these assemblies is as simple as adhering the flange on the drain to the membrane on the pan.

The downside to these systems is that they are more expensive than an old-fashioned mud job. The upside is that they open the door to nonpros who want to feel confident that the finished pan won't leak. Even though many manufacturers don't spend a lot of time promoting it, their bonded-flange drains can be integrated into more traditional (and less expensive) mortar-bed installations, too. Available from ACO Drain, QuickDrain USA, Schlüter.

ALTERNATE EXIT

JACLO AND QUICKDRAIN USA both offer linear drains with a side-outlet waste that allows for above-floor rough-ins or that can be used as an ace up the sleeve in remodeling situations.

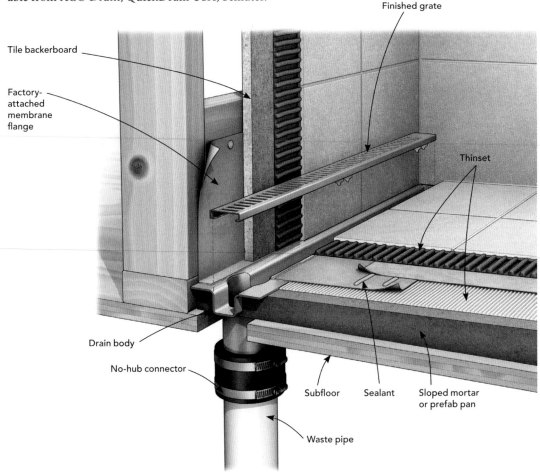

Tile backerboard

Factory-attached membrane flange

Finished grate

Thinset

Drain body

No-hub connector

Subfloor

Sealant

Sloped mortar or prefab pan

Waste pipe

4. METAL FLANGE

Instead of a traditional PVC membrane or even a modern thin-bed membrane, a metal-flanged drain body is designed to work with a liquid waterproofing membrane, such as Laticrete's HydroBan. After the drain is in place, a double layer of liquid is rolled onto the walls and floor of the shower; it also bonds directly to the drain body to create a waterproof seal. These systems install easily—if you can paint, you can use a liquid membrane—but as with fleece membranes, the waterproofing layer is far more expensive than the PVC membrane used with a mortar-bed installation. Available from Laticrete, Infinity Drain.

CUSTOM MAY COME STANDARD

A FEW LINEAR-DRAIN MAKERS fabricate custom drains to suit specific needs, but this is often limited to large orders. For Shower Grate Shop, every drain is made to order. You can specify length and width as well as outlet location and diameter. Plus, you don't have to wait for a quote; the pricing on the online order form updates as you tweak the specs.

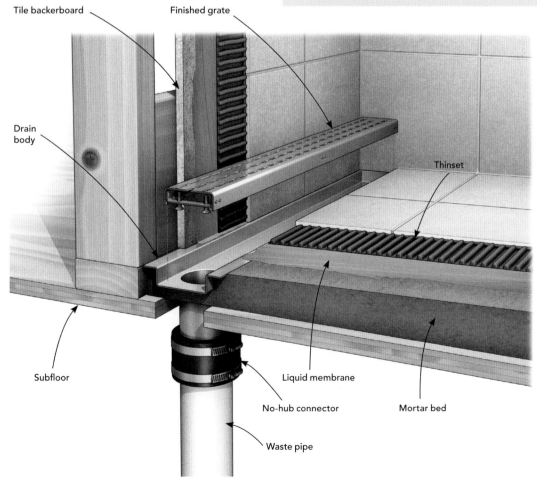

Tile backerboard

Finished grate

Drain body

Thinset

Subfloor

Liquid membrane

No-hub connector

Mortar bed

Waste pipe

How To

Install a Toilet

BY MIKE LOMBARDI

Ask a group of plumbers the proper way to install a toilet, and the conversation can get heated quickly. There are two major points of controversy: where to mount the flange and whether you should caulk the bottom of the toilet to the floor. When I install a toilet, I always make sure the closet flange is on top of the finished floor and anchored securely. This gives me the best chance for a sturdy, long-lasting, leak-free installation because the weight of the toilet and any occupant is transferred to the floor, not the connected piping.

Equally important, when the flange is on top of the finished floor, the outlet on the bottom of the toilet (the horn) is positioned so that it's below the top edge of the flange. This makes the wax seal last longer because the wax isn't being worn away by the constant flow of water. It also better protects the soft wax from the spiral-shaped hook at the end of toilet and drain snakes.

When connecting a toilet to the closet flange, I use plastic closet bolts made by Sioux Chief®. The bolts have chunky shoulders that help to hold them upright so that they're ready to accept the toilet as it's lowered into place. The bolts won't rust and will break if overtightened, a safeguard against cracking the toilet's base.

Caulking the bottom of the toilet to the floor is required by the International Plumbing Code and the International Residential Code.

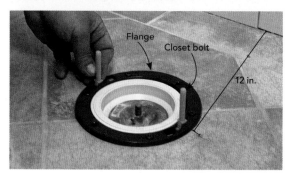

1 SECURE THE FLANGE. Dry-fit the flange so that when the closet bolts are at the end of the mounting slots, they will be 12 in. from the wall behind the toilet. When fitting is done, glue the parts together. Screw the flange to the subfloor with zinc-coated screws, and install the closet bolts.

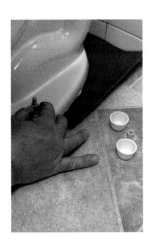

5 FASTEN THE BOWL. Lower the bowl over the closet bolts. Lean on the bowl, compressing the wax seal until the bowl is in full contact with the floor. Then, with the cap bottoms in place, tighten the two bolts a little at a time.

2 DRY-FIT THE BOWL. To identify installation problems early, always do a dry-fit. Because this bowl isn't quite level and has a slight rock, the author uses rubber-gasket material as a shim. Once he's satisfied, he removes the bowl and trims the rubber to fit around the flange.

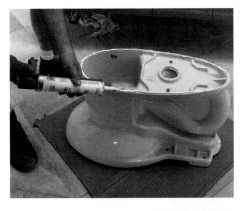

3 CAULK THE BOTTOM. With the bowl upside down, apply a bead of translucent adhesive caulk around the entire outside edge. This important sanitary measure is required by the IRC and the plumbing code.

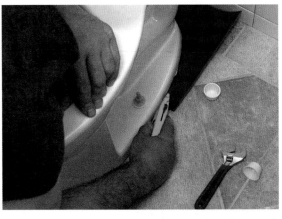

6 TRIM THE SHIM. Holding a utility knife so that the blade angles in, trim the rubber gasket flush with the bottom of the toilet. Use a fresh blade, and make the cut in several passes so that the blade doesn't slip and scratch the floor.

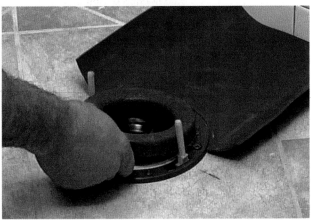

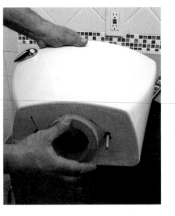

4 INSTALL THE WAX RING. After removing the plug, place the ring in the flange. This ensures that the wax seal is centered over the toilet outlet. The author prefers the plastic-horned Hercules® johni-ring®.

7 INSTALL THE TANK GASKET. In a conventional two-piece toilet, a soft rubber gasket seals the tank to the bowl. The brass bolts are tightened with a long socket provided by the toilet manufacturer. Go easy; overtightening can crack the tank.

8 CONNECT THE SUPPLY. The author likes to use braided supply lines with brass nuts at both ends. Choose one long enough to put a loop in the tubing. This puts less stress on the ends, which is where most leaks and breaks occur. Both ends have rubber washers, so the connections don't have to be tightened excessively.

9 CAULK AGAIN. Flush the toilet several times, inspecting the toilet and the basement for leaks. Once everything looks OK, apply another bead of caulk to seal the base to the floor, and smooth the joint with a moistened finger.

PROBLEM-SOLVING PRODUCTS

BEST BOLTS
Plastic closet bolts from Sioux Chief won't rust, and they'll break before they're tight enough to crack the toilet. Square shoulders keep the bolts upright in the flange.

SHIM STOCK
Rubber gasket makes an excellent shim for rocking bowls. This long-lasting material, available in the plumbing section of home centers, is impervious to water, is easy to cut, and molds to uneven surfaces.

SUPERIOR SEAL
The author likes translucent Phenoseal® for sealing the bottom of the bowl to the floor. The sealant prevents water from getting under the bowl.

Trouble-Free Toilets

BY MIKE LOMBARDI

I've installed, removed, and replaced more toilets than I care to count. In some cases, a toilet has to be replaced because the necessary repairs to the inner workings of the tank aren't worth the effort when compared to the cost of upgrading to a new fixture. There's not much I can do to predict how long these internal components of a toilet will hold up, but I certainly can ensure that the plumber or homeowner who pulls the toilet isn't faced with additional repairs to the bathroom. I've pulled lots of toilets that have been in service for 50 years or more yet had no evidence of wax-ring failure, leakage, or rot. The difference isn't in the quality of the toilet, but in the quality of the installation.

In my experience, the three essential aspects of a long-lasting and trouble-free toilet installation are a stable floor frame, a closet flange that's installed at the right height, and a bead of sealant or grout around the base of the toilet where it meets the floor.

The floor frame must be stable

From a framing perspective, there isn't anything special about the floor under a bathroom. If things go wrong, it's usually because somebody has reduced the strength of the floor by notching or drilling where they shouldn't, or because water damage has led to decay. Either of these problems will lead to movement in the floor, and that will affect the seal between the toilet and the closet flange.

Assess the condition of the floor by looking for loose tiles or feeling for sponginess. If there's access, always go below and look up for notched or drilled joists or for softness in the wood, which indicates rot. If the subflooring around the flange is rotten, it's best to cut out the old closet flange—either from below using a reciprocating saw, or from above with a specialty tool such as the Flange-Off (keco.com) or the Ram Bit™ (www.pascospecialty.com)—and replace it along with the section of flooring.

If you have to drill holes in the floor joists to route the waste line, do so through their center, and be mindful of the structural restrictions. Although not permitted by a strict interpretation of the building code, drilling waste-line holes through 2x8 and 2x10 joists is often approved by building inspectors if you agree to reinforce the joists. Reinforcement options include doubled joists, plywood gussets, angle iron, headers for transferring the load, and a support wall.

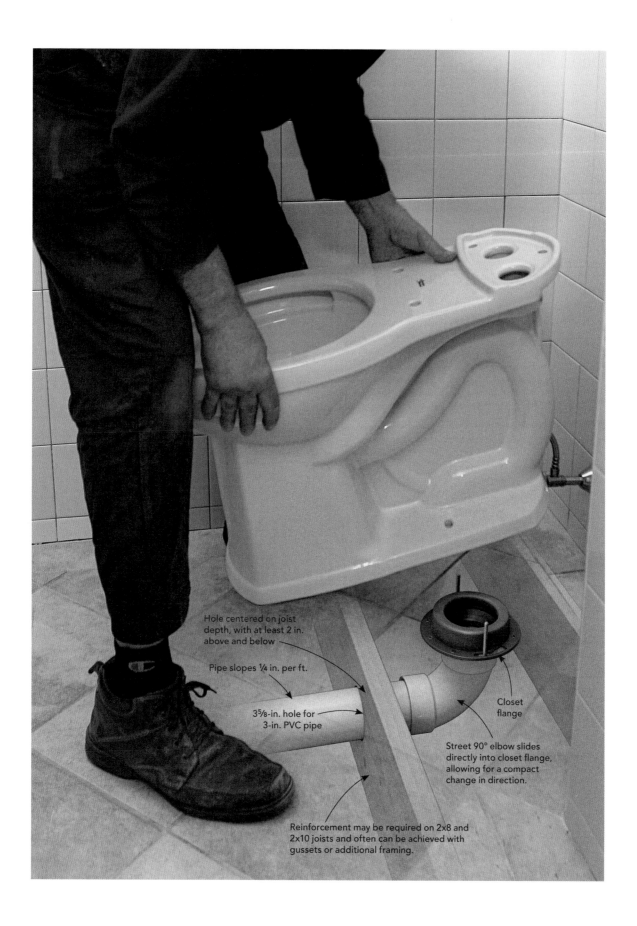

Hole centered on joist depth, with at least 2 in. above and below

Pipe slopes ¼ in. per ft.

3⅝-in. hole for 3-in. PVC pipe

Closet flange

Street 90° elbow slides directly into closet flange, allowing for a compact change in direction.

Reinforcement may be required on 2x8 and 2x10 joists and often can be achieved with gussets or additional framing.

Flange over the flooring

The underside of the closet flange should sit level and bear evenly on top of the finished floor. If new flooring has been added on top of the existing flooring, use spacer rings to extend the flange up. Although common, it's never OK to stack up wax rings to span the gap between a recessed closet flange and the horn of the toilet. A correctly installed wax ring is there to prevent sewer gas from entering the bathroom, not as a waterproof seal.

GOOD: FLANGE ON FLOORING

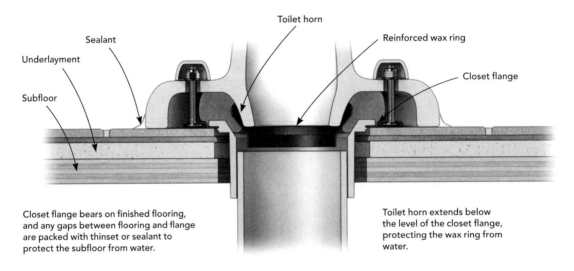

Sealant

Toilet horn

Reinforced wax ring

Underlayment

Subfloor

Closet flange

Closet flange bears on finished flooring, and any gaps between flooring and flange are packed with thinset or sealant to protect the subfloor from water.

Toilet horn extends below the level of the closet flange, protecting the wax ring from water.

BAD: FLANGE BELOW FLOORING

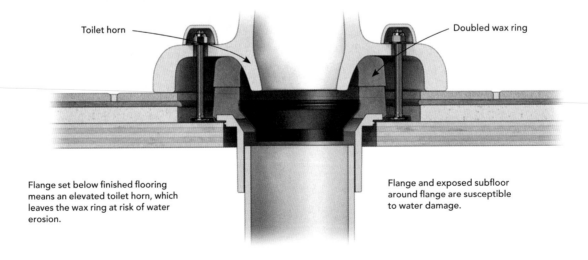

Toilet horn

Doubled wax ring

Flange set below finished flooring means an elevated toilet horn, which leaves the wax ring at risk of water erosion.

Flange and exposed subfloor around flange are susceptible to water damage.

If the hole in the subfloor is oversize, add a ¾-in. plywood support below to provide solid backing when setting the closet-flange screws.

Plywood support

Don't skip the sealant

Some plumbers argue that applying sealant where the toilet meets the floor will trap water and lead to rot if the wax ring ever fails. But sealant in this area is required by code, and for good reasons. The sealant prevents condensation on the outside of the bowl from wicking between the toilet and the floor, where it won't easily dry out. More importantly, it seals against soiled water following the same path if the toilet ever overflows. I always flush a newly installed toilet multiple times before sealing it to the floor with Phenoseal adhesive caulk.

A VITAL STEP. The floor, flange, and sealant can mean the difference between success and failure.

Cut a Laminate Countertop for a Sink

BY ANDY ENGEL

When you're building or remodeling a kitchen you can save time and money by using a ready-made laminate countertop. These tops, which generally have an integral backsplash and wraparound front edge, are durable and easy to find at home centers and lumberyards. Even if you have a laminate top custom-fabricated or you make it yourself, you can still use the sink-cutting methods described here.

Many sinks come with a layout template that makes marking the cut easy; you just trace the template with a pencil and cut out the hole with a jigsaw. If you don't have a template, trace around the sink rim with a pencil, and then adjust the line inward to get the proper fit. On dark tops like this one, I make the layout marks on light-colored masking tape so they're easier to see.

I cut most of the opening with a jigsaw equipped with a laminate-cutting blade. These blades cut on the downstroke to prevent chipping. If the countertop has an integral backsplash, there's usually not enough room for a jigsaw when making the rear cut (adjacent to the backsplash). I make this cut with an oscillating multitool.

After making the rear cut, I attach a cleat to the cutout with a single screw, which supports the cutout in place to prevent the countertop from breaking as the cut is finished. I use one screw so I can rotate the cleat out of the blade's path while cutting.

To make less mess, you might be tempted to cut the top outdoors or in your shop and then move the prepared top to the sink base. I generally don't do this, because with a large hole in the center it's very easy to break the countertop while moving it.

1 CENTER THE SINK. Use a combination square lined up between the cabinet doors to establish the side-to-side location of the sink. Make sure the front cut won't hit the cabinet rail below.

2 TRACE THE LINE. Trace the template or the sink rim as the starting point for layout lines. A layer of tape helps you see the pencil lines.

3 MOVE THE LINE INWARD. Without a template, the layout line must be moved inward so it will be covered by the sink rim. The margins vary by sink, but the minimum is about ¼ in. Make a mark at both ends of all four sides.

4 CONNECT THE DOTS. (left) Use a straightedge to connect the marks that correspond with the actual cutline (inset). Connect the corners at an angle for an easier cut and better sink support.

5 DOUBLE-CHECK THE LAYOUT. Confirm that the cuts will be covered fully by the sink rim, then cross out the original lines to prevent cutting on the wrong line.

MAKE THE CUT

TO PREVENT DAMAGING THE LAMINATE countertop, use a reverse-cutting jigsaw blade. These blades have teeth that cut on the downstroke instead of the upstroke. Go slowly, and apply steady downward pressure so that the saw doesn't bounce while cutting.

There's often not enough room to fit a jigsaw between the back of the sink and the backsplash. In these instances, use a fine-tooth blade in an oscillating multitool. Make the cut in several passes so you don't overheat the blade, which slows cutting and dulls the teeth.

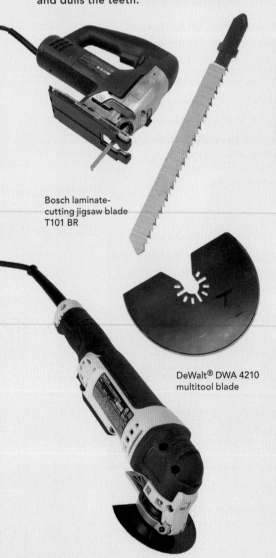

Bosch laminate-cutting jigsaw blade T101 BR

DeWalt® DWA 4210 multitool blade

6 DRILL THE CORNERS. Drill the insides of every corner with a ³⁄₈-in. spade bit. Make sure the holes are fully within the lines that mark the actual sink cutout.

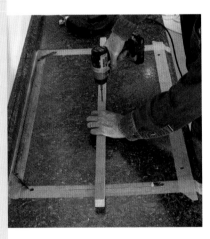

8 ATTACH A CLEAT. To prevent the top from breaking as you finish the cut, secure a cleat to the top. A single screw in the center allows you to rotate the cleat out of the way while cutting.

7 CUT THE BACK. Because of the backsplash, there's generally not enough room to cut the back side with a jigsaw. Instead, use a fine-tooth blade in an oscillating multitool.

9 FINISH UP WITH A JIGSAW. Use a jigsaw with a reverse-cutting blade to finish the sink cutout. Maintain downward pressure to keep the saw from bouncing as it cuts.

10 TEST THE FIT. After checking that the sink fits inside the cutout, clean all dust from the countertop, run a bead of silicone sealant around the rim, and install the clips that secure the sink.

Build a Floating Vanity

BY NANCY R. HILLER

As someone who prefers not to be vexed by job-related anxieties in the wee hours, I work hard to prevent foreseeable problems. On most jobs, gravity is the cabinetmaker's friend. When it comes to floating furniture, however, gravity poses certain challenges. If you don't take these challenges seriously, you may find yourself with a cabinet that wants to fall apart—or worse, one that falls off the wall.

Fine Homebuilding asked me to build a bathroom vanity for their Project House, and structural challenges were only one of the issues. Designed by architect Duncan McPherson, the cabinet's sleek, clean look depended on careful planning and on maintaining sharp lines. The vanity also was intended to be compliant with the Americans with Disabilities Act, so the center portion below the sink was to be removable for wheelchair access.

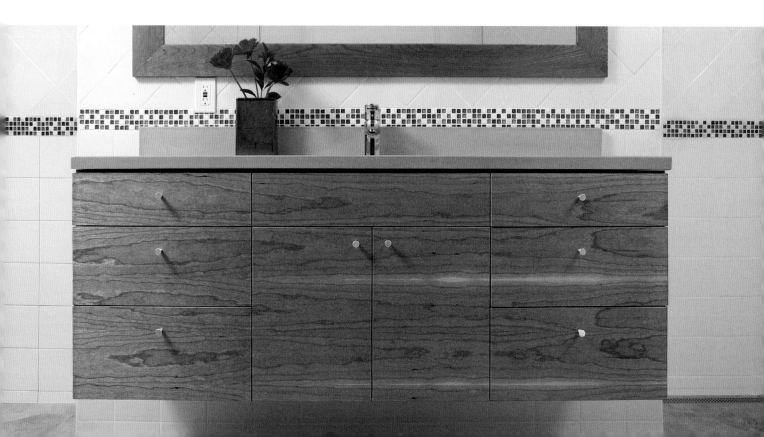

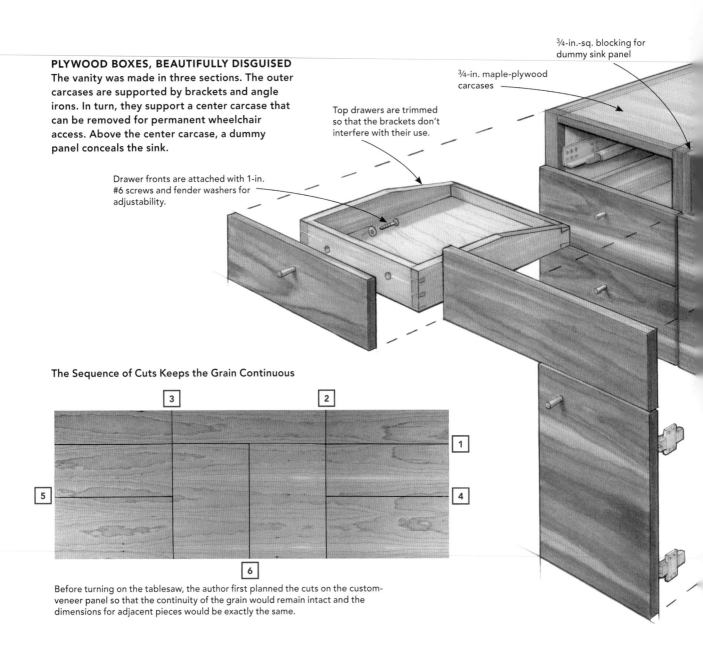

PLYWOOD BOXES, BEAUTIFULLY DISGUISED
The vanity was made in three sections. The outer carcases are supported by brackets and angle irons. In turn, they support a center carcase that can be removed for permanent wheelchair access. Above the center carcase, a dummy panel conceals the sink.

¾-in.-sq. blocking for dummy sink panel

¾-in. maple-plywood carcases

Top drawers are trimmed so that the brackets don't interfere with their use.

Drawer fronts are attached with 1-in. #6 screws and fender washers for adjustability.

The Sequence of Cuts Keeps the Grain Continuous

3   2
1
5   4
6

Before turning on the tablesaw, the author first planned the cuts on the custom-veneer panel so that the continuity of the grain would remain intact and the dimensions for adjacent pieces would be exactly the same.

To accentuate the horizontal shape, I wanted to wrap the exterior in the continuous grain of cherry-veneered moisture-resistant MDF; the carcases could be made from maple plywood. Solid maple drawers would be dovetailed for looks and strength.

Strength from fasteners and face frames

To build the cabinets, I began by cutting the case parts from prefinished ¾-in.-thick maple plywood. Because the sides of this cabinet were to have finished panels applied during installation, the ¼-in. plywood backs could simply be applied to the back of the cases, instead of housed in a groove or a rabbet.

To ensure the strength of these cabinets, I built them with biscuits interspersed with 2-in. Confirmat screws. After gluing and clamping the cases, I cleaned up glue squeeze-out and installed the screws.

Although the design is European-inspired, I added face frames to reinforce the structure of the cases and to have an alternative to veneer tape for covering the plywood edges.

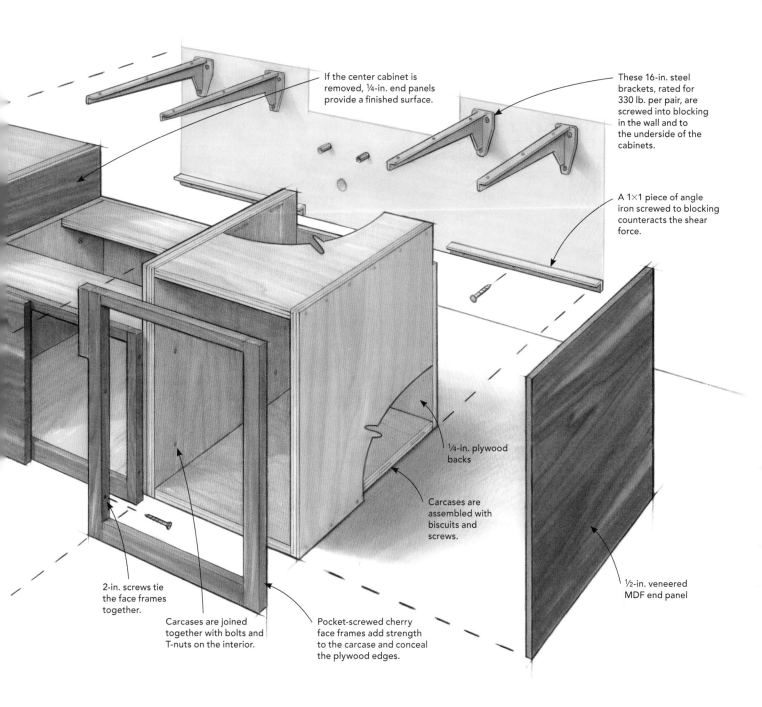

If the center cabinet is removed, ¼-in. end panels provide a finished surface.

These 16-in. steel brackets, rated for 330 lb. per pair, are screwed into blocking in the wall and to the underside of the cabinets.

A 1×1 piece of angle iron screwed to blocking counteracts the shear force.

¼-in. plywood backs

Carcases are assembled with biscuits and screws.

½-in. veneered MDF end panel

2-in. screws tie the face frames together.

Carcases are joined together with bolts and T-nuts on the interior.

Pocket-screwed cherry face frames add strength to the carcase and conceal the plywood edges.

I milled solid-cherry stiles and rails and joined the parts with pocket screws to make the face frames. I attached each frame to its case with glue and clamps, positioning the clamps inside the box so that pressure would be applied at the visible joints between case edge and face frame. After cutting the ¼-in. backs for all three cases, I test-fit the cases to each other in their final configuration, using T-nuts, bolts, and screws to attach the removable center case to the outer sections.

Dovetailed drawers are easy with the right jig

Once the cases were fitted with their face frames, I installed the drawer slides. This way I knew the exact dimensions of the drawer boxes. I also kept the hardware in mind when determining where to cut the grooves for drawer bottoms, because some types of drawer slides require a specific location relative to the bottom of the drawer side.

After cutting out the drawer parts from solid maple, I sanded the interior faces and set up the dovetail jig.

START WITH STRONG BOXES. Because the cabinets were fairly deep and cantilevered from the wall, the carcases had to be built to resist racking. The author first used biscuits to connect butt-jointed sides. Then she drilled pilot holes between the biscuits with a stepped bit and added beefy Confirmat screws (right).

CLAMPING UP SQUARE. At this point in the assembly, the carcases don't have backs or anything else that will keep the four sides square until the glue dries. As I clamp together each carcase, I measure the diagonals (above left). If the diagonals aren't equal, I offset the clamps on one side (above right) until the box is square.

Dovetails make a strong, beautiful drawer, but there was no reason for me to cut them by hand. Using a Keller jig (see the sidebar on the facing page), I can cut the four parts for one drawer in about 10 minutes. I cut the grooves for the ¼-in. plywood bottoms on the tablesaw and ripped the drawer backs at the grooves so that I could insert the bottoms into the grooves after the sides were assembled. Once the drawers were glued and clamped, I made sure that they were square and flat. I sanded the drawer boxes when the glue was dry, then inserted the drawer bottoms and fixed them each in place with two small screws.

TEMPLATES FOR PRECISION

WHEN I'M MAKING CABINETS I'm in a production mindset, so I use a router and a jig to cut the drawer dovetails. I've used several jigs, but the Keller jig is my favorite. It's incredibly simple and efficient, and it produces beautiful joints. The jig consists of two aluminum templates, one for the pins and one for the tails, which are clamped to the respective pieces. The set comes with top bearing-guided router bits.

Doors and drawer fronts from custom-veneer material

I could have bought a sheet of ¾-in. cherry plywood off the shelf to create the vanity front, but including the end panels meant that I'd need more than one sheet, and then the grain wouldn't be continuous. Luckily, there's a custom-veneer place in town where I was able to choose the veneer and how it would be laid up on three separate panels (see the sidebar on p. 116).

BOTTOM SLIDES IN LAST. After the glue had dried and the drawer assembly was square and flat, the author slid the plywood bottom into its groove and fastened it with small screws to the underside of the back.

CUSTOM VENEER IS A GAME CHANGER

I CONSIDER MYSELF LUCKY to live in Bloomington, Ind., because there's a world-class custom-veneer shop right in town. Although Heitink Architectural Veneer and Plywood supplies more than 120 species of veneered products to architectural millwork clients for enormous commercial projects (Las Vegas casinos, for example), it also makes small projects like this one possible. Pallets of veneer come into the factory and are trimmed, glued, and spliced into sheets. The sheets then are laminated to substrates of any size or type. Heitink can arrange the panels' grain patterns to match sequentially so that an entire room can be wrapped in a unique pattern of wood grain.

NOTHING GETS BY THE INSPECTOR. After the veneer sheets are glued up, each is checked on a big light table for cracks, imperfections, and other hidden defects.

I marked out the door and drawer faces on the plywood so that the grain alignment would be continuous across the face of the cabinet. I cut the drawer fronts and doors, then edge-banded them with heat-sensitive veneer tape and sanded the tape flush at the edges. I also drilled holes and mounted the European hinges on the doors. After locating the hinge plates on the inside faces of the center cabinet by holding the doors in position and placing marks directly on the inside of the case, I put the doors aside until the cabinet installation.

Finish for a wet area

Bathroom cabinets should have a water-resistant finish. If I were building more cabinets, I would have them sprayed with a conversion varnish; for this one cabinet, though, I brushed on several coats of oil-based polyurethane. To prepare the cabinet parts for the polyurethane, I vacuumed, then wiped it all down with a tack rag moistened with mineral spirits to remove any remaining dust.

After brushing on a coat of polyurethane, I let it dry thoroughly overnight. The next day, I scuffed up the surfaces with 220-grit sandpaper, tacked again, and applied a second coat. I repeated the whole thing for a third coat, too.

Putting it in place

Once on site, I began the installation by placing 2× blocking between the studs in the wall. Usually you have to remove drywall to access the stud bays, but if you're careful you can hide repairs behind the cabinet. (On this project I had access to the back of the tiled wall.) Using heavy construction screws, I attached one line of blocking to support brackets for the top of the cabinet and another line below for angle iron at the base.

Next, I found the centerline of the wall and marked a horizontal line for the top of the casework. I located the tops of the upper brackets by measuring down ¾ in. from the line. Each outside cabinet would be supported by two brackets positioned as close as possible toward the sides of each case to

DIAL IN A PRECISE FIT. To scribe each end panel to the wall, the author clamped the panel flush to the outside of the ¾-in. face frame, then used a ¾-in. scrap to mark the wall's contour.

MEASURE WITH COMMON CENTS. It's critical to maintain consistent spacing between drawer fronts, so rather than use a shim, the author used a pair of pennies between the faces to set the gap.

avoid taking up space that could otherwise be used for storage inside the drawer. I marked and drilled the positions of the holes, then installed the brackets and checked across all four to confirm that they were level.

I set the outer cabinets on the brackets and transferred the measurements for the plumbing onto the back of the center cabinet. After cutting the holes and checking the fit, I installed the center cabinet by carefully lowering it into place onto temporary supports. I then attached all three cases together by inserting bolts into the T-nuts. I screwed the outer cases onto the brackets and locked them into place. To draw the face frames tight, I also ran bolts through the face-frame edges.

I scribed the end panels to the wall and attached them with wood glue and brads. (The interior finished panels next to the center cabinet were cut and installed in the shop.) Now I was ready to finish the puzzle. I hung the doors, then attached each drawer face to its box with 1-in. #6 pan-head screws fitted through ¾-in. by ⅛-in. fender washers. I adjusted the faces until they were even across the entire assembly. (Placing coins between the faces is a great way to maintain even margins between the elements.) Finally, I fit the central dummy panel that will conceal the sink and attached it to the outside cases by screwing it to the blocks above the center cabinet.

IN A PERFECT WORLD, SCREWS WOULD BE ENOUGH

I CALCULATED THAT THE CABINET would weigh 207 lb. Add to this the concrete counter (which will sometimes be holding a full sink of water), the cabinet's contents, and the likelihood that someone, someday, will think that it makes sense to stand on the cabinet while changing a light bulb, and the total load could exceed 350 lb. For this job, I decided to use brackets rated for 330 lb. per pair, which I found at Häfele®, the cabinet-hardware supply company. To counteract the shear, I bought 1-in. by 1-in. steel angle iron from my local welding shop. After cutting it to the width of each side cabinet, I drilled holes into one side and screwed the pieces to the wall against the underside of the cabinet.

A New Approach to Concrete Countertops

BY BUDDY RHODES

Concrete countertops have become popular over the past 20 years, and with good reason. Of course, they look great. Because they're cast, they can be made in almost any shape or style, and unlike other counter materials they're practically bombproof. Best of all, almost anyone can make one with a few basic tools, which brings the price below that of most other materials.

I began working with concrete about 30 years ago. I made countertops, benches, big planters, and decorative tiles. Most of these were made either with a traditional aggregate mix or a dry-pack technique I devised that yields a variegated look. Made in molds, the objects were finished by hand-troweling or by rubbing with successively finer abrasive pads.

A few years ago I started fooling with a technique borrowed from the world of commercial concrete. For some time now, fabricators have made exterior panels for high-rise buildings with a mix that yields a strong, lightweight concrete. Their secret is to substitute fiberglass fibers and mesh for the traditional steel reinforcement. Because there's no need to bed the steel reinforcement in inches of concrete, the concrete can be made as thin as $1\frac{1}{4}$ in. Perhaps best of all, the finished surface is sprayed into the form before the rest of the concrete is added, which cancels the need for almost all the surface polishing and work at the end of the project.

Here, I'll show how I made a vanity counter and integral sink bound for *Fine Homebuilding*'s Project House. (I'd like to give credit to Brandon Gore for his inspiration and for teaching me how to fabric form a sink.) The first step in the process is to make the mold for the sink from fiberglass-resin-impregnated cloth and plywood, then attach it to the countertop form. Once it's complete, I use a drywall-texture spray gun to coat the form with a thin layer of tinted concrete, then mix a thicker batch with fiberglass fibers and hand-pack it to the final thickness. When the concrete has cured, the counter is nearly complete and needs only a light buffing and a couple of coats of sealer before being installed.

Start with the sink mold

The first step in making the mold is to determine the shape of the sink. You can make a sink in almost any shape or depth, as long as it directs water to the drain. The depth of the bowl is established by plywood ribs glued to a base that represents the sink rim. This frame then is covered with resin-impregnated cloth that hardens into a negative of the sink bowl. The trick here is to use different forms of

1 MOLD THE SINK. The first step is to build the sink mold, which represents the inside, rather than the outside, of the sink. It starts as a plywood structure that's then tightly wrapped with polyester cloth, coated with fiberglass and polyester resins, and sanded smooth. The sink mold begins with a base of ¾-in. melamine that's cut to the shape of the bowl's lip. Temporary backer ribs pocket-screwed to the back provide rigidity. The depth of the bowl is defined by ⅜-in. bending plywood hot-glued to the base. A length of pipe sets the location and depth of the drain.

2 NO WRINKLES. The foundation for the mold is a piece of polyester-fleece material (available from a fabric supply store) that's stretched tightly over the form and stapled to the edge of the base.

3 POLYESTER ON POLYESTER. The first base coat is a two-part fiberglass resin (3M®) that's applied with a brush over the form so that the material is coated. Be sure to wear an organic-vapor respirator when applying the resin. Set it aside to dry overnight.

4 BUILD A SMOOTH COAT. After sanding the base coat, mix auto-body filler (Bondo®) into a batch of the same fiberglass resin until it has the consistency of thick molasses. Pour it onto the form, and use a brush to coat the form evenly. Let it dry, then sand smooth.

CREATE THE COUNTER FORM. The counter form needs to be flat and smooth. The easiest way to make a form is to lay out the shape on a full sheet of ¾-in. melamine. Strips of melamine screwed to the sheet define the edges and depth of the counter. (The depth in this instance was 1½ in.) If needed, make the form for the backsplash at the same time.

polyester—polyester fleece cloth, two-part fiberglass resin, and auto-body filler—that bond together perfectly.

Here, I wanted a fairly conventional bowl, so I started with the shape of the rim, which was an oval with squared-off ends. After cutting out the shape from a piece of melamine, I attached 4-in.-wide reinforcing ribs to the form base with pocket screws. These ribs keep the shape from deforming during the resin's curing process.

After I determine the depth and profile of the bowl, I cut out four pieces of ⅜-in. bending plywood, one for each side of the bowl. I attach them to the base with small blocks and hot glue. I cover this structure with polyester cloth (otherwise known as fleece, the same stuff they make pajamas from).

After coating the sink form, then sanding and sealing it, I lay out the shape of the counter with 1 ½-in.-wide strips of melamine (the final thickness of the counter) screwed down on edge on a full sheet of ¾-in. melamine. While I'm at it, I make on the same sheet a form for a 4-in.-wide backsplash that's ¾ in. thick.

Remember that any imperfection in the form will be passed on to the counter, so everything should be as smooth as possible. Once I've placed the sink mold, I detail the form by filling all corners with silicone caulk and screw holes with modeling clay. Knockouts displace the areas meant for plumbing, such as the faucets and drain. Because wood absorbs water from the concrete and swells, it can't be removed once the counter has dried, so knockouts should be made from Styrofoam® or cast rubber. I make mine with VytaFlex® 40, a two-part urethane rubber from Smooth-On®.

ATTACH THE SINK MOLD. After trimming away any excess along the sink mold's bottom edge, mark the sink location on the counter form. Squeeze a bead of silicone caulk onto the sink bottom and press it firmly into position.

WAX EARLY, WAX OFTEN. There's no such thing as too much form release, so it's a good idea to apply three coats of butcher's wax to the completed form before spraying.

SHOPMADE BEADING TOOL

I USE THIS TOOL TO CREATE a consistent profile in the freshly silicone-caulked joints, which form the slight radiused edge of the counter. I made it by gluing a ¼-in.-dia. ball bearing with epoxy onto the end of a 3-in.-long bolt.

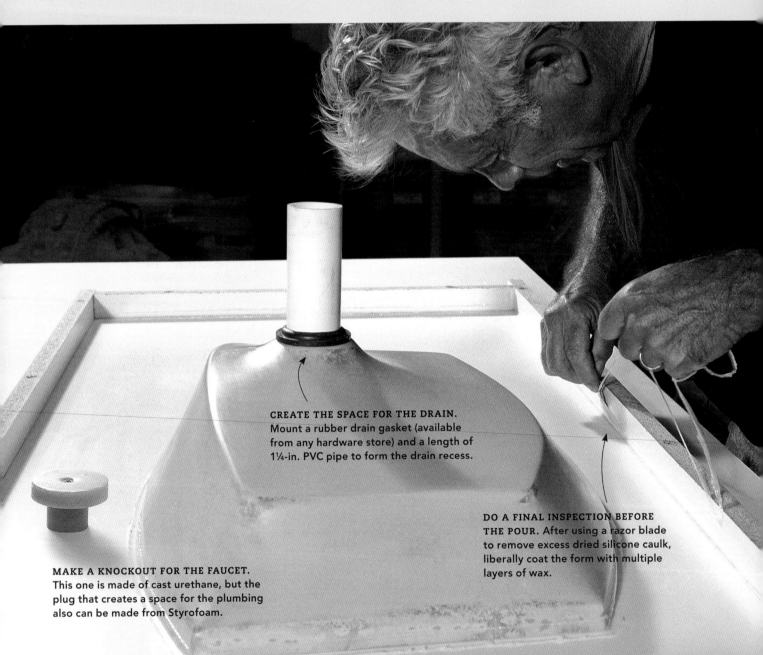

CREATE THE SPACE FOR THE DRAIN.
Mount a rubber drain gasket (available from any hardware store) and a length of 1¼-in. PVC pipe to form the drain recess.

MAKE A KNOCKOUT FOR THE FAUCET.
This one is made of cast urethane, but the plug that creates a space for the plumbing also can be made from Styrofoam.

DO A FINAL INSPECTION BEFORE THE POUR. After using a razor blade to remove excess dried silicone caulk, liberally coat the form with multiple layers of wax.

A BIG SPRAY GUN

TO GET AN EVEN, SMOOTH TEXTURE on the counter's surface, the first layers must be sprayed, and the easiest way to spray the mix is with a hopper-fed spray gun (see the photo at left), commonly known as a popcorn gun. It's typically used to apply plaster textures to ceilings, but it also will handle heavier mixtures. With a little practice, the gun is easy to use, but it requires an air compressor. I use a model called the SharpShooter®, which is made by Marshalltown®.

SPRAY IN THE COUNTER'S FINISH SURFACE. For this technique, the first layer of concrete in the form gives the sink its smooth surface. The mix is sprayed in two coats, each about ⅛ in. thick. For every 25 lb. of spray mix (portland-cement-to-sand ratio of 1:1), the mix uses 1½ qt. of water, ½ qt. of curing compound, 2 oz. of water reducer, and 220g of pigment. Mix in a 19-gal. bucket, liquids first, then add half the dry mix at a time.

Spray the first layers of concrete

The finished surface of the counter is made by spraying a thin mix of portland cement and sand with a popcorn sprayer. The most important thing at this stage is to make sure that the spray coats are applied uniformly to the surface of the form. When spraying, try to keep a consistent distance between the gun and the form, and sweep the gun back and forth in a slow, fluid motion. If you're not familiar with the technique of spraying, it's a good idea to practice on a piece of cardboard first to get a feel for the process.

The layer that gives the counter its strength is a mixture of concrete, glass fibers, and mesh. The fiberglass has been treated so that it won't break down in the highly alkaline environment of the concrete.

I apply handfuls of the fairly dry mix to make a 1-in. layer. After packing around the drain plug, I use a trowel to level the area directly at the base of the plug. I also check that I haven't left any voids, especially around the knockouts.

THIN AND WET. Because this layer is sprayed, it must have a thin consistency. Mix the liquids first in a 19-gal. bucket with a paddle in a ½-in. drill, then add the dry ingredients in stages. Note the shop-vacuum hose, which helps to control the dust during the mix. A dust mask is required equipment.

MAKE SURE THE SPRAY IS EVENLY DISTRIBUTED. After the first coat, use a chip brush to push the wet mix into any voids that might create air pockets in the surface.

FORM THE OVERFLOW DRAIN

To create the sink's overflow drain, first apply a 1½-in.-wide, ½-in.-thick strip of Styrofoam reinforced with packing tape on the side of the sink mold's outer edge so that it extends from the drain stub to about 1 in. from the sink rim. Cover the strip with the same depth of backing mix. After you remove the counter from the form, use a masonry bit to drill a ½-in. hole just below the sink rim where the end of the Styrofoam sits. Pour a few tablespoons of lacquer thinner through an empty caulk-tube funnel into the hole. The solvent dissolves the foam, leaving the open overflow drain.

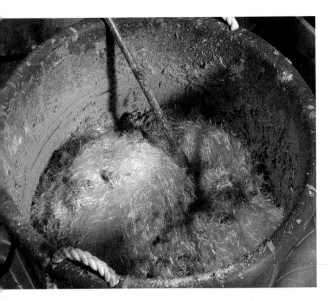

ADD CONCRETE, FIBER, AND MESH. This counter derives its strength from fiberglass fibers and mesh. Start the mix with 5 qt. of water, 2 qt. of curing compound, and 8 oz. of water reducer, then add 2 lb. of powdered dye and mix well. Next, add 100 lb. of the portland cement/sand mix (no aggregate), and when fully combined, fold in 2 lb. of alkaline-resistant fiberglass fibers. It's important not to break the fibers with excessive mixing.

ADD MESH FOR SUPPORT. Along the length of the counter, lay a piece of 4-in.-wide fiberglass mesh on each side of the sink, then cover it with the backing mix. The mesh should extend over the sink bowl.

After filling the form, I cover it with a plastic sheet, which keeps the concrete from curing too quickly, and leave it overnight. The next day, I remove the form sides and, with the help of an assistant, flip over the counter. We support it on two identically sized buckets, one on each side of the sink.

Finish touch-ups

The best part about this method is that once the counter is out of the form, there's little finishing to do. To fill the pin holes left by air bubbles, I make a paste of portland cement, dye, and water and squeegee it into the surface. When it's dry, I lightly buff the counter with a nylon abrasive pad. Finally, I apply three coats of sealer: first, a penetrating sealer; second, a satin sealer; and third, a coat of beeswax. They are absorbed into the surface and protect it.

PACK AND SMOOTH. Apply the backing mix by packing handfuls onto the form. The backing should have a consistent thickness of about 1¼ in. everywhere in the form. Use a float to smooth the final surface.

UNMOLDING THE COUNTER

WITH THE AMOUNT OF MOLD RELEASE USED, you'd think the counter would pop out in a hurry, but it rarely does. After driving two screws into the melamine sink-form top, we tried to lever it out, but the screws just pulled out. Compressed air didn't work either. Finally, I cut an oblong hole in the top and supported a short 2×4 with blocks on each side. We attached two short bar clamps to the 2×4 and underneath the hole, then tightened the clamps at the same rate until the mold popped out.

Build Your Own Bathroom Vanity

BY JUSTIN FINK

The details of a bathroom make a statement, and a vanity is often a focal point that ties those details together. The simplicity and clean lines of Shaker-style furniture appeal to me because they aren't adorned with excessive trim, appliqués, or other embellishments, yet they are more inviting and comfortable than modern pieces in a starker style. In addition, I think the Shaker style can work as well in a suburban raised ranch as it does in a 200-year-old farmhouse.

To build this vanity, you don't need a cabinet shop, and you don't need weeks of build time. With some common power tools and a slight increase in cost, you can build a vanity that is stronger and far more stylish than a production model, and that requires only a couple of weekends to complete.

SHAKER-STYLE VANITY

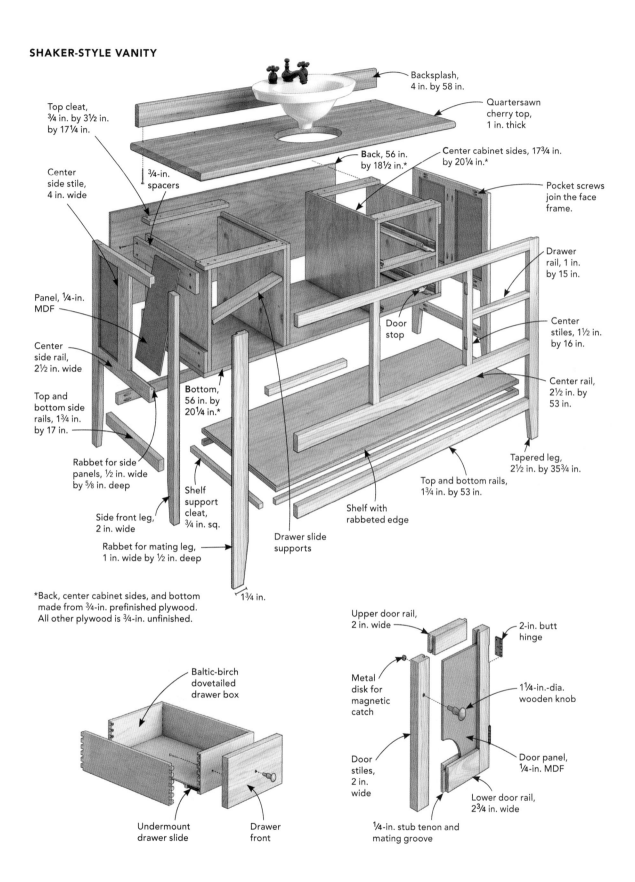

Top cleat,
¾ in. by 3½ in.
by 17¼ in.

Backsplash,
4 in. by 58 in.

Quartersawn
cherry top,
1 in. thick

Center
side stile,
4 in. wide

¾-in.
spacers

Back, 56 in.
by 18½ in.*

Center cabinet sides, 17¾ in.
by 20¼ in.*

Pocket screws
join the face
frame.

Panel, ¼-in.
MDF

Center
side rail,
2½ in. wide

Top and
bottom side
rails, 1¾ in.
by 17 in.

Rabbet for side
panels, ½ in. wide
by ⅝ in. deep

Side front leg,
2 in. wide

Rabbet for mating leg,
1 in. wide by ½ in. deep

Bottom,
56 in. by
20¼ in.*

Shelf
support
cleat,
¾ in. sq.

Drawer slide
supports

Door
stop

Drawer
rail, 1 in.
by 15 in.

Center
stiles, 1½ in.
by 16 in.

Center rail,
2½ in. by
53 in.

Tapered leg,
2½ in. by 35¾ in.

Top and bottom rails,
1¾ in. by 53 in.

Shelf with
rabbeted edge

1¾ in.

*Back, center cabinet sides, and bottom
made from ¾-in. prefinished plywood.
All other plywood is ¾-in. unfinished.

Baltic-birch
dovetailed
drawer box

Undermount
drawer slide

Drawer
front

Upper door rail,
2 in. wide

2-in. butt
hinge

Metal
disk for
magnetic
catch

1¼-in.-dia.
wooden knob

Door panel,
¼-in. MDF

Door
stiles,
2 in.
wide

Lower door rail,
2¾ in. wide

¼-in. stub tenon and
mating groove

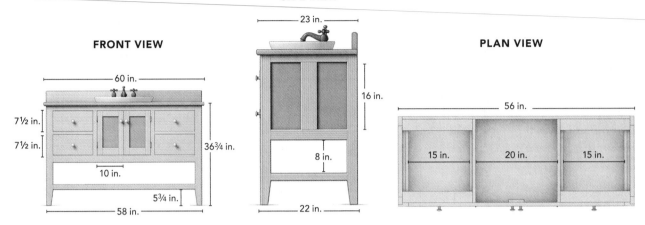

SIDE VIEW

FRONT VIEW

60 in.

7½ in.

7½ in.

10 in.

58 in.

5¾ in.

36¾ in.

23 in.

16 in.

8 in.

22 in.

PLAN VIEW

56 in.

15 in.

20 in.

15 in.

A classic look with a lot less effort

When designing this Shaker-inspired piece, I started with the same height, depth, and compatibility with standard plumbing fixtures that would be present on a store-bought vanity. From there, I added some details that you won't easily find, such as mortised butt hinges, full-extension ball-bearing undermount drawer slides, a solid-wood top, and a traditional milk-paint finish. Compared to the details on a production-line vanity, these small changes can make a big difference in the overall feel of the finished project, and they aren't that hard to execute. My goal in building this type of project is to respect the principles of traditional woodworking but challenge some of the techniques to make the building process a bit less fussy. Although the drawing on p. 127 may look intimidating, the necessary techniques for this build are basic, and I've included tips and tricks to increase your accuracy. The result is a vanity that looks and feels like a handcrafted piece of furniture, but one that goes together with more ease.

The most luxurious tools I used here were a track saw and a thickness planer, but even those are negotiable. If you don't have a track saw, then you can break down sheet goods with a circular saw and a homemade cutting guide. Also, even though

you may be purchasing rough lumber that requires planing on its face and edges, most hardwood suppliers will do this work for a reasonable rate (my supplier charges 25¢ per bd. ft.) if you don't have a thickness planer.

Materials chosen for their strengths

The build starts with the cabinet's plywood case, which is the foundation of the entire vanity—the part to which the rest of the components will be attached. The case consists of a continuous bottom piece, upright dividers to separate the center cabinet from the drawer sections that flank it, and a continuous back that locks everything into place. You'll need one sheet each of unfinished and prefinished ¾-in. plywood.

The unfinished plywood is used for the areas of the vanity that will either be painted or remain unseen. For water resistance and overall longevity of the undersink area, I prefer to use prefinished plywood. If you can't find a source for prefinished plywood, I recommend finishing both sides of a sheet of plywood with several coats of polyurethane and letting it cure before cutting the sheet into pieces. Otherwise, it can be a hassle to apply and sand clear coats of finish on the inside of an assembled box.

MAKE SHEET GOODS MORE MANAGEABLE. A track saw is ideal for dividing sheets of plywood into smaller, rough-size pieces. A sheet of 1-in.-thick rigid foam is a perfect sacrificial base and support for cutoffs. Run the parts through a tablesaw for final sizing to ensure that matching parts are the same dimension.

FASTENED, BUT LEFT LOOSE. After screwing together the two pieces of plywood for each center divider and attaching the spacers to each end panel, tack the subassemblies to the cabinet bottom with 16-ga. nails. Nailed sparingly, the case parts are loose enough for adjustment once the face frame is attached.

QUICK AND CLEAN TAPERS. The bottom of each leg stile receives a taper cut to give the finished vanity the look of a stand-alone piece of furniture. A plywood jig with an L-shape fence allows the piece to be safely supported for a clean-cutting pass on the tablesaw.

ONE PART SIZES THE OTHERS. A sacrificial miter-saw fence and shopmade throat plate ensure cleaner cuts. They also make it easy to register the stock, so you only have to measure the first piece in each group of parts, which can then be laid atop the next piece for repeat cuts.

FAUX FLOATING PANELS. To achieve the look of true floating panels without all of the complex joinery, assemble each of the vanity side-panel frames with pocket screws, and then cut a ½-in.-wide by ⅝-in.-deep rabbet in the back side of the poplar stiles and rails to accept a ¼-in. MDF panel.

AN IDEAL SPACER. When assembling the front face frame, use the drawer fronts—which are cut to the exact size of the opening—to help align the stiles and rails. Later, trim the drawer fronts to their slightly smaller finished size and you will have wasted no extra material on throw-away spacers.

THE ORDER MATTERS. Because they are only tacked together, the plywood parts have room for adjustment, which allows you to bring the case and assembled frame into alignment. First, flush up and fasten the two long rails, then the two outermost stiles. Follow up with the inner stiles and then the drawer rails.

The joinery used in the plywood case won't be visible in the final piece; for that reason, you can use a finish nailer to tack most of the parts together. After assembling the face frame and attaching it to the boxes, lock the plywood together permanently with 2-in. screws.

Aside from the plywood used for the bottom shelf, all of the surfaces of the vanity that will be painted are built from 5/4 poplar (1-in. finished thickness) and ¼-in. MDF. Both of these materials are readily available, inexpensive, and stable, and they take paint well.

For the top of my vanity, I decided to use solid quartersawn cherry. Compared to more conventional flatsawn lumber, quartersawn boards have relatively straight-running grain, an inherently stable orientation that minimizes movement across the surface of the wood as its moisture content changes.

Pocket holes are fast and strong

The parts for the face frame, side-panel frames, legs, doors, and drawer fronts are all cut at the same time. All are crosscut to 1 in. longer than their final desired lengths, ripped ⅛ in. wider than their desired width,

and then run through the thickness planer on all four sides to bring them to their final dimension before crosscutting them to their exact length.

Anywhere that I can, I use pocket-screw joinery as a fast and strong solution for hidden fastening. A pocket-hole jig is quick to set up, a cinch to use, and with hardly any moving parts, it just never seems to let me down. The only places on this project where I used a more traditional form of joinery were on the two doors.

Because the doors incorporate floating panels, the surrounding poplar pieces need to be grooved on a tablesaw to accept the ¼-in. MDF panels. But pocket screws won't work when driven through a groove-edge board, and even if they did work, the exposed grooves and pocket holes would be visible when the cabinet doors were open.

Instead, cut stub tenons on the edges of the doors' top and bottom rails, allowing them to fit into the same groove that is already being cut to accept the MDF panel. All of this joinery can be cut on the tablesaw, provided you carefully set the fence and blade height for each step. After glue up and sanding, trim the doors to fit using a standard step-by-step door-fitting.

ONE SETUP, TWO PASSES. Door stiles and rails receive ½-in.-deep grooves made by cutting to one side of a marked centerline, then flipping the piece to widen the ⅛-in. kerf into a ¼-in. groove. A featherboard ensures that parts stay firmly pressed against the fence.

NIBBLE THE TENONS. A stop block attached to the fence of a miter gauge registers each end of the door rails to create the shoulder cut of the ½-in.-long stub tenons, which are created by making a series of successive passes and testing the fit in the mating groove.

NOT LOOSE OR TIGHT, BUT SNUG. The panel and tenons should slide snugly into the grooves. If the tenons are too thin, glue shims to their cheeks. If they're too fat, hit them with a sanding block. After glue up, trim the door to final height.

MORTISES MADE EASY. After trimming the top and bottom of the doors, rout the hinge mortises on the doors and assembled face frame using a T-shape plywood template and bearing-guided mortise bit.

ONE DOOR MARKS THE OTHER. With the first door sized, hung, and clamped in the closed position, temporarily hang the second door, and mark a line on the backside where the doors overlap.

DOUBLE-STICK SLED. The safest way to trim the second door, especially if the cut needs to be a slight taper, is to attach the door to a plywood sled with double-stick tape so it can be cut on the tablesaw.

TACKLE THE GLUING IN STAGES. Rather than trying to glue up a 23-in.-wide countertop all at once, glue up pairs of boards. This makes it easier to get parts clamped and misalignments corrected before the glue starts to set up. Join the pairs to make the whole top.

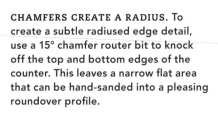

CHAMFERS CREATE A RADIUS. To create a subtle radiused edge detail, use a 15° chamfer router bit to knock off the top and bottom edges of the counter. This leaves a narrow flat area that can be hand-sanded into a pleasing roundover profile.

PERFECT DRAWER FACES. With the drawer boxes fixed to their slides and pushed into the cabinet, apply double-stick carpet tape to the back of the drawer face, and carefully press it into place. The tape is strong enough to allow the drawer to be opened so that the front can be fastened from the inside of the box with 1¼-in. pan-head screws.

Know when to buy rather than build

Drawer boxes aren't much harder to build than any other part of this vanity. But when I compare the convenience and low cost of ordering dovetailed drawer components with the steps and amount of time involved in making them myself, it's a simple decision. I buy my drawer components online from Barker Door, where the parts are cut to my specifications and arrive ready for glue up and finishing. For this project, the parts for all four drawers made of Baltic birch (a type of tightly veneered plywood) cost me $143, including shipping to my doorstep. Had I bought the plywood and built the boxes myself, I would have spent $116 for materials alone, and I consider my time worth more than the $27 savings.

For drawer slides, don't skimp. It's the one part of this cabinet that gets used daily, so it's the last place you want to save a buck. I use Blum® undermount slides. They aren't cheap, but they install easily, ride smoothly, and have a soft-close mechanism.

Step up to a solid-wood top

For the top of my vanity, I bought rough-dimensioned 6/4 cherry boards and planed them to a 1-in. finished thickness. After gluing up and sanding

SOURCES

DRAWER BOXES
dovetailed Baltic birch, unassembled
www.barkerdoor.com

KNOBS
1¼-in.-dia. Shaker knob
www.shakerworkshops.com

DRAWER SLIDES
563H undermount slides
www.barkerdoor.com

HINGES
2-in. rolled barrel butt hinges
www.horton-brasses.com

FAUCET
Kingston Brass KS395.AX
www.faucetdirect.com

SINK
Kohler K-2075-8-0 Serif®
www.amazon.com

PAINT
Milk Paint Soldier Blue
www.milkpaint.com

the top, I cut the hole for the sink using a template and a jigsaw before applying the polyurethane finish. This sequence is important because it allows me to apply finish to the visible surface of the countertop and also to the edges of the sink cutout, which are likely to get wet at some point in the life of the vanity.

This vanity took about 30 hours to complete and cost me about $850 in materials—comparable in cash outlay to many commercially available vanities of this size and style. In fact, this vanity was less expensive than many similar models being sold online. Plus, I know mine is built solid in a classic style that I believe will remain timeless, and it has a handmade touch that you can't get from a factory-built vanity.

Perfecting the Tiled Tub Surround

BY TOM MEEHAN

Over my 35 years of installing tile, I've done well over a thousand tub surrounds. Take it from me: Tiling a tub surround might seem like the kind of remodeling project you can jump right into, but it's not. It takes quite a bit of planning and proper follow-through to get quality results; this is not a job I would recommend for a first-time installer. To this day, I still treat each new installation the same as the first. The key lies in knowing how the last tile will fit before the first tile touches the wall. This means knowing how well the tub was installed, where each course of tile will land, and how the cut tiles will lay out.

A STORY POLE ELIMINATES SURPRISES

UNLESS YOU'RE REALLY LUCKY, you'll have to cut some tiles to make the layout work. The key is planning where those cuts should land so that they are less noticeable. When properly laid out, cut tiles should be no less than half the size of a full tile. There are times, of course, when small pieces are unavoidable, but the problem can be minimized with a little effort and imagination. Layout can be determined with a tape measure, but it's far easier to skip the math and just make a story pole.

A STICK TELLS THE STORY. Cut a piece of wood for the vertical layout and another for the horizontal layout, each a bit shorter than the distance between tub and ceiling or wall and wall. Place the tiles one at a time, including a space for grout between each if the tile isn't self-spacing, and mark the layout on the stick.

KNOW YOUR TUB INSTALLATION. It would be nice if every tub installation were dead level, but that's rarely the case. Before you can begin the tile layout, lay a level across the top of each side of the tub. The bottom row of tiles can be cut to follow the contour of the tub or to account for high spots, so the goal here is to find the low point, which becomes the starting point for the rest of the layout.

UP FROM THE BOTTOM. Set the end of the story pole on the tub's lowest spot, then draw a mark at least halfway up the wall that corresponds to the joints of your story-pole layout.

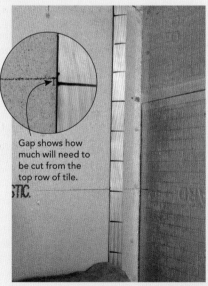

Gap shows how much will need to be cut from the top row of tile.

ESTABLISH A BENCHMARK. Transfer the halfway mark across all three walls of the tub surround, making sure it's level. This is your benchmark line.

PLAN FOR THE BAND. It's also a good idea to use the story pole to determine the position of the accent band and the way it will relate to the shower hardware, and the position of niches or shelves in the tub surround.

FLIP IT FOR THE CEILING. Turned end for end and placed against the ceiling, the story pole indicates the amount that needs to be cut from the top row. Here, the cut will leave almost an entire tile, which is perfect.

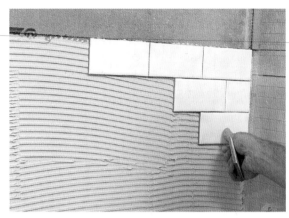

AN EVEN SPREAD. Working from the benchmark line down, start with the lower part of the back wall, spreading the thinset cement with a ¼-in. square-notched trowel. Use a sag-resistant latex-modified thinset such as Laticrete 255 for tub surrounds because it reduces the chance that tiles will slide out of position before the cement sets up.

THE FIRST TILE ESTABLISHES THE PATTERN. On this job, the story pole confirmed that a full row of uncut tiles could fit along the back wall, so the first row begins with a full tile, followed by a half-tile below it to establish the running bond pattern. If a full row of uncut tile won't fit, it's better to start in the center of the wall and have the same cut on each end.

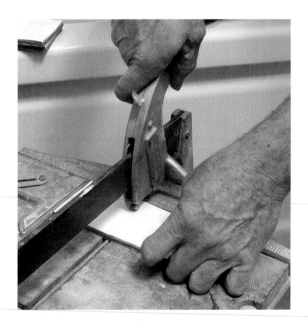

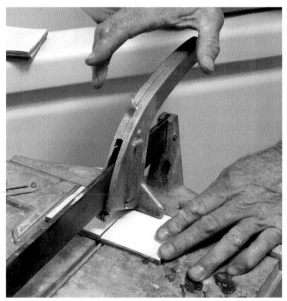

SCORE AND SNAP. Simple straight cuts can be made as you go, but tile as much as possible before slowing down to make the more complicated cuts, like those around plumbing fixtures. For all straight cuts, a basic snap cutter works quickly and makes a clean cut. Score across the top of the tile, then give the handle a quick bump with the palm of your hand to break the tile at the score line. If the cuts are difficult, small, or notched, a tile saw is a better choice.

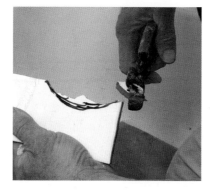

CURVES REQUIRE NIPPERS. After installing as many full tiles as possible around the showerhead and mixing valve, you can use a pair of nippers to fit in the remaining tiles. Holding the tile in place, use a permanent marker to outline the area that needs to be cut. Carefully nibble up to the marked line with a set of tile nippers. The cuts don't have to be pretty; just get close enough so that the tile easily fits the open spot in the layout. The gap will be covered by the fixture's trim plate.

KEEP CUTS TO THE BOTTOM. Compensate for an out-of-level tub at the bottom row of tile. After using a straightedge to ensure that the highest completed row is straight, fill in the tiles at the tub. These cuts, which are often tapered and can vary from tile to tile, can be done on a snap cutter, but a wet saw is more accurate.

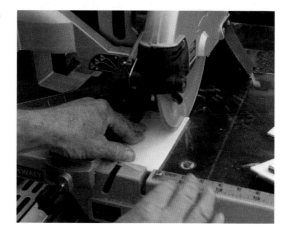

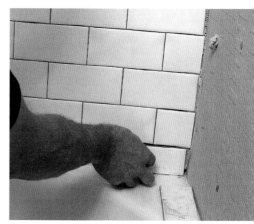

KICK UP THE CHARACTER WITH CUSTOM FEATURES

I LIKE TO OFFER SIMPLE UPGRADES that make an impression but don't cost much or add much time to the job. I often include a built-in shampoo niche, but two of my other favorite upgrades are a corner shelf and a band of contrasting mosaic tile.

CORNER SHELF

Typically, I make a corner shelf from a 12x12 stone tile. Here, I cut a piece of marble in half diagonally and then rounded over the edges with a rub brick. Installation is easy: Butter the back edge of the shelf with thinset and rest it atop a course of tiles. Trim the next course of wall tiles as needed. To keep water from pooling on the shelf, put a few temporary plastic wedge spacers under the shelf, all the way at the back of the corner, so that it sets up with a slight pitch.

ACCENT BAND

As long as you're not using glass tile, which requires a slightly different approach, you can install an accent band without changing your approach too much. Use a utility knife to cut sheets of mosaic tile into strips, set them into the thin-set with firm pressure, and adjust individual tiles as needed to keep things even.

For this job, the customer asked for classic 3x5 white subway tile, which has never gone out of style in all the years I've been on the job. To give the tub surround a bit of a kick, I incorporated a band of mosaic tile into the layout and installed a marble corner shelf for shampoo bottles and a bar of soap. Neither of these little changes added much cost for materials or much time to the installation, but both help this space to stand apart from a typical tiled tub surround.

As is the case in any wet area, the tile substrate should be cement backerboard or another approved backer that will not deteriorate or harbor mold.

In this case, because the tub surround met wall paneling on one side, I used standard ½-in.-thick Durock cementboard for most of the job, but installed ¼-in.-thick HardieBacker cementboard, a fiber-cement product, on the wall that needed to be flush to the paneling.

Strategies for success

I start all of my installations by making a story pole to help me in planning the horizontal and vertical layout. On the back wall of the tub, which is seen first and most frequently, I want the tiles laid out so that any necessary cuts land in the two corners and are of equal size. On the sidewalls, where symmetry is not as important, cuts can be hidden in the back corners.

If the tile will stop short of the ceiling, then you won't need to cut the top row. I usually run my tub surrounds right to the ceiling. I'd rather not end up with a small piece at the top, but I also want a full tile at the tub.

Determining the size of each course can require a little compromise. If it looks as though the course of tile at the ceiling will be too narrow, I try reducing the size of the pieces on top of the tub. Also, if the tub is significantly out of level, a line of cut tile at the tub will make the problem less obvious. On the job shown here, the tub was out of level by about ¼ in. from end to end, which is a very common situation. I accounted for this by planning the bottom row so that full-height tile starts at the lowest point and is gradually adjusted and cut as needed to absorb the high spots.

Installing tile is the fun part

Once the layout has been determined, the hard part of the job is just about done. There will still be some tiles that need to be cut and some holes to be made for plumbing, but as long as you follow the plan and keep the tiles level, the next step will be the fast and gratifying part of the installation.

I always spread an ample amount of cement to get a full bond rather than skimping and leaving a few voids on the wall. When there's a good coating of thinset on the wall, I comb it with the teeth of the trowel in one direction. This makes a big difference in achieving a complete bond. Making sure that trowel lines all go in one direction reduces the possibility of voids in the thinset behind the tile. I also make sure to push each tile into the cement and give it a ¼-in. slide to achieve a good bond. Subway tiles often have self-spacing nibs to keep grout joints consistent. Regardless of the tile, though, you should always check with a level to ensure that the tiles are

running at the same height and that joints are lining up at the corners.

I usually tile the lower half of all three walls of a tub surround before moving any higher. A pro can install about 25 sq. ft. of tile in 20 to 30 minutes. If you're a DIYer, plan on no more than half that square footage.

Cutting the tiles is the hard part of the job. The cut pieces have to fit properly and the grout joints must be spaced evenly so that everything blends together smoothly. Most ceramic, porcelain, and even some glass tiles can be cut with a snap cutter, which is a fast, portable, and nearly silent tool. Notches, curves, and other fairly simple nonlinear cuts can be handled with a pair of nippers. Almost all stone tiles, and even some handmade tiles, have to be cut with a wet saw, which is also indispensable for more complicated cuts or when working with fragile tiles.

Grouting for consistency

If I'm using more than one package of grout, which in most surrounds will be a nonsanded grout, I mix everything together dry to ensure that the color is consistent. Then I mix the grout with clean water—that's a must. Generally, I spread the grout over the entire tub surround; by the time I finish spreading the last section, the first section is ready to clean. On hot days, grout will set up more quickly. In rainy weather or on humid days, the grout will take longer to firm up.

After spreading the grout, I wash the excess off the surface of the tile. It is important to wring out the sponge and not to use too much water. Also, when mixing the grout, I don't make it too watery. This weakens the strength of the grout in the long run. The next day, I wipe on a coat of sealer heavy enough to saturate the grout joints. I typically use a foam brush, but a rag also can work. I then wipe down the tiled area with a clean white cloth, leaving no sealer residue.

GROUTING CAN MAKE OR BREAK THE JOB. As with laying out and setting the tiles, there's a right way and a wrong way to tackle a grout job. My father used to say, "A grout job can make a mediocre tile job look great or a great tile job look mediocre." Crisp, clean, and even grout lines are the goal, and there are a few key things to focus on.

PREGROUT CLEANUP. Before mixing up the grout, spend a few minutes looking over every joint in the tub surround. Even a day after it's been applied, the thinset is still fresh enough to be removed easily with a utility knife.

SPREAD AND SCRAPE. Use a margin trowel to load grout onto a rubber float, and then use the float to apply it to the wall. Spread the grout in broad, arcing strokes. Start with your arm extended, and pull the float toward your body. The first pass packs grout into the joints; the second pass scrapes away most of the excess.

PACK AND TOOL THE JOINTS. Once the grout has firmed up but before you wash down the tile, use the butt end of a Sharpie® marker as a grout stick to strike the grout joints. This packs in the grout tightly and makes the joint consistent.

WIPE AWAY THE HAZE. Once the tile has been washed down and all excess grout removed, let everything dry for about 15 minutes, or until a light haze develops on the surface of the tile. Then use a clean cloth or quality paper towel to wipe the haze off the surface of the tile, buffing it to a finished shine.

Old-School Path to a Wide-Open Bath

BY TOM MEEHAN

Life is full of uncertainties. You can count on a few things, though, and here's one of them: Water runs downhill. In a bathroom, the trick is to keep water going toward the drain. Porcelain vessels are good at containment, but switching from a tub to a shower stall changes the game. Curbless showers, which make life easier for folks with special needs, also complicate the issue of the drain.

Before the advent of tile backerboard, tile was set on a substrate of troweled cement mortar, known in the tile world as a mud job. I've learned to apply this mud-and-tile method to a curbless shower so that the water goes where it's supposed to. For this job, I also installed a linear drain along the far wall, which means that the shower floor is pitched in only one plane, rather than in a bowl shape around a circular drain.

Prep the subfloor first

I begin by lowering the subfloor in the area of the shower so that I don't have to use as much mortar. There are three options for this step: (1) add an additional layer of ¾-in. plywood around the shower area; (2) notch the floor joists and resheathe the floor; or (3) add cleats to the joists. Whatever option I use, the idea is to lower the floor in the shower area

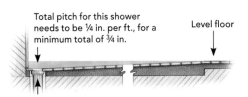

Total pitch for this shower needs to be ¼ in. per ft., for a minimum total of ¾ in.

Level floor

Because the tile mortar bed needs to slope about ¼ in. per ft. and the curbless shower needs to be about 1 in. deep around the room, the subfloor in the shower area must be lowered. Here are three ways the author has accomplished this.

Subfloor is built up ¾ in.

1. BUILD UP THE SURROUNDING FLOOR. A layer of ¾-in. plywood added around the area of the shower increases the pitch to the drain. Factor in a ¼-in. drop per ft. when planning the shower.

2. NOTCH THE FLOOR JOISTS. Certain situations, especially remodels, call for dropping the subfloor level by notching the joists (usually by ¾ in.) in the shower area. Reducing the width of floor joists can weaken the floor, so it's recommended that the notched joists be doubled across the area of the notch.

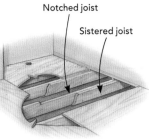

Notched joist

Sistered joist

3. ADD CLEATS AND DROP THE SUBFLOOR. The author's favorite method is to remove the subfloor in the area of the shower, fasten cleats to each side of the joists at the thickness of the plywood (½ in. or ¾ in.) below the top of the joists, and then fill in the spaces between the joists with plywood.

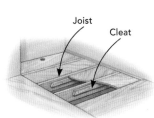

Joist

Cleat

by ¾ in. (Larger showers may require more pitch.) On this job, it was easier to add another layer of plywood to the subfloor.

Next, I put down a layer of #15 builder's felt, followed by galvanized 2.5-lb. diamond-mesh wire lath to anchor the mortar to the floor. I start nailing in the middle of the room, then push out the mesh to the perimeter as I nail so that the wire doesn't buckle in the middle.

The floor needs a proper mix

It's extremely important that the mortar have the right consistency. If it's too wet, it has no strength; too dry, and it won't pack down. I start with 25 full shovels of sand for every bag of portland cement. This basic batch unit will cover about 35 sq. ft. at a depth of 1½ in. To arrive at the correct consistency, I use about 5 gal. of water, added in small amounts as I mix.

Establish the perimeter

After I've mixed the mortar, I fill a 5-gal. bucket and start to dump the mortar around the perimeter of the room, up to the shower area. I tamp it down hard with a steel trowel and use a wooden float to pack the edges, especially the corners. (Be aware of the toilet flange's location. You don't want to cover it over and tile it—unfortunately, I know this from experience.) As I pack down the perimeter, I keep checking to make sure that it's level all the way around the room. I'll deal with the pitch in the shower once I have this level line as a reference.

At the door threshold, I nail a strip of 1x as a stopping point. When installed, the tile should come flush to the top of the strip. To establish the correct height of the mortar, I create a point ⅜ in. below the top of the strip, then check the height with a tile once I've laid the mortar. It all depends on how level the floor is, but I usually aim for a perimeter depth of about 1 in. and no less than ¾ in.

READY THE FLOOR FOR MORTAR. The first layer of the tile floor consists of overlapping pieces of #15 builder's felt, which prevents the subfloor from absorbing moisture from the mortar.

GROUND THE MORTAR. Galvanized diamond mesh gives the mortar an attachment point on the floor. Cut into pieces with a 2-in. overlap, and nail with 1½-in. galvanized roofing nails every 6 in. to 8 in.

THE RIGHT MIX

ONE TRICK TO MIXING MORTAR is to use a chopping motion, bringing the hoe up high so that gravity helps to pull it through the dense sand and portland-cement mix. I mix the ingredients twice, once from each side, then add water and mix three more times.

NOT TOO WET OR TOO DRY. The mortar is just right when it holds together.

LAY THE MORTAR BED

Using a mortar underlayment makes pitching the floor toward the drain possible. While round drains require the surrounding floor to be bowl-shaped, a linear drain is positioned against the shower's back wall, so the shower floor needs to slope only in a single plane to the drain.

DUMP THE MORTAR. Use a 5-gal. pail to distribute piles of mixed mortar evenly around the perimeter.

1 PACK AND LEVEL. On the level part of the floor, use a steel trowel to pack down the loose mortar so that it forms a level perimeter about 1 in. thick around the room.

2 FILL AND SCREED. Dump more mortar in the middle of the floor, and pack it down. Use a level as a screed, resting one end on the perimeter as a reference for the floor's center.

3 CREATE THE PITCH. In the shower area, extend the level floor grade to the high end, then create a single slope to the drain. The total difference in grade should be about ¾ in. for a 3-ft.-long shower like this.

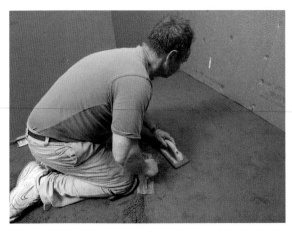

4 SMOOTH TRANSITIONS. Once the pitch is established, use a wooden float to grade the transition from the level floor to the shower along the side.

Fill and screed to the drain

When the perimeter is packed and level, I start to fill in the interior with mortar. Using the perimeter as a guide, I screed the mortar with a straightedge. The key to pulling the straightedge is not to pull it straight but at an angle from the perimeter. I pack everything down with the steel trowel, then smooth the surface with a wooden float in an orbital motion as I go. If there are any low points, I fill them in and pack them down again. I use a steel trowel for a last finishing pass. It's a good idea to work from inside the room toward the door.

Once I've established a level plane in the rest of the room, I start working on the pitched floor of the shower. Here, the outside edge of the shower is level with the rest of the room. Inside the shower area, I pitch the mortar down to the drain, aiming for a ¾-in. difference in grade from one end to the drain. I use 2x2 tiles in the shower to ease the transition in grade from the shower to the floor, which will be covered in 12x12 tiles.

With the pitched floor established in the shower, my next task is to set the drain. For this job, I'm installing a linear drain. Unlike a traditional round

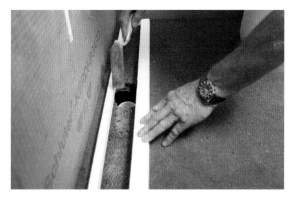

DOUBLE-CHECK WITH A TEMPLATE. Use the drain's foam spacer as a template to check the excavation. Remove any excess mortar with a narrow trowel, then check the drain's fit.

MARK THE LOCATION. Position the linear drain and its integral membrane flange over the drain hole, and push it into the mortar. The resulting shallow depression marks the basic outline that can be excavated.

GLUE IT IN PLACE. Fill the cavity and cover the immediate area with thinset; then place the drain and membrane. Firmly press the membrane into the thinset with a trowel.

CHECK THE HEIGHT. Before the thinset is dry, it's a good idea to make sure that the drain will lie just below the surface of the tile. The finished height of the drain grate is adjusted with screws.

drain flange that's installed before the mortar, this drain is tied into the membrane overlay. Besides its shape, the main difference in a linear drain is that it doesn't require a flange. Once installed in the floor, it's tied directly to the drainpipe with a flexible coupling. When the drain fits, I finish the rest of the floor and allow the mud to dry overnight.

Protect the floor with a waterproof membrane

Now that the mortar has set up, I can set the drain and then install a waterproof membrane that seals the porous mortar layer. (I used Schlüter's Kerdi membrane on this job, but Noble's NobleSeal and Laticrete's Hydro Ban are two alternatives.) Using the drain template, I check to see that the space is the right size. The mortar is still relatively soft, so it's easy to make adjustments with a small trowel. I vacuum up the crumbs, apply the thinset, and install the drain. This whole trough should be level so that water will go to the center drain evenly.

Once the drain is in, I start the membrane process by installing the 5-in. band around the room's perimeter, splitting it between the wall and the floor. I use a $3/16$-in. V-notch trowel to spread the thinset, lay out the band, and squeegee out the excess thinset with a drywall knife whose corners have been rounded off. The preformed corners are installed the same way, and I am especially careful to make the inside corners tight against the wall. Next, I cut sheets of membrane and dry-fit them around the room, making sure that I have at least 2 in. of overlap on all seams. I draw a line at the edge so that I apply the thinset only where I need it.

With the sheet back down, I start at the center and work my way toward the outside, first with my hands, then with the drywall knife, pressing out all the voids and air pockets. The joints should be nice and tight. The worst thing you can do is start on the outside from each direction and have the whole thing buckle in the middle. Whatever excess is out-side, I flatten down with the trowel. Voids will eventually cause cracks in the tile. In the shower area, I overlap the entire drain flange with the membrane.

Tile is the easy part

When I first spread the thinset, I use the back side of the trowel and burnish it over the membrane. I also do this over plywood or any other surface, because rubbing the thinset deeper into the membrane with the back of the trowel gives you a much better bond. When it's set and done, I turn over the trowel and use the toothed side, which creates a consistent height for the tile and at the same time allows me to even out any highs or lows that might be in the membrane.

Once the first tile is set in place, the placement of every piece of tile in the room is determined. I use a rubber grout float to pack the tiles down to set the bond and flush up the corners. For this project, the shower area was to be covered with 2x2 tiles, with 12x12 tiles used for the remainder of the floor. Behind the drain, rather than put in a few small pieces with the 2x2s, I cut down 12x12s; I think that's a better look.

The final step in the floor installation is grout. The grout should be mixed so that it's workable, but fairly stiff. Too much water weakens grout and can cause color variations. I start in the far corner and spread the grout across the whole floor, let it set for about 15 minutes, then come back and wash it off. The key to trowel work is to hold the trowel at about a 30° angle to the floor so that the grout really gets pushed down into the joints. A second swipe at 60° cleans off the excess. There's no problem leaving a little bit of excess, because that helps in the cleanup.

START WITH THE BORDER. Spread thinset into the corners a few inches up the wall and onto the floor. Fold the corner strips in half, press them into the thinset, and squeeze out any excess.

COVER LOTS OF GROUND. After dry-fitting sheets of membrane to overlap the edges, spread thinset out for each piece individually. Keep the trowel tight to the floor so that it cuts through to the concrete and leaves a consistent surface.

START IN THE MIDDLE AND WORK OUTWARD. Once the membrane is pressed into the thinset, start in the center of the sheet, and begin troweling any excess thinset out toward the edges.

IN A PERFECT WORLD, TILE WOULD BE FLEXIBLE

TILES, ESPECIALLY LARGE TILES, must be installed so that they're fully supported on a flat surface, or they'll crack. In situations where the floor is not flat (in a shower stall, for instance), small tiles conform more easily. In this bath and curbless shower, both conditions exist, and rather than use small tiles throughout, I made a transition from large field tiles to small tiles in the shower with intermediate-size tiles that could handle the switch between level and sloped floors. I decided to go with a diagonal layout bordered by 4-in.-wide strips. After bringing the small shower tiles to the edge of the transition, I cut 4-in.-wide strips from the 12x12 tiles and mitered each corner. Next, I cut the big square tiles in half diagonally, which established the pattern for the rest of the floor.

Fix a Failing Bathroom Floor

BY MIKE LOMBARDI

In a perfect world, there would never be a battle between framing and plumbing. The reality, though, is that bathrooms are often small, and there frequently is precious little space to fit all the incoming and outgoing plumbing necessary for the tub, shower, vanity, toilet, and other fixtures. Without forethought in the design phase, upfront communication between subcontractors in the rough-in phase, and a willingness to do the job right in remodels, sacrifices are often made.

These problems usually are found in the floor system: Joists are notched carelessly, cut through, or drilled incorrectly, sometimes directly under a bathtub or toilet, where there is an added load on the framing. In the bathroom shown here, water leaking from the joint between the tile floor and the tub apron had rotted the floor sheathing, the original joist below, and a new joist that had been "sistered" in place to rescue the original. To make matters worse, the adjacent joist had been notched almost two-thirds of the way through to accommodate the tub's waste line. These framing nightmares aren't uncommon, and though nobody likes to hear it, proper repair often means a full demolition of the bathroom.

The plans for this project included expanding the bathroom's footprint, so we had the luxury of removing the partition walls on both ends, which gave us lots of room to work. We had a full-height basement below the bathroom, which also made our work easier. Often, the ceiling below the bathroom has to be opened up or part of the rim joist removed so that new joists can be slid into place. The plans also called for a barrier-free shower, which meant lowering the floor so that the tilesetter could create a sloped mortar bed, a decision that has its own structural complications.

In the end, we elected to install doubled floor joists under the whole bathroom. Damaged joists were cut out and replaced with new lumber spanning from plate to carrying beam, and joists that were still in good condition were beefed up with new joists sistered alongside them. After notching the joists in place for the lowered floor, the whole assembly was tied together with ¾-in. subfloor sheathing.

Know the signs of trouble

The first signs of structural inadequacies in a bathroom floor usually show up in the form of cracked grout joints in floor or wall tile, or even cracks in

the tiles themselves. Most fixtures in the bathroom are heavy, are used frequently, and can shed or leak enough water over time not only to wet the floor below, but also to wet it repeatedly so that it doesn't dry out. That's the perfect recipe for rot. These problems most often occur near the toilet, the bathtub, and the shower stall.

The toilet requires a large drainpipe connection (3 in. or 4 in. dia.), and in older homes, it was common for the plumber to notch the floor joists rather than to bore a clean hole through the framing to run the pipe. This notching can cause settling of the finished floor and can disturb the toilet flange's watertight connection. The damage in this case may be from a leak so small that it does not immediately show up, even when you're looking at the ceiling below the bathroom, but continuously wets the subfloor and framing to a point of decay and rot. Condensation also can contribute to floor and wall damage near the toilet. A toilet that is continuously running, especially during hot, humid conditions, will cause condensation to form on the tank, bowl, and cold-water supply piping. Although usually in small amounts, the constant drip of water causes damage to nearby subflooring, wooden trim, and eventually framing.

POOR MAN'S PRY BAR. Used against the floor joists, a long 2x makes a great pry bar to help lift tongue-and-groove floor sheathing.

OPEN THE FLOOR. Depending on the plans for the remodel, you can sometimes remove partition walls, which makes cutting the floor with a circular saw a quick task (photo far right). Most of the time, the walls are staying in place, though, so use a reciprocating saw (photo right) to cut the flooring flush to the plates.

MAKE WAY FOR THE NEW WOOD. With the old subfloor removed, it's time to remove all nails from the tops of the joists and to remove or reroute any plumbing, electrical wiring, or ductwork that will interfere with the installation of the new subfloor and joists.

GET THE SAG OUT. It's not uncommon for an old floor joist, especially one that's been notched deeply, to have sagged over time. Before sistering a new joist to the old, string a line between the joists' two bearing points (photo right), and use a piece of framing lumber and a small sledgehammer to lever the joist up until the sag has been removed (photo far right).

CUSTOM SIZING. If you're spanning between a mudsill and a carrying beam, you often can leave the joist long, sliding one end over the carrying beam while the opposite end is lifted into position. If you're spanning between two walls or rim joists, the joists must be shorter to maneuver them into place. The old joists may not be the same height as new lumber, but you can notch the bottom edge if needed.

PREP FOR A MORTAR BED

THE PLANS FOR THIS BATHROOM include a barrier-free shower, so the floor had to be lowered in preparation for a sloped mortar bed. A plywood cleat screwed to the side of the joist serves as a guide for the circular saw. At each end, an oscillating multitool or reciprocating saw finishes the cut.

ROLL 'EM UPRIGHT. Slide one end of the joist over the top of the carrying beam so that the other end can be lifted and slid toward the rim joist. Start with the lower edge of the joist roughly in position, then roll the joist into place and persuade it into its final upright position with a small sledgehammer. The joist may need to be raised slightly to ensure that it's carrying the load from the wall above. Use a pry bar to create space between the mudsill and joist, and then slide in opposing shims (photo right).

Temporary support

A HELPING HAND. Demolition should be an orderly operation, so rather than randomly cutting the joists and letting them fall, work carefully. Cut the damaged joists into 3-ft. to 4-ft. sections, making them easier to uninstall and carry out. To keep the unsupported ends of a damaged joist from falling as you make cuts, screw a scrap of wood to the top of the joist at a point just beyond where you will make the cut.

A bathtub uses a smaller drainpipe connection than a toilet, but the tub drain assembly (the trip waste and overflow) and the trap can interfere with the floor framing. A cast-iron tub is heavy. Add in 40 gal. to 80 gal. of water, and it's not hard to imagine the stresses being placed on the joists. The weakened floor can cause the tub to settle, which leads to cracked tile and fractured grout joints that allow water to wick into the subfloor below. I've also seen floors deflect enough that water from the showerhead has begun following the inclined tub rim into the grout joint fissure or onto the floor.

The demo phase informs the rebuild

When planning for a bathroom remodel, good preparation helps to prevent the possibility of future water damage. The demolition phase of the project usually reveals the areas that have been affected by moisture penetration and guides what needs to be corrected during the rebuild. Take pictures, make notes, and pay attention to details. Each job is different, but experience has taught me to focus on a few key areas.

First, know where your fixtures will go and how they will be installed. You may have to fur out walls, box out floor framing, adjust joist layouts, or even tweak the position of a fixture to avoid problems. Also, remember that solid, reinforced floor framing under the tub and toilet guarantees sturdy, level installations. It also pays to explore all fixture options. Often, you can find a tub or toilet with different rough-in requirements that may fit better with your floor framing.

Second, don't just seal around the fixtures after they're in place. Waterproofing should start with the subfloor and underlayment. Apply a good-quality silicone sealant where the tub apron meets the subfloor, where the tile backerboard meets the tub rim, and around all the shower faucet/fixture penetrations before, during, and after the tile is installed. The toilet flange should be sealed where it meets the finished floor, and the toilet bowl should be caulked or grouted to the floor.

Toilet tanks can be purchased with an insulated liner that helps to prevent condensation from forming, an option that I always recommend when the bathroom has a history of water damage from condensation.

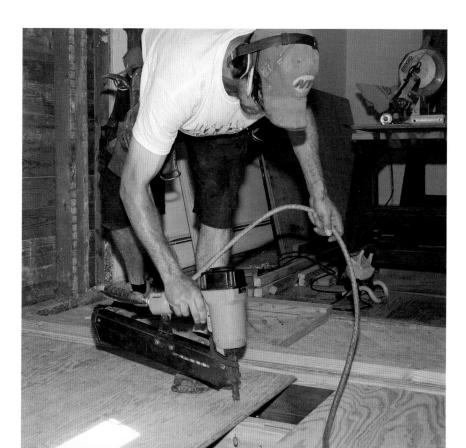

A SOLID SUBFLOOR SEALS THE DEAL. With the notches complete, the floor is tied together with ¾-in. tongue-and-groove subfloor sheathing laid in a bead of construction adhesive and fastened with screws or ring-shank nails.

14 Tips for Bathroom Plumbing

BY MIKE LOMBARDI

I've been a plumber for almost 40 years. I learned the trade from some really good plumbers, but I've also learned from making mistakes and seeing the mistakes of other pros and amateurs. This experience has made me a better plumber and has helped me to build a loyal clientele. A recent job, a full bath remodel at *Fine Homebuilding's* Project House, offered the perfect opportunity to share some of my favorite hard-earned lessons for better and easier bath plumbing.

The job included moving the sink and the toilet to make room for a new barrier-free tile shower, so we tackled all the typical full-bath rough-in tasks. We used as many cost-saving strategies as we could think of—provided they didn't sacrifice the quality or the longevity of the job.

One thing that always makes jobs like this go easier is to have locations for fixtures, tile, and plumbing decided well before rough-in starts. Changes and rework can quickly blow any budget. Plumbers and tilesetters don't like redoing their own work, and they will charge accordingly to fix problems resulting from poor planning.

1 ASSEMBLE WHAT YOU CAN. It's often easier to dry-fit and assemble fittings before tucking them into a stud or joist cavity. For example, attaching the supply lines and shower arm before putting the mixing valve into the wall provides more room for turning wrenches and pliers.

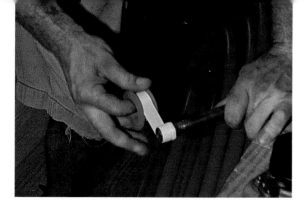

2 USE THE RIGHT NUMBER OF WRAPS. Start threaded connections by covering the male side of the fitting with three wraps of Teflon® tape. Larger pipes will take up to six wraps. Wrap the tape in a direction that follows the pipe or fitting as it's tightened.

3 USE PIPE DOPE, TOO. Thread-sealing compound lubricates the tape so that it doesn't shred, and it also provides extra insurance against leaks. The author prefers Hercules Megaloc® nonhardening thread sealer.

4 WEAR YOUR SAFETY GEAR. Spattering solder, dripping PVC primer and glue, and general overhead work contribute to the high incidence of on-the-job eye injuries among plumbers, so it's important to wear eye protection. Pro-quality plumbing torches are loud, so wear hearing protection when soldering.

5 WIPE SOLDERED JOINTS. Best practice is to wipe soldered joints after you sweat them, but it's not just about looking neat and clean. Soldered copper connections depend on a layer of flux, but flux is corrosive and should be removed while it's still hot. Always use a dry rag to remove flux. A wet rag cools the joint too suddenly, resulting in a weaker connection.

6 KNOW THE WALL FINISH. The difference in thickness between one type of tile and another can determine if a shower valve's handle and trim ring will fit. You often can order different trim kits to compensate for thick wall tile, but it's easier to set the valve in the right spot.

7 MIX AND MATCH. PEX tubing saves labor and works great, but the author prefers the added rigidity of copper for supplying shower valves, shower arms, and valve stub outs. Insulating the copper reduces noise, saves energy, and prevents condensation, which can lead to mold growth.

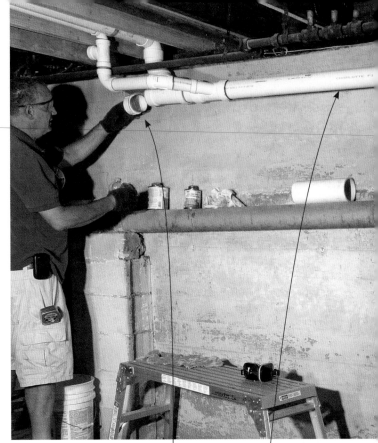

8 SECURE VENTS AND STACKS BEFORE CUTTING. Existing waste lines and vents may be perfectly serviceable, but you often need to add, move, or eliminate pipes during remodeling work. Secure existing pipes with two-hole straps before cutting into them, or risk bringing down all the pipe above you.

11 INCLUDE CLEANOUTS. Code requires cleanouts where pipes transition from vertical to horizontal.

9 REAM PIPE CUTS. The little burrs left when you cut plastic drain pipe tend to snag whatever nastiness is passing through the pipe. Eventually, the rough edge creates a clog big enough to require professional drain clearing. Deburring also makes dry-fitting easier. Copper supply lines also should be reamed.

12 USE THE RIGHT SLOPE. Sloping waste lines from 1/8 in. to 1/4 in. per ft. allows proper drainage and keeps solid waste moving along.

10 USE THE RIGHT GLUE. PVC and ABS use different cements for joining pipe and fittings. ABS piping doesn't require primer, but you should prime both male and female sides of any PVC connections. Ensure a neater job by holding the pipe or fitting so that excess primer drips off instead of running down the side of the pipe. Apply two coats of glue to the male side and a single, light coat to the female side of the connection.

PVC primer and cement

ABS cement

13 USE DISH SOAP FOR FLEXIBLE COUPLINGS. Plumbers often depend on flexible couplings for making repairs and connecting the different kinds of pipe used in waste lines and vents. Make it easier to slide the tight-fitting couplings onto the pipes they're joining by first adding a few drops of dish soap.

14 AAVS ARE YOUR FRIEND. Air-admittance valves (AAVs) allow air into drain lines while preventing sewer gas from escaping. They're great for remodeling work, as they can replace many feet of vent piping. Just make sure they're accessible. Covering them with HVAC return registers in what otherwise would be inaccessible locations allows them to breathe and provides future access.

A NEW PLUMBER'S TOOL KIT

YOU MAY ALREADY HAVE A RECIPRO-CATING SAW or a handsaw that you can use for cutting plastic waste lines and vents, but you'll need some new tools for working with copper and PEX supply lines. Nonpro plumbers might balk at spending $45 for an aluminum pipe wrench when steel versions cost half as much, but aluminum wrenches are easier to carry and do less damage when you drop them. You can get cheaper torches, too, but self-lighting versions free a hand for wiping joints and other tasks.

Self-lighting torch

Tubing cutter

12 in. tongue-and-groove flat-jaw pliers

Compact tubing cutter

14-in. aluminum pipe wrench

Ridgid 23468 ½-in. and ¾-in. PEX crimp tool

4-in-1 fitting brush

Solder and flux kit

Remodeled Baths

A Bathroom where East Meets West

BY TERRY HERNDON

I t's always a pleasure to reconnect with a previous client. Recently, one such client contacted my company, UpStream Construction, to renovate and combine two bathrooms and an enclosed porch in his 1956 home. We had remodeled his kitchen previously, and because of that, we had a great relationship with him.

Our client explained that on a business trip to Japan, he had met a woman and fallen in love. He proposed marriage, and she accepted. He knew it would be shocking for his fiancée to move from a Japanese city with a population of 13 million to a small town in the United States with fewer than a thousand residents. In an effort to make his new bride-to-be feel at home, he planned to convert the bathrooms and porch into a Japanese-style bath. In addition to our firm, he also contacted Karen Turner, the designer with whom we had worked on his kitchen.

The existing space consisted of two symmetrical bathrooms with windows overlooking a common

FIGURING OUT THE FLOOR

ONE OF THIS PROJECT'S BIGGEST CHALLENGES was the removable teak-panel floor system in the bathing area. The panels cover a recessed slab on grade that slopes from all four walls to a central drain that captures water from the shower as well as overflow from the soaking tub.

To maintain a level surface, each of the 16 panels had to be tailored to a specific location in the room. Each panel measures 29½ in. by 24 in. and consists of four teak slats and three runners made of ipé; we chose these woods for their durability in wet environments.

To get accurate dimensions for the panels, project manager Donny Clinedinst and I used stringlines set at the finished-floor elevation to make a grid over the floor corresponding to each individual panel. We then measured down at each intersection and midpoint of the string to give us the vertical elevations of the corners and the midpoints of each panel.

In our woodworking shop, we milled 1x6 teak stock to ¾ in. by 5¾ in. for the slats, and 2x4 ipé stock to 1½ in. by 2 in. for the runners. We then ripped the ipé to the corresponding elevations taken from the stringline, minus the thickness of the teak slats, with a bandsaw. We affixed the slats to the runners with marine resorcinol glue and stainless-steel screws with ipé plugs.

Back at the site, we used an electric planer, hand planers, and a belt sander with various grades of sandpaper to fine-tune the runners to the profile of the shower floor. To cushion the walking surface, we adhered EPDM to the bottom of the runners.

Teak slat — Stainless-steel screw — Plug — EPDM — Ipé runner

sunporch (floor plan, p. 161). The floors and most wall surfaces of the baths were tile, and there was hydronic heating in slabs under the floor tile. Overall, the space was in good condition considering the age of the home.

A marriage of two spaces

Karen envisioned combining the two baths and the sunporch, as well as an adjacent hallway closet, into one bathroom. This gave us a space measuring 15½ ft. by 15 ft. Within that footprint, Karen devised a plan to create five different spaces: a traditional Japanese prewash/soaking-tub area; a standard shower; and a sitting area flanked by two separate spaces, each with a commode and a vanity sink. Her design had to allow the space to function as a shared bathroom that also provided individual privacy for our clients. It also had to adhere to Japanese culture and customs.

How does a Japanese bath differ from what we're accustomed to in the United States? In Japan, taking a bath involves much more than simply washing oneself. To many Japanese, soaking in their ofuro is as essential a part of their daily routine as eating or sleeping; it is viewed as a necessary part of a healthy, happy life. It is also considered a social activity, and parents often bathe with their children. With regard to size, Japanese soaking tubs are much deeper than most American tubs, allowing the bather to sink down in water up to chin level. The water also tends to be much hotter than in a typical American bath.

A soaking tub is usually installed in a large area and faces a glass wall that allows the bather to look out onto a garden or natural area. The sole purpose of the tub is for therapeutic relaxation, not hygiene. Prior to entering the tub, one must take a thorough, cleansing shower so that other family members can share the same tub of water. A typical Japanese bathroom has two segregated areas. One includes a changing area near the shower and tub, the other a water closet. The water closet is never in the same room where bathing takes place.

Modifying the space

Our client's new wife wanted the tub and shower area to feel as though it were actually outside. To do this, and to achieve optimal natural light and the best view of the Japanese garden that would be directly outside, we installed a 12-ft. Pella® sliding-glass door with integral blinds for privacy. This space houses a linen cabinet, a shower, and a Lydia freestanding soaking tub. The floor is constructed of removable teak panels placed over a heated slab with a floor drain (sidebar on the facing page).

Adjacent to the tub and shower area, we created two mirror-image spaces, each with its own sink vanity and toilet. The spaces are separated by a common shower with two washing stations and a vanity table flanked by two shoji screens handcrafted by Roger Sherry, a local artisan. Sherry constructed the screens using teak and acrylic panels that simulate traditional rice paper without the risk of damage from humidity. The panels can be closed for privacy or opened to provide a communal bath area. Because the common vanity area would be used primarily for dressing and getting ready for the day, we added a floor-to-ceiling mirror framed with teak.

The opportunity to work with such a variety of materials was one of the most rewarding aspects of this project. We are all skilled carpenters, so being able to work with such exotic woods as teak and ipé was a treat. The cabinets, fabricated by Gaston & Wyatt of Charlottesville, Va., were constructed of teak, as was all the interior trimwork: baseboard, wall caps, beam work, and thresholds. Cogswell Stone fabricated the countertops from marble spotted with fossils. We installed travertine tiles on the floor and in the common shower, and a 3-cm travertine slab in the prewash shower area. One of

CROSSING CULTURES. Dual bathroom spaces create a mirror-like image when viewed from the prewash-shower area.

A SHARED, PRIVATE PLACE

The original intent of this master-bath remodel was to create two separate spaces that would allow privacy while embracing the natural light and open feeling of a Japanese bath. The option also exists to use the entire space as one bath, simply by opening the sliding shoji panels on each side of the central dressing table.

Because one entrance to the bath opens from a guest-room hallway and the other from the master suite, it's also possible to use one-half of the space as a guest bath for visiting family and the other half as a private bath for the homeowners.

Both sides open to the traditional Japanese bathing area located on the footprint of the former porch. Whether open or closed, there exist throughout the bath subtle visual barriers and sightlines that extend a sense of privacy.

—Karen Turner, owner of KTK Design in Charlottesville, Va.

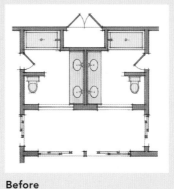

Before   After

the most fascinating items we installed was the Toto Washlet S400. Like most toilets in Japan, this unit has a sophisticated array of electronic functions: It opens, closes, and flushes automatically, and it is outfitted with a seat warmer, multiple bidet settings, water-temperature control, a dryer, and an air purifier. The combination of a high-tech toilet with Robern® medicine cabinets, Amba® heated towel warmers, and contemporary lighting makes this bathroom both modern and efficient.

SOURCES

FLOOR AND WALL TILES
Italian crème honed marble
www.cogswellstone.com

HEATED TOWEL BARS
Amba Jeeves E Curved
www.ambaproducts.com

LAVATORY FAUCETS
Hansa Stela
www.hansaaust.com.au

LAVATORY SINKS
Kohler Camber® in bouclé tweed
www.kohler.com

SHOWER SLAB
Walnut Vecchio travertine
www.cogswellstone.com

SOAKING TUB
MTI Lydia MTCT-124
www.mtibaths.com

VANITY TOP
Fossil brown marble
www.cogswellstone.com

ALL THE ELEMENTS. An emphasis on natural materials within a narrow color palette preserves tranquility in the functional areas of the bath. Left: Acrylic panels serve as a durable but convincing stand-in for traditional rice paper in the teak shoji doors that separate the bath's two sides. Between the doors is a shared vanity table. Below: Topped with fossil-laden marble (right), identical sink vanities flank each side of the shared shower. The fossils reference the homeowner's career as a biologist.

A Half-Bath, Fulfilled

BY GREGOR MASEFIELD

When Bill and Kris Gerson called me to remodel their home, their thoughts were only on improving their dysfunctional, outdated kitchen. But the house's boxy layout and the Gersons' impending status as empty-nesters quickly led to conversations about their home's other shortcomings and how we might take advantage of this opportunity to transform it to meet their changing lifestyle.

We started work on a plan to open the compartmentalized living spaces on the first floor. Scheme after scheme for the new designs involved borrowing or stealing space from the home's first-floor bathroom—most often from the shower that no doubt had been included in the original plan so that the builder could boast two full baths. The fact was that in all the years the Gersons had spent raising their four boys in the house, the shower had never been used. It's not hard to understand why: Not many people would choose to shower in close proximity not only to the kitchen but also to the home's entry, both areas of high traffic and public activities. The Gersons needed a first-floor bathroom, but they needed one suitable for public, not private, use.

What worked, and what didn't

Despite the ill-conceived shower, the existing bathroom's assets included a skylight and a window. Also, its toilet was nicely off to the side, allowing the window wall to serve as a focal point. Its location off a hallway was suitable to a public bath, allowing friends and family to take leave of public activities, disappear, then reappear in a discrete place between the home's larger spaces.

We soon arrived at a design direction for the adjacent spaces and determined that the bathroom would remain, but as a powder room. We decided to remove the unused but tired shower and to replace the toilet and sink with new units. To enhance privacy, we created an alcove between the bath and the hallway. The linen closet—no longer needed for shower supplies—would be removed to add space to the entry. The bath would be considerably smaller, but much better.

To improve the bathroom space, we decided to use design elements to create an experience removed from the rest of the first floor. If the open plan we designed for the rest of the house communicated a sense of being together, the design concept for this bath would communicate a sense of being alone.

SOURCES

Duravit® Starck 3
www.duravit.us

VESSEL SINK
Stone Forest honey-onyx Urban
Vessel Sink
www.stoneforest.com

FAUCET
Eurostyle Knick Stick
www.eurostyleinc.com

SINK TRAP
Mountain Plumbing Products round-
style decorative lavatory trap
www.mountainplumbing.com

PENDANT LIGHT
The Lighting House parchment and
leaves design
www.vermontlightinghouse.com

A SEPARATE PIECE. To make the new powder room distinctive, a dramatic live-edge slab of cherry serves as a vanity top.

A space unto itself

To promote this separate experience, we added material elements that harmonized with the surrounding spaces but at the same time stood out. For example, because the wood trim used in the rest of the first-floor space was square, milled stock, we wanted the bathroom sink and whatever it sat on to come together in a simple composition that was honest, natural, and beautiful in and of itself. We also wanted the vessel to glow.

A live-edge cherry plank was the perfect surface to mount the honey-onyx vessel sink Kris chose. Grounding the space with its natural form, it would also tell a story of how wood forms and grows. We called Larry "The Logger" Altman of Altman Custom Timber Products in Burlington, Vt., for a live-edge cherry slab, preferably with knees, or the sweep of the trunk at its base.

Larry found a beautiful piece of wood, and our general contractor, Sean Flynn of Silver Maple Construction, cut and attached it with concealed fasteners. Sean's willingness to troubleshoot design details contributed in no small way to the success of the project.

While earlier concept sketches included a towel compartment below the slab that played off other rectangles in the room, this feature was abandoned in favor of clean simplicity. Instead, the homeowners used a cutoff from the slab as a shelf where the old shower had been. The solution was quick and simple, keeping with the room's independent spirit.

A sink solution

This dramatic sink and vanity demanded to be a focal point. Placing the sink beside the window and below the skylight would allow it to have a strong

EVOLUTION OF A POWDER ROOM

THE POWDER-ROOM REMODEL came as a result of changes made to the entire first floor, and its design options were influenced by the changes proposed around it. Here's a look at some of the scenarios the author and the homeowners considered along the way as they shifted rooms and explored various options for the space that once housed the unused shower.

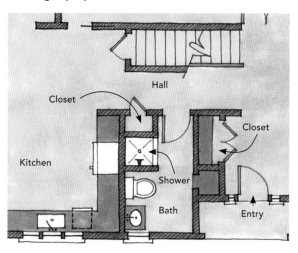

1. FIRST FLOOR BEFORE. The original floor plan was compartmentalized, with the kitchen adjacent to the original full bath. A utility closet opened into the hallway; another closet opened into the bathroom.

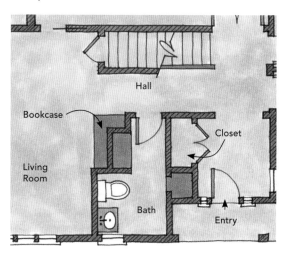

2. MOVE THE LIVING ROOM. One proposal involved the living room switching places with the kitchen. In this scenario, the closet moved into a mini-hallway leading to the bathroom, and the living-room side of the wall accommodated a built-in bookcase.

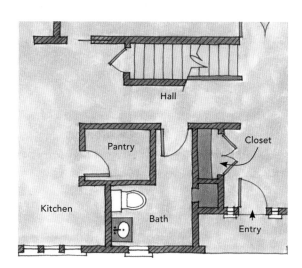

3. SPACE FOR A PANTRY. Another idea was to leave the kitchen where it was, and create a pantry in the area of the unused shower and the utility closet.

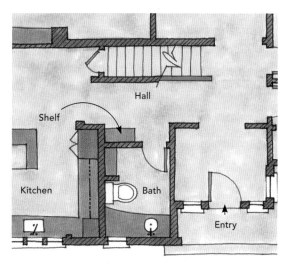

4. FINAL PLAN. Thoroughly remodeled, the kitchen stays where it is. The shower is removed and replaced with shelving; the hall closet blends into an alcove that backs the powder room off the hall. Removal of two closets, including one that served the bath, widens the front entry.

relationship to those two natural-light sources. At night, a single light source above the sink would create an effect that was perhaps even more dramatic. The complicating factor here, however, was that this plan required placing the sink on an exterior wall. In Vermont's cold climate, we rarely consider plumbing in an exterior wall. The solution was to build a shallow chase within the exterior wall in which to house the sink pipes. Rectangular in shape, the podiumlike chase is faced with dark slate to provide a subdued background against which the lively sink pops visually. The minimalist space now has an engaging focal point that shines with the bathroom's two natural-light sources.

BLANK BACKGROUND FOR A BRIGHT BOWL. Light from the skylight above makes the honey-onyx vessel sink glow against a background of slate. The design isn't all about looks, however; the rectangular box keeps the pipes from freezing in the outside wall. The chase was framed with 2x4s before the vanity-top slab was fitted around it. Once the slab was in place, the box was finished with top and side pieces of Douglas fir (screwed from the inside) and faced with backerboard, which then was tiled with 4x4 slate.

HOW TO FLOAT A VANITY TOP

SEAN FLYNN'S INVISIBLE FASTENING SYSTEM involves supporting the slab with steel angles attached to studs on each sidewall. After templating the top for a snug fit, he routed a thin slot on each end, starting at the back and stopping about 2 in. short of the front edge. He then held the slab horizontally, sliding both ends over the angles simultaneously. This method worked because the room's slightly-out-of-square walls narrowed toward the window. Had that not been the case, Flynn had an alternative (below right).

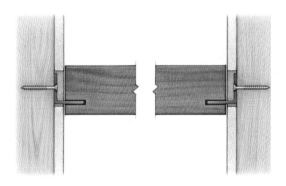

Slotted on both ends, the vanity slab is held in place with 1½-in. by 1½-in. steel angles screwed directly to the studs. Drywall is cut back just enough to accommodate the hardware. The split side of the slab is held up with two angles, one on each side of the crack.

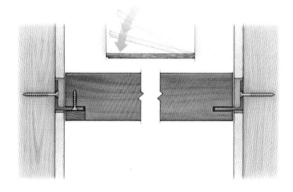

Had the walls' orientation been more problematic, an option would have been to cut a slot on one end and a rabbet on the other, allowing the slotted side to be fitted onto the angle and then dropped into place, with the opposite angle resting in the rabbet. A small glued-in patch would complete the invisible installation.

Two Rugged Baths

BY CHARLES MILLER

Pounded by surf and raked by prevailing winds and relentless tides, the geological chopping block known as the Northern California coast is merciless. At the place called The Sea Ranch, the cliffs are scoured clean, and the cypress trees grow at an angle, espaliered by the wind. Geologists point out that a 30,000-ft.-thick layer of stone has disappeared here over the past 10 million years, lost to erosion. The only way to make a building that holds up in this harsh environment is to assemble it with the toughest materials available. Concrete, stainless steel, stone, tempered glass, tight-grained redwood, and copper are all on that list.

Ninety years ago, an Austrian architect used a similar menu of materials in a house that changed the course of residential design in California. In West Hollywood, Rudolph Schindler designed and built the Kings Road House, a duplex that defied convention. With an open plan that included a courtyard with a fireplace, concrete walls on the inside, and unadorned materials used as finished surfaces, the Kings Road House became the quintessential indoor/outdoor California residence.

Back on the north coast in 2004, Gabriel Ramirez acquired one of the premier bluff-top lots at The Sea Ranch. Perched above a sheltered cove, the site was perfect for the kind of house pioneered by one of Ramirez's most-admired architects: Rudolph Schindler. Ramirez asked two Southern California architect/educators steeped in Schindler's work— Judith Sheine and Norman Millar—to collaborate on what Ramirez describes as "the only house I plan to build from scratch."

Millar and Sheine updated Schindler's list of preferred building materials, adding corrugated Cor-Ten® steel, ipé, and marine-grade Douglas-fir plywood. They devised a system of horizontal and vertical grids for orchestrating the intersections of the structural and finish materials, inside and out.

Baths epitomize Schindler's style

The two upstairs bathrooms, modest in scale and low-key in their colors and their composition, demonstrate this seemingly effortless rigor. They adhere to the approach that Schindler described in his assessment of his Kings Road House: "The traditional building scheme, by which the structural members of the house are covered onionlike by layers of finishing materials: lathe, plaster, paint, paper, hangings, etc., is abandoned. The house is a simple weave of structural materials which retain their natural color and texture throughout."

AS RUGGED AS THE LANDSCAPE. With rafter tails breaking it into illuminated squares, a room-length skylight casts a soft light across the east wall. Just beyond the showerhead, a tall casement window admits the prevailing breeze and the sound of the surf. The board-formed cast-concrete walls are both structural and stylish.

The two upstairs baths are on the east side of the house, in separate bump-outs that stand proud of the house's wedge-shaped footprint. The north bath (photo above) has the taller ceiling, with a shower along the north wall. The south bath has a tub along the south wall (photo on p. 171).

Initial plans were to use concrete for the shower pan and tub, but concrete's weight in upstairs installations and its potential for cracking argued against it. In searching the web for fixtures and fittings, Ramirez discovered Diamond Spas, a Colorado-based fabricator of custom metal tubs, spas, and pools. He commissioned a copper hot tub from them and was so pleased with the results that he ordered a copper shower for one bath and a copper tub for the other.

A palette of materials in the spirit of Schindler and the site had emerged. The warm tones of the copper, the wood, and even the concrete echo the cliffs and buckskin meadow grasses that border the house. For consistency in the materials' roles and relationships, the architects established guidelines: Ceilings are marine-grade Douglas-fir plywood; cabinets are also Douglas fir, but with a more refined

SOURCES

TOILETS
Duravit Starck X
www.duravit.us

FAUCETS AND SHOWER MIXER
Hansgrohe Axor® Starck
www.hansgrohe-usa.com

SINKS
Sonoma Stone
www.sonomastone.com

TUB AND SHOWER PAN
Diamond Spas
www.diamondspas.com

LIGHT FIXTURES
David Weeks
www.davidweeksstudio.com

SQUARED OFF. Rectilinear shapes at different scales abound in the baths, from the end-grain Douglas-fir flooring to the Duravit Starck X toilets. Practical issues included the need to create custom copper sleeves to extend the pipes for the tub mixer (inset).

PRECIOUS METAL. Prized on the coast for its longevity in a salty environment, copper steps inside as a faceted jewel of a tub framed by a wood and concrete backdrop.

vertical-grain pattern; walls that are likely to get wet are either copper or concrete; walls in dry areas are ipé.

Simple? Not!

By design, the baths are calm and orderly. Everything lines up. There are no gaps unless there are supposed to be gaps, in which case they measure ³/₁₆ in., period. There's no trim. Of course, nothing is harder for a trim carpenter than not to have trim to cover the gulf between what was drawn and how it turned out. Projects like this don't get built without a talented ringmaster. In this case, that ringmaster was Sam King.

King had to solve scores of unforeseen problems to make these baths look effortless—for example, how to attach copper panels to the walls with no visible fasteners. The obvious choice would be a sealant/adhesive, but what kind? No one knew. King ran a series of tests until he found a sealant (Dow Corning® 795) that didn't react with copper.

In another "solve this" puzzle, the position of the tub mixer had to be extended from the wall to reach its target. The solution: custom-made copper sleeves that look like they came with the tub (bottom left photo, above).

At one point, King was so deep in concentration while securing a trimless towel bar to a concrete wall that he didn't realize that Ramirez was standing at the door a few feet away. Ramirez recalls that as King dialed the towel bar into its final position, he stood up, surveyed the installation, and said to himself under his breath, "Sweet. Now walk away."

Guided by Schindler, Gabriel Ramirez and his architects knew when to walk away from the drawing board and start building.

AN ARCHITECT AHEAD OF HIS TIME

TRAINED AS AN ARCHITECT IN VIENNA, Rudolph Schindler came to America in 1914 to work with Frank Lloyd Wright as an unpaid draftsman. For Schindler, learning everything he could from the master made a salary pale by comparison. Schindler planned to learn from Wright and return to Austria. It didn't work out that way.

At 31, Schindler settled into the dynamic of Taliesin East in Spring Green, Wis., and quickly became an important member of Wright's staff. He found himself caught up in the energy of the place and met his bride to be, Pauline Gibing of Evanston, Ill.

At the same time, Wright's commissions were coming from clients in far-off places, spreading him thin. He needed somebody to oversee the ones he couldn't attend to on a regular basis. Among them was a significant commission from Aline Barnsdale, an oil heiress who had hired Wright to design the Mayanesque Hollyhock House in East Hollywood. Schindler moved to Los Angeles in 1920 to oversee its construction; in doing so, he fell into the rhythms of Southern California. Unlike Austria, where an oppressive architectural conservatism stifled fresh thought, Los Angeles was wide open to new ideas. An incorrigible, free-spirited Bohemian, Schindler had found his greener pastures.

By 1921, the Hollyhock House was finished, and the Schindlers took a High Sierra vacation in Yosemite. Their campsite—with its granite boulders for a backdrop, a campfire ring for warmth, and a thin canvas tent for shelter—stoked Schindler's imagination. Why not combine these contrasting elements in a house? The result is the house he built for himself on Kings Road in West Hollywood. Its slab floors and tilt-up concrete walls stand in for granite, the courtyard fireplaces are the campfires, and the second-floor canvas "sleeping baskets" are the tents. None of these elements entered the mainstream, but the exposed structural elements of the Kings Road House and the indoor/outdoor nature of its plan charted a new course for California residential architecture.

Schindler lived and worked in the Kings Road House until his death in 1953, his practice kept afloat mostly by small residential commissions. An exception was the Lovell Beach House, a magnificent cast-concrete arrangement of pure-white rectangles elevated above the street. Although Schindler's innovative design baffled critics during his lifetime, by the 1960s, influential architecture critics such as Esther McCoy and David Gebhart saw the genius in Schindler's work, and said so. Prominent architects such as Charles Moore sang Schindler's praises.

Today, the Kings Road House remains, a living museum open to students who want to see firsthand a house still standing at a fork in the road of residential design.

Echoes from a landmark. The bathroom of the Kings Road House showcases Schindler's innovative use of materials. The house is open to the public through a branch of the Austrian Museum of Applied Arts (makcenter.org).

The Stay-at-Home Spa

BY ROB BRENNAN

I f you were from Finland, you might use sauna as a verb. Apparently, there is a scientific technique to using these cedar-clad hot rooms to promote health and vitality. The process involves showering, heating up slowly, cooling down quickly, and drinking plenty of water. Tom and Denise Genuit are busy parents, professionals, and snowboarders who learned how to take a traditional sauna from their European neighbors. When they called my firm to talk about some remodeling work, they already knew that someday, they wanted a master bath where they could retreat from the stress of their careers as a doctor and a nurse. They knew it would include a sauna. What we ended up designing was a master bath that offers a full spa experience with a direct connection to the garden terrace and hot tub a story below.

The master retreat

This remodel actually began as a landscape project. Tom and Denise wanted to improve their private backyard by tearing off an existing deck and replacing it with a patio. They also knew, however, that they wanted to connect the interior of their home with the landscape in a more meaningful way. When they started talking to their landscaper about adding a porch or sunroom, he referred them to us.

Very quickly, we came to the conclusion that now was the time to remodel their second-floor master bath, which was not particularly small, but was dated. What they really wanted was not so much a new master bath, but more of a master retreat: a sunlit spa with separate shower and tub, a water closet, a double vanity, a sauna, and a real connection to the backyard.

An addition was in order. In this case, a second-floor addition meant a first-floor addition, so we designed a sitting room below the master bath with a fireplace and a bank of windows that look onto the new patio. We also included a stairway from the bathroom to the patio, which was one of the more challenging aspects of the design.

We initially considered an outdoor stair. Because the clients wanted year-round access to the backyard hot tub, though, we decided that exterior stairs could be dangerous. We settled on a closed stair with lots of awning windows for a visual connection with the exterior and to allow fresh air into the transitional space. An additional benefit of the stair is that guests can use the master retreat without going through the bedroom.

Inside-out materials

When it came to choosing materials for Tom and Denise's bath, we drew spiritual inspiration from the baths at Peter Zumthor's Vals Spa in Switzerland. These baths are timeless in quality and materials.

SUNLIGHT FALLS ON A SUSTAINABLE MATERIAL PALETTE. Recycled IceStone® counters sit atop a bamboo vanity and tub surround. A wavy backsplash from 3form® is made from a polyester resin and is GreenGuard-certified to promote healthful indoor-air quality. The sauna kit from SaunaFin® was a DIY project for the homeowners and their son.

FROM GOOD TO GREAT

WHILE THEIR ORIGINAL MASTER BATH did not want for space, these homeowners wanted a full, spalike retreat from their stressful professional lives. Four distinct areas orbit the spacious circulation area: the vanity, the tub, the sauna, and the shower.

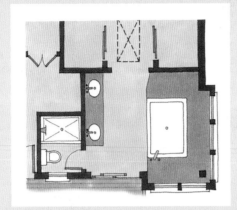

SECOND FLOOR BEFORE

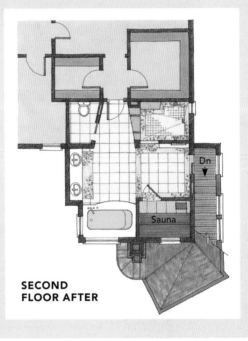

SECOND FLOOR AFTER

LIGHT AND FUNCTION IN A LAVISH SHOWER. The walk-in shower has a window and hardworking walls. Teak shelves are used for storage and display. A bench and a towel warmer add function and comfort. A frosted-glass door to the stairwell offers light and privacy.

We wanted to bring that same natural quality to this project: the immutability of stone, the warmth of cedar, the freshness of bamboo.

With plenty of sunlight from windows on all three of the bathroom's exterior walls, even in the shower and sauna, we were able to extend the ephemeral quality of light reflecting on these materials through the whole day. We wanted to bring more than just sunlight in from outside, because this was an outdoor project as well. We also wanted to use some modern, sustainable, and playful materials.

The river-stone tile border mimics the stonework of the chimney and retaining wall, and comforts Tom and Denise's feet as they stand at the vanity. Knowing that the bath would have a cedar-clad sauna, we used cedar as an exterior accent for siding the stairwell and bump-out. The IceStone glass and

THE INDOOR CONNECTION. The materials used outside the addition reflect the bath, including the cedar siding that mimics the sauna walls, and the stone patio and chimney that reflect the river-rock floor-tile accents inside.

mother-of-pearl counters, serpentine 3form Varia Ecoresin backsplash, bamboo vanity, and tub and sauna surrounds add a modern touch with sustainable sensibilities. The teak shower shelves are traditional and durable.

Tom and Denise decided to install the sauna themselves. We specified a curb, a rubber-membrane floor, a blueboard wall, and an exhaust fan for ventilation, and they ordered a kit from SaunaFin. Tom had a great experience assembling the kit with his son and has high praise for the customer service at SaunaFin.

Reflecting a trend

Although Tom and Denise still have one child at home, this project aligns with a remodeling trend that we have been noticing: empty-nesters and midcareer homeowners looking to personalize their colonials, ranches, and bungalows for their current lifestyle as well as life changes on the horizon. It's not uncommon to hear homeowners say things like, "Yeah, the whirlpool tub is nice, but honestly, we never use it." Tom and Denise use every bit of their new bathroom, year-round. It seems remodeling with lifestyle—not resale—in mind was the right thing for them to do.

BEYOND THE BATH

THIS MASTER-BATH REMODEL included a new space on the first floor and a new landscape design. The homeowners' desire to have the hot tub be part of the bathroom experience meant creating a direct path from the indoor bathroom to the patio outside.

BEFORE

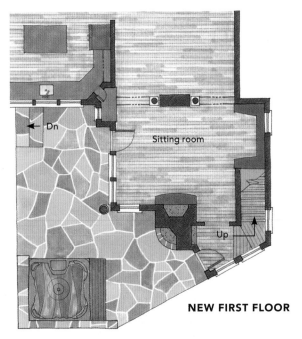

Dn

Sitting room

Up

NEW FIRST FLOOR

A SPECIAL SPACE TO SIT. The lower level of the addition is another sanctuary for the homeowners. The away room has a cozy fireplace, a sleek wall-hung TV cabinet, and some simple bookcases. Like the bathroom, the sitting room is lush with sunlight.

A Porch Becomes a Bath

BY DONNA WAX

When looking for a home for our family, my husband and I did not shy away from houses in need of updating. This historic home certainly fit the bill. Our house dates to 1910 and is known as the Pipes Family Home, historically significant for being the family home of Wade Pipes, a prominent local architect famous for his residential work in many Portland, Ore., neighborhoods.

Typical of the Craftsman-style homes designed at the turn of the century in Portland, the bedrooms were small, and the entire extended family shared the one bath in the house. The Pipes house had a similar layout and had survived previous homeowners' minor remodels. It still needed to be brought into the 21st century, however, by enhancing the functionality and comfort of existing spaces. High on our to-do list was adding a master bathroom that would simultaneously create a master suite and relieve the congestion in the home's sole bathroom.

REDESIGN THE INTERIOR, AND PRESERVE THE EXTERIOR

WITH RESPECT TO THE SURROUNDING HISTORIC NEIGHBORHOOD, the goal was to have as little impact on the exterior elevations of the home as possible while improving the usefulness of the existing floor plan.

To create a private master suite, the author blocked the hallway entrance at the top of the stairs, eliminated a closet in the existing master bedroom, and created a new doorway to the bathroom. This new doorway created the suite she was looking for and made the entrance to the bath less intrusive on the circulation areas within the bath. The bathroom windows, which fill the voids of the old sleeping porch, are of a proportion reflective of the other windows around the house. A new, larger closet inhabits the top half of an 8-ft.-sq. two-story addition.

All this work was done in an effort to maintain continuity on the exterior and to improve functionality and comfort in the interior.

Architect Donna Wax, donnawaxarchitect.com
Tile contractor Todd Robinett
Cabinetmaker Eric Wolf, wolfandson.com

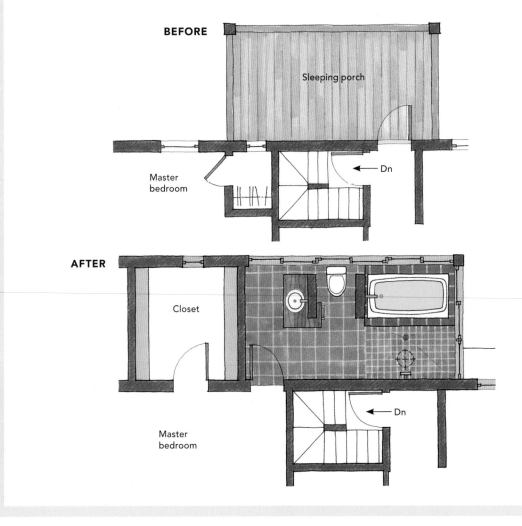

BEFORE

Sleeping porch

Master bedroom

Dn

AFTER

Closet

Master bedroom

Dn

EXTERIOR IMPACT. New sliding windows fill the old openings in the sleeping porch. They're designed to blend into the existing home by maintaining the original look of the exterior elevation.

Reinventing the porch

On the second floor of the house, I combined two small bedrooms to make a master bedroom large enough for a king-size bed and a sitting area around an existing fireplace. The seldom-used sleeping porch adjacent to the master bedroom was the perfect size for a master bathroom. To capture this space, I eliminated the existing porch access from the common hallway and added a doorway in the master bedroom.

The footprint of the old sleeping porch was an elongated rectangle measuring 8 ft. wide by 15 ft. long with a finished floor 6 in. below the existing second-story floor. The difference in floor levels created an opportunity to install radiant heating in the bathroom and to build a curbless shower, which makes the bath feel larger than it is.

With little need for privacy between the various functions of the bathroom, I had 3-ft.-long walls built to separate the areas for the vanity, the toilet, and the shower. I stopped the walls 6 in. shy of the exterior windows to allow the sliding windows to run continuously along the bump-out and to preserve the lines of the original sleeping porch. Not only do these walls define functional zones, but I also used them as chases for the plumbing supply and drain lines and for the HVAC ducts. As a result of this arrangement, the bathroom space feels continuous even though each bathroom element has a clearly defined area.

A CURBLESS SHOWER IMPROVES FUNCTION AND FLOW. Curbless showers are an incredibly efficient way of integrating a separate shower and tub arrangement into a small space. When the shower rain head is not in use, the shower disappears, in essence, and the area simply serves as circulation space around the bathtub. The author reduced the size of the floor tiles from 12 in. by 12 in. to 4 in. by 4 in. in the shower area to obtain the proper slope to the floor drain.

A Craftsman look with an Asian twist

The new bathroom is influenced by Japanese architecture in its use of space, light, and materials. In this case, the Japanese aesthetic helps to create a modern interpretation of Craftsman interiors and to distinguish new construction from old, which I thought was important.

The sleeping porch had large openings on two of its walls, which made privacy from the neighbors and the street a challenge. My solution was to fill the voids with obscure-glass windows much in the way shoji screens are used in Japanese architecture. The windows are operable sliders placed 30 in. above the floor. When the windows are fully opened, the tub area simulates the experience of being in an open-air hot tub while maintaining privacy for the bather. I selected stock Marvin® sliders with double glazing that had been acid-etched on the inner face of the interior glazing. The frames are made of pine, but I had them stained to match the Douglas-fir ceiling and trim in the rest of the bathroom.

I made an effort to save the original painted-fir ceiling of the sleeping porch, but not enough of the material was salvageable. I ended up having a new Douglas-fir beadboard ceiling installed and put the salvageable portions of the old ceiling to use in new exterior soffits.

I chose to tile the two interior walls of the bathroom—those that share a wall with the main house—with 8-in. by 16-in. honed Jerusalem limestone tiles that were cut from 16-in. by 16-in. tiles. The narrower tiles play up the horizontal lines of the space. I used complementary rubble-limestone tiles on the screen walls. On the floor, tub deck, and exterior walls, I opted for black Brazilian slate, another nod to Japanese architecture.

The master bath has increased the livability as well as the resale value of our house. While the space has clean lines, the light and warm interior finishes make for a calm, inviting space. The only downside of the renovation lies in the extra effort it now takes us to leave the bath. It has become something of a family retreat in our house.

SOURCES

WINDOWS
Wood Ultimate Glider
www.marvin.com

WALL TILE
Jerusalem honed limestone
www.oregontileandmarble.com

SCREEN WALL TILE
Chinese rubble limestone
prattandlarson.com

SHOWER FIXTURE
12-in. rain head
www.opella.com

TUB
Amiga®
www.jacuzzi.com

TOILET
Carlyle®
www.totousa.com

FLOOR TILE
Brazilian black slate
prattandlarson.com

FAUCET
Designo series
www.kwcamerica.com

SINK
Stainless-steel Rhythm®
www.kohler.com

WOODWORK DISPLAYS JAPANESE AND CRAFTSMAN INFLUENCE

HISTORICALLY, CRAFTSMAN ARCHITECTURE borrowed heavily from the Japanese vernacular. Both Craftsman and Japanese architecture emphasize materials and the skill of the builder. The wood in the bathroom is a combination of pine, Douglas fir, and Honduras mahogany. The conversion varnish used on all the wood highlights its beauty and helps it to withstand wet locations.

The custom mahogany medicine cabinet and floating vanity wrap the screen wall to which they're anchored—a detail that highlights the artistry in the construction of the space.

BUILT-IN JOINERY. The floating mahogany vanity and the mahogany medicine cabinet wrap the screen wall to create an elegant detail that is also functional. A combined magazine rack and toilet-paper holder is easily mounted to the back of the wood vanity.

Half-Baths Full of Function

BY LYNN HOPKINS

Much of my work involves renovating and reconfiguring houses in New England, many of which date back to a time when half-baths were nonexistent. If a house did have an original half-bath, it was likely located in a small shed in the backyard—not exactly the kind of space contemporary homeowners are looking to renovate. Updating these houses can be challenging, and integrating a half-bath can take some creative thinking. Designing a half-bath—often called a powder room here in New England—usually involves figuring out how to shoehorn it into an existing plan. Whether in a remodel or a new home, you have to consider who will use it even before you determine its location.

Create privacy in public spaces

The original intent of the half-bathroom was to create a facility for guests. Traditionally, these bathrooms were located near the entry foyer to keep guests from wandering too deeply into the private areas of a home. The same reasoning holds true for modern-day half-baths.

With this in mind, determining an appropriate location can be challenging, because a half-bath has two requirements that can be in conflict. First, it should be convenient to the social spaces of the house—the living, dining, family, and kitchen areas. It also must provide sufficient privacy. Locating a powder room off an entry, hall, or other circulation space is ideal. Entering and exiting a half-bath that opens into a room where people are eating, cooking, or having a conversation is awkward at best and embarrassing at worst.

Finding space in the desired location can be a challenge, but because this room is generally not used for an extended period of time or a variety of tasks, the area requirements can be minimal. I have tucked powder rooms into closets, hidden them under stairs, and squeezed them out of adjacent rooms. When a small house increases substantially in size, a full bath may no longer be needed in its current location and can be replaced with a smaller and/or more gracious half-bath. The right location often trumps room size.

Make it compact

Because this type of bathroom is going to be used more for hand washing than bathing and grooming, the sink doesn't need to be very large, and the towels can be smaller. Wall-hung or pedestal sinks require only a small area and result in a more spacious-feeling room. Storage requirements in a powder room aren't the same as in a full bath, either. Hand soap, a bottle of aspirin, a few spare rolls of toilet paper, and some bandages are often all that need to be accommodated, not the voluminous range of toiletries found in a full bath. These items often can be placed in compact wall cabinets, on shelves, or in canisters. Recessed or built-in storage can steal a few valuable inches of space from the walls without enlarging the footprint of the room.

A wall-hung toilet is another way to save space; because the tank is concealed within the wall, the fixture doesn't project too far into the room. Servicing the fixture occurs through the actuator plate and doesn't require dismantling the wall. Still another space-saving trick is to tuck a toilet below a sloped ceiling, such as the underside of a stair, as long as the ceiling height in front of the toilet is adequate to meet code. Section R305 of the

FINE FINISHES. Because the shower and tub were removed, moisture is no longer a problem in the bath, so vertical-grain Douglas-fir-clad walls could be installed without concern. Glass tile adds durability and reduces maintenance in the wet area around the sink. The floor is made of slate tiles.

RETHINKING A FULL BATH

BEFORE

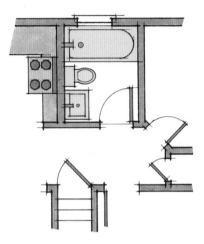

The minimal-size full bath was necessary when the house was a little Cape with two small bedrooms on the first floor. As the house grew, however, additional bathrooms elsewhere made the tub in the original bath unnecessary. The window in the shower was problematic, too.

AFTER

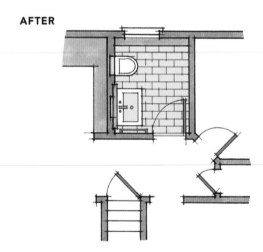

Eliminating the tub freed the room to take advantage of the window. Condensation and moisture issues were eliminated, expanding the range of finish options drastically. A two-fixture bath configuration eliminates much of the shampoo/shaving/makeup clutter that accompanies a full bath, effortlessly keeping the room tidy and ready for guests.

IRC requires a minimum of 6½ ft. of ceiling height at the centerline of the 21-in. clearance area in front of the toilet—that is, 10½ in. beyond the toilet's front edge.

Small still can be custom

Because its spatial demands are not as great as those of a full bathroom, a powder room can have greater finish options and custom details. Humidity and moisture levels are less than those in a full bath, so wood and all kinds of wallpaper can be practical choices for wall finishes. Moisture-proof materials such as tile are still the best choices where water spray is inevitable, such as around the sink area. Another advantage of a powder room is that even the most expensive finishes may be affordable because the space is so small. Splurging for that beautiful but costly tile won't feel quite so excessive.

SUBSTAIR SOLUTION. Tucking the half-bath under a set of stairs makes efficient use of otherwise useless square footage. The toilet is ideally located beneath the sloped portion of this small space.

BARE ESSENTIALS. A small vanity holds all that is required of this half-bath, which is located near the front entry and is used predominantly by guests. To elevate the aesthetic of the small space, the homeowners chose this bronze 17-in. undermount sink by Kohler.

TUCKING A BATH UNDER THE STAIRS

BEFORE

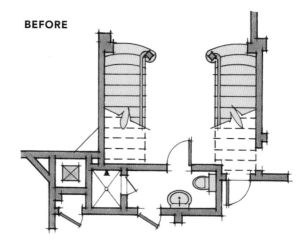

The house has a wonderful double staircase that is visible as soon as you walk through the front door. At some point, previous owners installed a powder room behind the small door centered below the stair landing. Not only was this an overly public location for such a private room, but it also cut the kitchen and family room off from the rest of the house.

AFTER

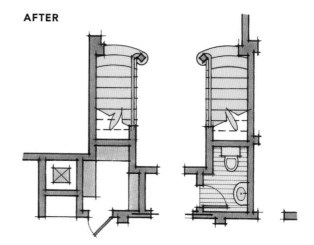

Moving the powder room to the area under one of the stairs made it possible to open up a sightline through the house to the back garden. Tying the expanded family room and reconfigured kitchen in with the public front rooms of the house dramatically improves the flow between all rooms. The powder room is still centrally located but is discreetly accessed off a small vestibule.

Bed, Bath, and Beyond

BY PAUL DEGROOT

As it happens, the home Jen and Pierre bought had been recently remodeled. The home's location near town and great schools was hard to beat. Mature trees filled the big yard. However, the house didn't fit their needs well in several areas, including the master suite.

The master bedroom opened directly off the bustling living room and kitchen, making a peaceful rest or a quiet read impossible. With no alcove or hallway as a buffer, the bedroom door was within five easy steps of the stove. When the door was open, you could plainly see into the bedroom while snacking at the kitchen counter. If the bathroom door was open, it was even possible to see the master-bath tub from the dining table. And the troubles didn't stop with layout.

A poorly pitched drain line below the slab caused the shower and tub to back up occasionally. It's no surprise that Jen and Pierre chose not to fix the tub motor when it broke: The installer entombed it behind tile with no access panel.

Move the bedroom first

When they could stand it no longer, Jen called to see if I could improve their situation. Luckily, there was plenty of room to expand into their backyard.

We agreed that extending a new master suite into the yard, though expensive, was the only cure. Placing the bedroom outboard gave it three exterior walls and abundant windows, perfect for natural ventilation and balanced light. A concrete patio stood in the way, but no sobs were heard when the Bobcat® dug it up. To the contrary, the addition gave me the opportunity to design better outdoor-living space right outside the living room where it was needed most.

We all agreed that sloped ceilings in both bedroom and bath were must-haves, mimicking the vaulted ceiling of the living room, a handsome feature from an earlier remodel. Boosting the feeling of airiness in the bedroom, I used 9-ft.-tall walls to raise the eaves above those surrounding the 8-ft. walls of the original construction. The old bedroom became an office and library, and created a transition zone between the living room and the master suite.

I reshuffled the deck on the old closet and bathroom space. None of it was worth saving, and moving walls is relatively easy when there's attic space above to hide headers and beams. I moved the closet to an inland position so that the new bathroom could run lengthwise along the existing exterior

REFLECTING THE LIGHT. Centering the tub and windows on the exterior wall with a clerestory above delivers lots of daylight to the room. Mirrors opposite the windows spread the light farther and enlarge the space (inset photo, above). Using frameless glass to enclose the shower makes it as invisible as possible. Black grout gives the wall tile a dry-stack appearance. Playful bubbles of glass surround the tub as an accent.

PRIVACY, PLEASE

THE OLD MASTER BEDROOM opened to the busy living room. With doors ajar, it was possible to see from the dining table into the bedroom and bath. Converting the old bedroom into an office and building into the backyard solved space and privacy problems. A short hallway links, and separates, the office and bedroom. Moving the closet to an interior position freed the exterior wall for the new bathroom, where windows are essential. Pocket doors from the bath to the closet allow for circular flow and keep morning fender benders to a minimum.

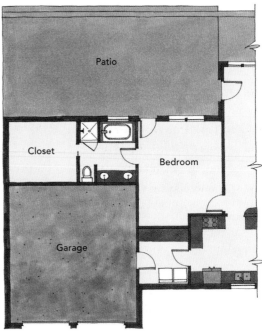

BEFORE

AFTER

wall. I gained extra length by stretching the bath 50 in. beyond the old slab line. Doing so afforded the wide, low-pitch vault and high clerestory windows that I sought to replicate in the windows and ceiling of the new bedroom.

It's all about the tub

When space is tight, I try to talk folks out of having a big tub in their bath because it hogs lots of floor space and is often used infrequently. When there is plenty of room, though, it's a rare client who doesn't want me designing both a tub and shower in the mix. It's a no-brainer in such cases that the tub be positioned below windows. There isn't a better use of the exterior-wall space, and extra daylight in a bath is always welcome. Having a vaulted ceiling in this bath made it even more obvious that the tub and its windows would be centered on the outside wall.

Pierre did his homework and found a tub for serious relaxation: A BainUltra®, model Amma® 7242, sporting a turbine motor to push heated air through 58 jets. I placed the 72-in.-long tub below double-hung windows so that fresh air could enhance the bathing experience on mild days. For privacy, Jen opted for pleated window shades, matching those in the bedroom, over obscured glass. When down, the shades block views inward while allowing muted daylight to pass.

The drop-in tub rests on slabs custom-made by John Newbold, a local expert in glass-fiber reinforced concrete. Extremely dense and fine-grained, his concrete work is a beautiful, durable alternative to natural stone for about the same cost. The raised ledges on each end of the tub are topped with the same concrete and are perfect for shampoo bottles and coffee mugs. Jen and Pierre chose a bone-white color for the slabs so that the glass tile could be their main accent in the room. Directly surrounding the tub is a band of circular glass tiles evoking images of stones worn smooth by a clear, cool stream. Large glazed tiles in earthy browns extend up from this band to the sills of the clerestory windows and clad the tub platform as well.

SINK AND COUNTER CAST AS ONE. Although it appears to hang off the wall, the vanity cabinet is installed with a deeply recessed toe kick. You can't see it, but it allows the cabinet to support the concrete countertop and sinks. A 24-in.-deep cabinet leaves ample room behind the sink to mount a faucet without crowding the backsplash. Setting back the banks of drawers that flank the vanity gives the cabinet a furniturelike quality.

NORTHERN LIGHTS. The vaulted ceiling and north-facing windows in the new master bedroom recall those in the existing living room. North glazing in Austin's air-conditioning climate is a perfect way to scoop up light without too much solar-heat gain.

BEYOND. Seen on the right, the new master bedroom extends into the backyard with a roofline and high windows similar to those in the existing living room. A new patio links the indoors and the beckoning lawn.

Not-so-public toilet

This is the first time I've used glass panels for a water closet. Although it seems odd at first, it's akin to a toilet stall in a public restroom, but with frosted glass for the panels and door. The owners wanted visual privacy, yet didn't want a dim, claustrophobic water closet hemmed in by solid walls. Frosted glass lets light through, making the stall feel bigger and less confining. This sense is reinforced by the open-air top. While an opaque partition between the tub and toilet would yield more privacy, we agreed that it would detract from the openness conveyed by the vaulted ceiling. Book-ending the tub with the glass shower, the glassed-in water closet is the answer for this particular room and this particular family.

Vanity flair

Two sinks form a vanity across the aisle from the tub. Molded and poured integrally with the countertop, the 8-ft.-long slab of glass-fiber concrete is monolithic magic. A cabinet with flush-fitted doors and drawers supports the heavy concrete.

I deeply recessed the cabinet toe kick to lend the appearance of a floating vanity while still carrying the substantial weight to the floor. Varying the cabinet depth on the ends helps to ease walking space around the corners, but mainly, I just think it looks better. The drawer banks on the ends are 21 in. deep. I specified a 24-in. depth for the sinks, which leaves plenty of space for mounting faucets. The extra inches around the faucet make cleanup easier and give more room for personal items.

I picked rift-sawn white-oak veneer for the cabinet and ran its tight linear grain pattern horizontally. We finished it in a midnight espresso stain to mimic the tone of the owners' bedroom furniture. The dark wood sandwiched between the white floor tile and countertop is a dramatic contrast. Borrowing from the tub surround, the circular-glass-tile backsplash gives a dash of color and character. Above that, big frameless mirrors reflect light from the windows opposite them. Behind each sink, the mirror is actually an M Series recessed medicine cabinet from Robern. The mirror glass is set off from the

SOURCES

CONCRETE
Newbold Stone
www.newboldstone.com

WALL TILE
Porcelanosa® Shine Dark
www.porcelanosa-usa.com

ACCENT TILE
Porcelanosa Moon Glacier Metallic
Cremas

FLOOR TILE
Porcelanosa Nieve Nature

MEDICINE CABINETS
Robern M Series
www.robern.com

GLASS HARDWARE
C.R. Laurence Co.
www.crlaurence.com

FROSTED GLASS CONCEALS THE TOILET. The home-owners were willing to sacrifice some privacy to gain a water closet not claustrophobic to use.

wall by ½ in., forming a finger pull along the edges for easy opening and no glass smudges. The center mirror is fixed to the wall on spacers to make it flush with the medicine cabinets. Always a stickler for excellence, contractor Eric Harrison saw to it that this detail and the dozens of other particulars of this project were carefully executed.

Bathroom Reborn

BY DAVE MULDER

A few years ago, I completed the remodel of a bathroom that was part of a larger renovation of a kitchen. Both rooms were products of their age and of benign neglect, but the dim clutter and the bad design in the bathroom were more concentrated and harder to live with than the problems in the kitchen. In addition to its other sins, the bath had an awkward fixture arrangement. Worst of all, the room's only window was hidden in the linen closet, which took up nearly a quarter of the floor space.

After gutting the space, I moved one end wall about 18 in., then closed off the doorway that opened to the living room and created a new doorway to the kitchen. The closet became the new shower stall, and I replaced the old window with a smaller casement unit that I pushed up near the ceiling for privacy. I also added a skylight over the vanity, which really brightens the room.

As in the kitchen, I built all the cabinets from bamboo plywood that I finished with water-based Enduro® satin poly from General Finishes®. The room has electric-radiant heat that I installed beneath the tile.

BEFORE

CHAOTIC AND DARK. The window at the end of the room was hampered by the linen closet and louvered doors that were built directly in front of it.

Learning from our experiences

Rick, the homeowner, has lived in the remodel for three years now and has provided me with valuable feedback. To create more lighting options, I added dimmers to all three light fixtures. I also installed a timer for the ceiling fan, which is so quiet that it's tough to remember to turn it off. I found that it's important to mount the wall-hung sink faucet exactly level, because the mirror magnifies any deviation. Also, I've had to add another coat of polyurethane to the counter. All in all, these details are fairly minor issues for a much better bath.

SPACE-SAVING DOOR. Rather than take up valuable real estate with a swinging door, the author applied bamboo veneer to a 1⅜-in. slab of MDF and hung it from heavy-duty track hardware. The dense slab not only matches the cabinets, but it also keeps noise to a minimum.

MOVE THE ENTRANCE, THEN REDESIGN

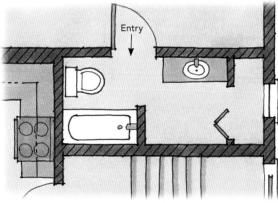

BEFORE
The toilet and bathtub were right in front of the door, which opened to the living room. To get to the linen closet, you had to squeeze between the vanity and the tub.

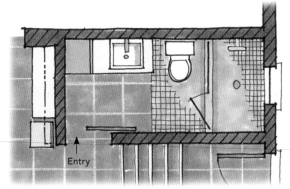

AFTER
After closing off the living-room entrance, the author moved the bath entrance to the kitchen side. The shower was relocated to the end of the room, with the toilet between the sink and the shower.

Tailoring a Full Bath for Empty Nesters

BY JENNIFER JONES

Our clients, a couple of empty nesters with a charming Bay Area house built in 1914, asked us to create a beautiful but functional master bathroom that would complement the architectural details of their home. We wanted this to be the one and only remodel of this bathroom. Creating a timeless design that would remain stylish and functional for many years was our top priority. We achieved this through smart space planning and by using classic materials and fixtures, and a soft, muted palette.

Four Details Worth Replicating

This project illustrates the potential in reimagining existing spaces with light remodeling work. Combining layout improvements with updated fixtures and finishes has resulted in an absolutely new bath within the old bath's footprint. Here are the changes that had the greatest impact.

1. REMOVING THE EXISTING TUB

This simple remodel made way for a large light-filled shower defined by a glass partition and curb. The partition, as well as a recessed shower niche with glass shelving, helps bridge the gap between the traditional and the contemporary styles of the space.

2. THE CARRARA-MARBLE BASKET-WEAVE FLOOR

This floor evokes a traditional quality. Keeping the flooring consistent throughout the compact space helps tie the design together and make the space feel cohesive.

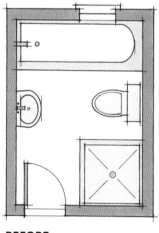

BEFORE

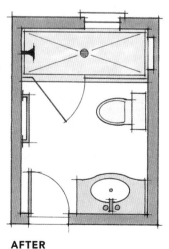

AFTER

3. THE FREESTANDING WEATHERED-OAK VANITY

Replacing the old vanity provides a textural contrast to the muted-gray ceramic tiles and light dove-gray walls while providing plenty of storage. The Carrara-marble top and cross-handle faucet controls add a traditional touch that blends well with the home's original details.

4. APPLIED PANEL MOLDING

This toned-down detail simulates traditional wainscot, is inexpensive, and adds another layer of traditional detail to the bath. Adding tile to these walls would have overwhelmed the small space.

FORMED TO FIT

Paying attention to the dimensions in this project yields insight into what arrangements may work in your own bath designs. Here are some of the author's recommendations, which exceed code in some instances, when it comes to spatial planning.

- Shower width: 30 in. minimum
- Shower-door width: 28 in. minimum
- Space on each side of toilet tank: 10 in. to 12 in.
- Clear space in front of toilet: 24 in. minimum
- Clear space in front of vanity: 30 in. minimum

SOURCES

VANITY CABINET
Empire Rosette Single Vanity
www.restorationhardware.com

VANITY TOP
Carrara marble
www.restorationhardware.com

FAUCET
Lugarno® 8-in. widespread
www.restorationhardware.com

LIGHTS
Lugarno Sconces
www.restorationhardware.com

FLOOR TILE
Tribeca™ New White Basketweave
www.walkerzanger.com

WALL TILE
Elements tile, color 915
www.annsacks.com

SHOWER FIXTURES
Symbol
www.kohler.com

TOILET
Eco Promenade®
www.totousa.com

Two Baths for a Vintage Home

BY ANN MCCULLOCH

Taking on a remodeling project in an old house requires a careful balancing act. Ideally, the remodel will improve the way the house looks and functions but won't sacrifice its old-house charm. I recently had the chance to work with great clients in Portland, Ore., who understand that there's more to remodeling than simply swapping old for new.

The Schulers' home is an exemplary Tudor revival. Such homes, which had their heyday in the 1920s and '30s, have distinctive steep roofs, stucco exteriors, and attention-grabbing Arts and Crafts–inspired interiors.

A NEW MASTER BATH THAT LOOKS OLD

The recently remodeled bathrooms in this vintage home combine modern amenities such as walk-in showers and large vanities with period-appropriate fixtures and finishes such as a claw-foot tub and faucets with cross-handle valves. The result is baths that look old but that work for today's lifestyles.

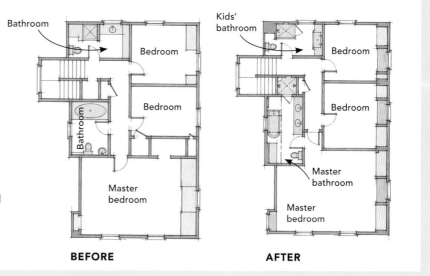

BEFORE

AFTER

The Schulers, who bought the house three years ago, contacted me about a comprehensive update of their home that included remodeling the two upstairs bathrooms. The Schulers were excited about the prospect of remodeling to make their home more functional, and were particularly concerned about getting the details right. They had good reason for concern; a past remodel wasn't kind to this house.

Specifically, the master bathroom is where the greatest remodeling atrocities had occurred. Redone in the 1980s, the master bath had brown fixtures and mauve wall-to-wall carpeting that clashed with the house's period details. Even worse, the previous contractor created structural problems when he removed load-bearing walls while changing the original floor plan.

The Schulers asked me to update and expand their master bath and to undo the damage done during the past remodel. Also on their list was a fun and functional bath for their three kids. The Schulers were clear that they didn't want alterations made to the exterior of the house, so any space added to the bathrooms would have to be carved from the existing floor plan. They also requested that the baths be styled appropriately and not clash with the house's traditional roots.

Choose finishes and fixtures wisely

It's likely that the previous owner of the Schulers' house loved the new master bath. The fixtures and color palette would have been at the height of fashion. However, not many years later, these once-trendy selections were showing their age.

Rather than choose the latest and greatest materials, I encourage my remodeling clients to go with a simpler style and more timeless fixtures. This prevents the design from looking outdated before its time.

CALMING, NOT BORING

Often dominated by shades of white, period baths can be boring and have an institutional feel that's not relaxing. The cool colors on display in this bath are soothing without being boring. Paint is from Miller Paint® (www.millerpaint.com).
Wall: Evolution® Marseilles flat
Ceiling: Acro Pure, Sugar Dust flat
Vanity: Acro Pure, London Road semigloss

FUN FOR THE KIDS

LARGER THAN MOST VANITY SINKS, the farmhouse sink in the kids' bathroom keeps water contained and provides enough room for sharing. The glass pulls on the vanity help to maintain a period look.

In the Schulers' baths, we used classic white subway tile on the walls and porcelain mosaic tile on the floor. Both types would have been common when the house was built. To make the otherwise plain white floor more interesting, we added a decorative border and accents with contrasting colors, an idea inspired by a floor I once saw in a beautiful old hotel.

In the master bath, we opted for a cast-iron, free-standing claw-foot tub and a white-marble vanity top with undermount sinks. Once again, we chose fixtures that would have been common in the 1920s and '30s.

In the kids' bath, I designed a vanity that looked like an old piece of furniture, but we gave it a fun twist by installing a farmhouse sink with two faucets. With a pair of faucets, two kids can get cleaned up or ready for bed together, and the huge sink means less water on the countertop. Of course, a farmhouse sink would have been relegated to the kitchen when the house was built. Because the sink is appropriate to the period and highly functional in this bath, however, we considered it to be an acceptable departure from the norm.

Mixing old and new

The remodeled baths in this house are a good example of mixing old and new styles. For example, the Schulers wanted tiled showers, but a modern, glass-enclosed shower can look really out of place in a period-inspired bath. For the kids' bath, we chose a simple rectangular design with basic door and mounting hardware. Keeping the shower simple and unobtrusive helps it to blend in with the period-appropriate bath fixtures nearby. We also used inexpensive industrial-looking light fixtures over the more period-looking vanity. The pairing works because the lights and the vanity have simple lines and similar finishes. In the master bath, we installed the shower in a separate space, so only the shower

KID-FRIENDLY AND BRIGHT
Light-green walls and a darker-green vanity are examples of fun and playful colors that kids like. Paint is from Miller Paint (millerpaint.com).
Wall: Evolution, Saw Grass Cottage flat
Ceiling: Acro Pure, Sugar Dust flat
Vanity: Acro Pure, French Pear semigloss

KEEP IT SIMPLE. The glass shower's clean lines and simple hardware don't compete with the period-style fixtures nearby. The white subway tile and mosaic floor were features common to many Tudor homes of the time.

TIMELESS TUDOR. With its steep roof, massive chimney, and stucco exterior, this home is typical of American Tudor-revival architecture. The inside of the house has lots of built-ins, decorative mosaic tile, and ornamental plaster.

door is visible from the rest of the bath. This provides extra privacy and allows the more period-appropriate bath fixtures nearby to define the dominant style of the space.

Making more space

By modern standards, both bathrooms were cramped, so we used a variety of strategies to gain space. For the kids' bathroom, we took over a closet in the adjoining bedroom, which became the new shower. We replaced the lost storage with built-ins that include a window seat for reading and relaxing. The shower is 3 ft. 6 in. by 3 ft. 10 in. Compared to a code-minimum shower (3 ft. by 3 ft.), it feels spacious.

In the master bath, we added a new tiled shower and a toilet alcove. The alcove was created by stealing space from the master bedroom (floor plan, p. 201). This required moving a bedroom wall. The lost space wasn't used much, so making the room a little smaller was a sensible compromise.

The whole family loves the new baths, and I'm pleased with how well they fit in with this wonderful old house.

DETAILS

THE RIGHT FINISHES can help a contemporary bath to fit better in an older house. Even though they're brand new, these products contribute to the look and feel of an original bathroom.

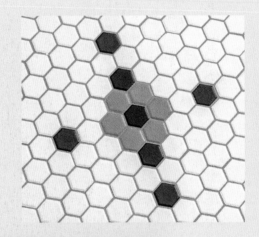

MOSAIC FLOOR TILE
Daltile mosaic tile in Arctic White, Garden Spot, and Cityline Kohl (www.daltile.com)

MASTER-BATH LIGHT SWITCHES
Rejuvenation, Inc.®, push-button switch with brass wall plate (www.rejuvenation.com)

MASTER-BATH FAUCET
Belle Foret™ N315 02, cross handle, chrome (belleforet.com)

Small-Bath Serenity

BY ANNI TILT

This bathroom was designed to be part of a whole-house remodel that aimed to create a place of meditation: a spot to gather with friends and family or just to gather one's thoughts in the Zen tradition. In the tiny upstairs bath, for example, my firm added a skylight and pale-blue tile and paint, creating a sky focus. In contrast, this remodeled downstairs bath is earth-focused, with deep, rich colors, wood details, and intimate garden views.

Hunting for a plan

While the remodel of the old house was extensive, we decided to leave the bath in its existing location, which still worked in the new plan and would reduce plumbing complications.

Working within the existing footprint required that space-saving tricks be implemented to make the new bathroom functional. The sliding door and an added bay keep the bath open without disrupting adjacent spaces. Putting the tub in a new window bay adds space to the room while providing a grand view of the garden. The bay was less costly and complicated

STEP UP AND IN. The tansu-inspired tub surround offers storage in its steps and lets bathers slip comfortably into the Kohler Tea-for-Two® tub, which is surrounded by large casement windows.

CRAFTSMANSHIP ON DISPLAY. The custom fir vanity with its bamboo sink sets the tone for the Japanese-inspired bathroom and is just one of several details worthy of attention. Another, reflected in the vanity mirror, is the bathroom door, carved by local artist Jordy Morgan.

than building a full addition with foundation; it has the extra benefit of breaking up the exterior facade. As in the rest of the house, we looked to Japanese design for inspiration around the tub. We set the tub into a tansu-inspired surround made of salvaged fir. In the style of traditional tansu cabinets, the steps that access the tub double as storage space.

The elevated tub in this half of the bath reinforces the Japanese ritual of bathing, in which the bathtub is as much a place for relaxation as it is a site for daily cleansing. The large windows of the bay focus the whole bath on the garden view, expanding the small room. This reflects the Japanese landscape technique of borrowed scenery.

Custom style

Choosing finishes and fixtures for such a design demands commitment to the chosen aesthetic. It all has to work together. With that in mind, we had hoped to find an antique Asian chest for the sink cabinet, but the space requirements were too exacting. Instead, we had Eastern Classics, a Berkeley-

SOURCES

FAUCET
Hansgrohe
www.hansgrohe.com

LIGHTS
Barn Light Electric Raindrop Sconce
www.barnlightelectric.com

SINK
Stone Forest Moso Bamboo Vessel
www.stoneforest.com

TUB
Kohler Tea-for-Two
www.kohler.com

TUB FAUCET
Price Pfister™
www.pfisterfaucets.com

VANITY CABINET
Eastern Classics
www.easternclassics.net

VANITY TOP
Custom concrete by Bohemian
Stoneworks
www.bohemianstoneworks.com

WINDOWS
Loewen™
www.loewen.com

based company that builds Japanese-style furniture, provide a custom fir vanity to fit our specifications.

The sliding door was carved on both sides by a local artist. It echoes totem-like sculptures in the owners' garden, reinforcing the connection between the house and the garden. The slatted salvaged Douglas-fir ceiling, which provides texture as well as acoustic dampening, continues through to the adjacent entry space, fusing the new bath to the rest of the home.

A Master Bath Carved Out of Closet Space

BY JOHN BOATMAN

Over the past few years, John Boatman has been hard at work teasing out the charm in his 1911 Washington, D.C., town house. Foremost on his priority punch list was to remedy a dysfunctional second-floor layout and to add a master bathroom where no bath had existed.

Looking at the floor plan, John took stock of his storage needs and the potential that lay in the existing closet spaces. By moving a few nonbearing walls and relocating two bedroom closets, he not only created enough space for a cozy, spalike master bathroom but also made the second floor a much more functional and pleasing place to be.

Creative Solution

It took more head-scratching to figure out how the existing floor plan was intended to work than it did to envision a newly designed space. A pass-through between the master bedroom and the middle bedroom was awkward and redundant given the main hallway,

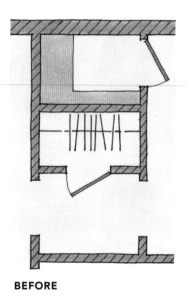

BEFORE

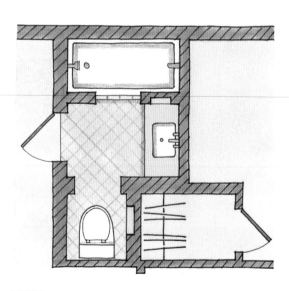

AFTER

SOURCES

FAUCET
Kohler Purist®, brushed-nickel finish

SHOWERHEAD
Kohler Purist, single function

BACKSPLASH
Ceramica Magica Perla mosaic in keshi gold; Boyce & Bean sea-green mosaic accents

FLOOR
Casa Dolce Casa® glazed Tuscania tile

VANITY TOP
Custom crema-marfil marble by Stone & Tile World in Rockville, Md.

SINK
Kohler Kathryn®

TUB
Kohler Tea-for-Two

TOILET
Kohler San Raphael®

and it could easily be jettisoned from the new layout. Similarly, John realized he didn't need the existing master-bedroom closet because he could move storage to custom built-in closets along the north wall of the bedroom. The bath walls were thickened to accommodate utilities and storage niches.

MAXIMIZE SPACE. A water closet occupying a footprint of only 36 in. by 42 in. houses a toilet and a 7-in.-deep storage recess for bathroom items and towels.

COOL DETAIL

A CLEAN, UNINTERRUPTED TILE BACKSPLASH is made possible by hiding GFCI outlets and light switches in a false vanity drawer.

MAKE THE MOST OF YOUR ROOM. A site-built vanity holds a sink that was selected for its width and narrow depth and allows for as much open floor space as possible.

Steam Spa

BY ALEXANDRA IMMEL

The original bathroom in this circa-1987 home had pink 4-in. by 4-in. tile on the floors and walls, outdated fixtures, and a dark, undersize shower. The tub, oversize and underused, sat in the nicest corner of the bathroom. The design was not uncommon for the era in which the house was built, but the homeowners—like many who have lived in and remodeled older homes—were ready for a master-bath upgrade. We took three primary steps to transform this dated space into a spalike bath. We carved out space for a large walk-in closet, added a steam shower, and finished the new bath in a modern style that better reflects the owners' contemporary way of life.

211

STEAM SHOWER PRIMER

INTEGRATING A STEAM SHOWER into a project isn't as daunting as one might expect. Here are some general considerations and a couple of lessons learned.

- The shower ceiling should be sloped to prevent condensate from falling on bathers.
- Waterproofing demands are the same as with a conventional shower, including an appropriately pitched shower pan.
- The steam generator can be placed within 60 ft. of the shower, depending on the unit, but the most practical placement is in a nearby cabinet.
- Standard bathroom ventilation outside of the shower is sufficient for managing moisture.

LESSONS LEARNED

- A small gap around the door doesn't have a significant impact on the loss of steam in the shower.
- The teak bench seats in this shower perform well, but the initial teak oil finish did not. The seats had to be refinished with five coats of spar varnish, which has held up nicely.

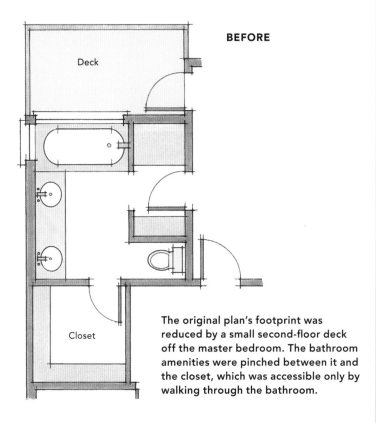

BEFORE

Deck

Closet

The original plan's footprint was reduced by a small second-floor deck off the master bedroom. The bathroom amenities were pinched between it and the closet, which was accessible only by walking through the bathroom.

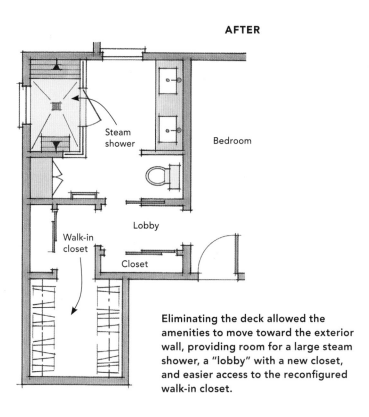

AFTER

Steam shower

Bedroom

Lobby

Walk-in closet

Closet

Eliminating the deck allowed the amenities to move toward the exterior wall, providing room for a large steam shower, a "lobby" with a new closet, and easier access to the reconfigured walk-in closet.

SOURCES

SINKS
Kohler Kathryn
www.kohler.com

SINK FAUCETS
Zucchetti ON
www.zucchettikos.it

SHOWER FIXTURES
California Faucets Tiburon
Collection
www.calfaucets.com

Hansgrohe handheld shower
www.hansgrohe-usa.com

STEAM UNIT
Mr. Steam® generator with MS
Butler package trim
www.mrsteam.com

FLOOR TILE
12x24 Marazzi SistemN
www.marazzi.it

WALL TILE
4x16 Contract Series Matte Biscuit
www.arttileco.net

COLORED GLASS IN SHOWER
Blazestone recycled-glass tile
www.bedrockindustries.com

VANITY TOP
Caesarstone® concrete
www.caesarstoneus.com

VANITY CABINET
Canyon Creek Cabinet Company®
www.canyoncreek.com

A Three-Quarter Bath in Half the Space

BY STEVE WILMOT

Architect Steve Wilmot and his family live in a Craftsman-style house in Northfield, Minn. The house was built in 1911 by a Swedish carpenter who occupied it for the next 50 years. Afterward, the house endured a long line of owners who neglected it over several decades. The Wilmots bought the house at a garage sale. (The owner had included the house in the list of items for sale in her newspaper ad.) It needed work, but it was a solid structure with plenty of character that had lots of potential.

While remodeling the upstairs bathroom was at the top of their priority list, the Wilmots also wanted a more complete bath to replace the quasi-powder room that occupied a closet in the first-floor bedroom. (The closet, approximately 3 ft. by 8 ft., contained a toilet but no sink.) After studying the space and making preliminary drawings, Wilmot realized that the space was just big enough for a sink, a shower stall, and a relocated toilet.

"Aha!" moment

Access on the long side of a rectangular room is generally easier, all the more so in a tiny room. Wilmot realized that the existing door's location wouldn't work, and he considered opening the wall below the first stair landing so that the entrance would be from the kitchen. However, that arrangement would provide only enough space for a half-bath. Instead, he moved the door to the middle of the bedroom side, which left enough room for both a toilet and a shower stall. The one downside: Wilmot had to choose a small sink to create enough clearance at the doorway.

LET IN THE LIGHT. Rather than install a new exterior window, Wilmot opted for a cabinet above the toilet to store towels, toilet paper, and medicine-cabinet items. To provide natural light and to reduce the tight feel of the room, he replaced the wood panels in the door with translucent glass that gives the added benefit of showing when the room is occupied.

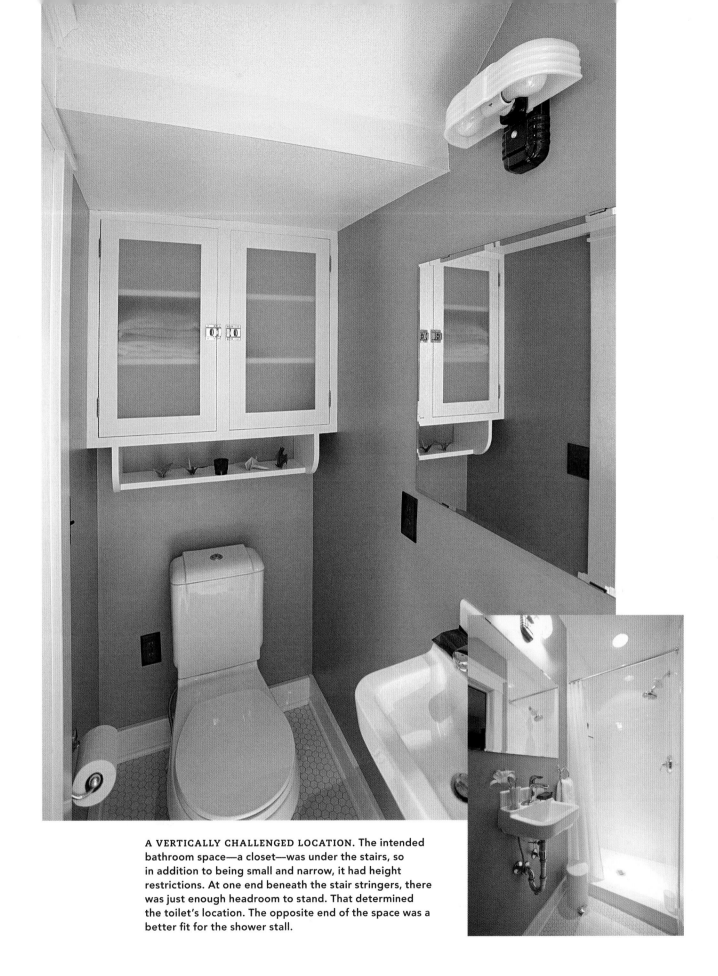

A VERTICALLY CHALLENGED LOCATION. The intended bathroom space—a closet—was under the stairs, so in addition to being small and narrow, it had height restrictions. At one end beneath the stair stringers, there was just enough headroom to stand. That determined the toilet's location. The opposite end of the space was a better fit for the shower stall.

CEILING DETERMINES FIXTURE LOCATIONS

According to code, at least 50% of any room with a sloped ceiling must be at or above the minimum height of 84 in., and no portion may be below 5 ft. Code also specifies a minimum ceiling height of 80 in. over fixtures. The ceiling height below the stairs was just high enough to satisfy code with the minimum height at the front of the toilet.

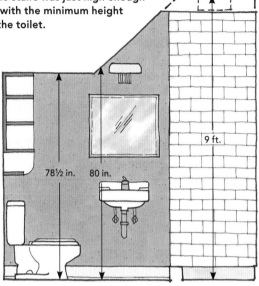

SOURCES

LIGHT FIXTURE
Rejuvenation, Inc.
www.rejuvenation.com

TILE
Subway Ceramics®
www.subwaytile.com

DUAL-FLUSH TOILET
Sterling® Plumbing
www.sterlingplumbing.com

ANTIQUE SINK
Garage sale

BEFORE

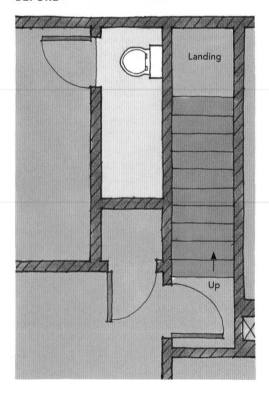

AFTER

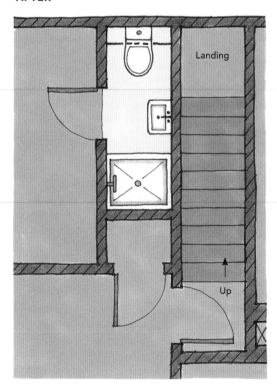

CONTRIBUTORS

John Boatman is a home designer and builder.

Rob Brennan, AIA, is the principal of Brennan + Company Architects (www .brennanarch.com) in Ellicott City, Md.

Don Burgard is the *Fine Homebuilding* senior copy and production editor.

Paul DeGroot (www.degrootarchitect. com) is an architect who designs custom homes and additions in Austin, Texas.

Andy Engel is a senior editor at *Fine Homebuilding*.

Justin Fink is the *Fine Homebuilding* Project House editor.

Jamie Gold, CKD, CAPS, is a Certified Kitchen Designer in San Diego and the author of *New Kitchen Ideas That Work* (Taunton Press, 2012) and the upcoming *New Bathroom Idea Book* (Taunton Press, 2017). You can find her designs and blog online at www.jgkitchens.com.

Sean Groom is a *Fine Homebuilding* contributing editor and lives in Simsbury, Conn.

Russell Hamlet is a principal at Studio Hamlet Architects (www.studiohamlet. com), an innovative and environmentally focused architecture firm based on Bainbridge Island, Wash.

Terry Herndon is owner and president of UpStream Construction in Crozet, Va.

Nancy R. Hiller (www.nrhillerdesign. com) is a professional maker of custom furniture and cabinetry based in Bloomington, Ind. She specializes in period-authentic furniture and built-ins for homes and offices from the late-19th through mid-20th centuries.

Martin Holladay is a senior editor at *Fine Homebuilding.*

Lynn Hopkins (www.lhopkinsarch. com) is an architect working and living in Lexington, Mass.

Alexandra Immel is the creative heart of AIRD, a Seattle company that designs home remodels and custom new homes. Using empathy, talent, and experience she guides clients through the collaborative design process. She studied architecture in Oxford and Brighton, and became a registered Architect in the UK in 1991. Zoltan Farkas is a talented Seattle Contractor who translates drawings into beautiful spaces.

Jennifer Jones is the owner and principal designer of Niche Interiors in San Francisco.

Jefferson Kolle is a freelance writer living in Bethel, Conn.

Maria LaPiana is a freelance writer who writes about home design, health, and wellness.

Kurt Lavenson (www.lavensondesign. com) is an architect and writer in Oakland, Calif.

Mike Lombardi is a plumber in Danbury, Conn.

Gregor Masefield, AIA, NCARB, heads Studio III Architecture (www .studio3architecture.net) in Bristol, Vt.

Ann McCulloch is a designer in Portland, Ore.

Duncan McPherson is an architect and Principal with Samsel Architects (www .samselarchitects.com) in Asheville, N.C.

Tom Meehan and his wife, Lane, are owners of Cape Cod Tileworks, a full-service store in Harwich, Mass.

Charles Miller is an editor at large for *Fine Homebuilding.*

Dave Mulder runs a design/build company in Grand Rapids, Mich. His website is www.fourbyeight.com.

Matt Nauman is vice president of UpStream Construction in Crozet, Va.

Buddy Rhodes has been at the leading edge of concrete design in both residential and commercial applications for the past 20 years. Lately, he's been working with a new lightweight concrete mix that doesn't need traditional reinforcement, so the material can be much thinner. His company Buddy Rhodes Products (www .buddyrhodes.com) merged in 2012 with Delta Performance and Blue Concrete to provide the most up-to-date concrete products.

Cathy Schwabe, AIA, is an architect in Oakland, Calif. Her website is www. cathyschwabearchitecture.com.

Debra Judge Silber was the *Fine Homebuilding* design editor.

Matthew Teague is a professional furniture maker and the editorial director of Spring House Press.

Anni Tilt is principal of Arkin Tilt Architects (www.arkintilt.com) in Berkeley, Calif.

Donna Wax (www.donnawaxarchitect. com) is an architect in Portland, Ore.

Steve Wilmot is an architect and home designer.

CREDITS

All photos are courtesy of *Fine Homebuilding* magazine © The Taunton Press, Inc., except as noted below.

The articles in this book appeared in the following issues of *Fine Homebuilding*:

p. 5–8: Bathroom Sightlines for Privacy and Grace by Kurt Lavenson, issue 215. Drawings by the author.

p. 9–12: Remodel a Bath for Accessibility by Duncan McPherson, issue 228. Photography by Ken Wyner. Drawing by the author.

p. 13–17: Better Bathroom Storage by Jamie Gold, issue 217. Photography by Brian Pontolilo. Drawings by Martha Garstang Hill.

p. 18–20: Invisible Ventilation for a Better Bath by Russell Hamlet, issue 223. Drawings by the author.

p. 21–23: Finishes for a Master Bath by Duncan McPherson, issue 231. Photography courtesy manufacturers; p. 22, from left to right: Benjamin Moore, Toto USA, Samsel Architects, Grohe; p. 23, clockwise from top left: Charles Bickford, Fong Brothers, Cindy Black, Charles Miller. Drawings by the author.

p. 24–29: Light a Bathroom Right by Russell Hamlet, issue 223. Drawings by the author.

p. 30–33: How to Daylight a Bathroom by Cathy Schwabe, issue 231. Photography by David Wakely. Drawings by the author.

p. 35–42: Low Flow by Sean Groom, issue 215. Photography courtesy the manufacturers, except for the photos p. 38, p. 40, and the top left photo p. 41 by Dan Thornton.

p. 43–51: Bath Sinks with Style and Sense by Maria LaPiana, issue 239. Photography courtesy the manufacturers.

p. 52–55: Seven Basic Styles of Bathroom Sinks by Don Burgard, issue 231. Photo p. 52 courtesy Restoration Hardware®, left photo p. 53 by Charles Bickford, right photo p. 53 courtesy Swan Corp., left photo p. 54 and left photo p. 55 by Brian Pontolilo, right photo p. 54 by Rob Yagid, right photo p. 55 courtesy Restoration Hardware.

p. 56–59: Tubs for Small Spaces by Jefferson Kolle, issue 223. Photography courtesy the manufacturers. Drawing by Trevor Johnston.

p. 60–65: Freestanding Tubs by Maria LaPiana, issue 247. Photography courtesy the manufacturers, except for the left photo p. 63 by Rob Yagid.

p. 66–68: The Basics of Bath Fans by Martin Holladay, issue 248. Photography courtesy

the manufacturers. Drawing by Dan Thornton.

p. 69–74: Backerboard Options by Martin Holladay, issue 225. Photography by Dan Thornton, except for the photo p. 69 and the left photo p. 72 by Lane Meehan.

p. 75–81: Miles of Tile by Debra Judge Silber, issue 234. Photography courtesy the manufacturers, except for the photo p. 75 by Ryann Ford, the bottom right photo p. 77 by davidduncanlivingston.com, and the photo p. 81 by Olson Photographic.

p. 82–91: Smart Choices in Bathroom Flooring by Matthew Teague, issue 215. Photography by *Fine Homebuilding* staff, except for the linoleum photo p. 82, the left photo p. 86, and the photo p. 88 courtesy Mannington; and the left photo p. 91 by Dennis Anderson.

p. 92–97: Linear Drains for Custom Showers by Justin Fink, issue 231. Photo p. 92 courtesy Infinity Drain; photo p. 93 courtesy ACO; photos p. 94, p. 95, and p. 96 by Rodney Diaz; and photo p. 97 courtesy Shower Grate Shop. Drawings by Christopher Mills.

p. 99–101: Install a Toilet by Mike Lombardi, issue 237. Step-by-step photography by Patrick McCombe.

Product photography by Dan Thornton.

p. 102–105: Trouble-free Toilets by Mike Lombardi, issue 254. Photography by Justin Fink.

p. 106–108: Cut a Laminate Countertop for a Sink by Andy Engel. Step-by-step photography by Patrick McCombe. Product photography by Dan Thornton.

p. 109–116: Build a Floating Vanity by Nancy R. Hiller, issue 236. Step-by-step photography by Charles Bickford. Product photography by Rodney Diaz. Drawings by Bob LaPointe.

p. 117–123: A New Approach to Concrete by Buddy Rhodes, issue 234. Photography by Charles Bickford.

p. 124–131: Build Your Own Bathroom Vanity by Justin Fink, issue 252. Photography by Rob Yagid. Drawings by John Hartman.

p. 132–138: Perfecting the Tiled Tub Surround by Tom Meehan, issue 237. Photography by Justin Fink.

p. 139–145: Old-school Path to a Wide Open Bath by Tom Meehan, issue 233. Photography by Charles Bickford.

p. 146–151: Fix a Failing Bathroom Floor by Mike Lombardi, issue 232. Photography by Justin Fink.

p. 152–155: 14 Tips for Bath Plumbing by Mike Lombardi, issue 234. Step-by-step photography by Patrick McCombe. Product photography courtesy the manufacturers.

p. 157–160: A Bathroom where East Meets West by Terry Herndon, issue 239. Photography by Allen Russ. Drawing p. 158 by Dan Thornton; p. 159 by Martha Garstang Hill.

p. 161–165: A Half-Bath, Fulfilled by Gregory C. Masefield Jr., SIP 35. Photography by Susan Teare, except the top photo p. 165 by the author. Floor plan drawings by Martha Garstang Hill. All other drawings by Christopher Mills.

p. 166–169: Two Rugged Baths by Charles Miller, issue 237. Photography by the author, except photo p. 169 by Charles Bickford. Drawing by the author.

p. 170–174: The Stay-at-Home Spa by Rob Brennan, issue 231. Photography by Anne Gummerson. Drawings by Martha Garstang Hill.

p. 175–181: A Porch Becomes a Bath by Donna Wax, issue 231. Photography by Rob Yagid, except photo p. 177 by David Papazian. Drawings by Martha Garstang Hill.

p. 182–185: Half-baths Full of Function by Lynn Hopkins, issue 241. Photography by Rob Yagid. Drawings by Martha Garstang Hill.

p. 186–191: Bed, Bath, and Beyond by Paul DeGroot, SIP 35. Photography by Ryann Ford. Drawings by Martha Garstang Hill.

p. 192–194: Bathroom Reborn by Dave Mulder, issue 231. Photography by Charles Bickford, except for before photo by author.

p. 195–197: Tailoring a Full Bath for Empty Nesters by Jennifer Jones, issue 247. Photography by Thomas Kuch. Drawings by Martha Garstang Hill.

p. 198–202: Two Baths for a Vintage Home by Ann McCulloch, issue 239. Photography courtesy David Hiser, except bottom right photo p. 202 by Dan Thornton. Drawings by Martha Garstang Hill.

p. 203–205: Small-Bath Serenity by Anni Tilt, issue 239. Photography by Ed Caldwell.

p. 206–208: A Master Bath Carbed Out of Closet Space by John Boatman. Photography by Rob Yagid. Drawings by Martha Garstang Hill.

p. 209–211: Steam Spa by Alexandra Immel, issue 247. Photography by Tucker English. Drawings by Martha Garstang Hill.

p. 212–214: A Three-Quarter Bath in Half the Space by Steve Wilmot, issue 223. Photography by Charles Bickford. Drawings by Martha Garstang Hill.

INDEX